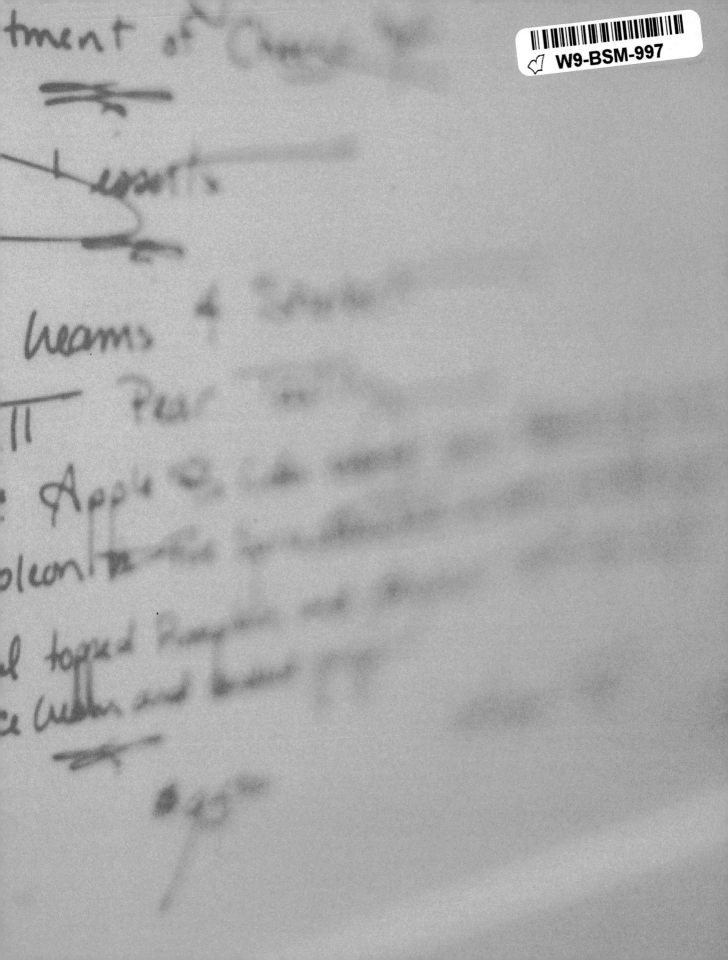

WITHDRAWN

EAT

THE SWEET LIFE

THE SWEET LIFE
Desserts from Chanterelle

KATE ZUCKERMAN

PHOTOGRAPHS BY TINA RUPP

Bulfinch Press

NEW YORK ✳ BOSTON

CONTENTS

INTRODUCTION 6

A Note About Ingredients,
Tools, Terms, and Procedures 10

ONE / TARTS 13

Hazelnut Tart Shell 14

Sweet Tart Shell 15

Flaky Tart Shell 16

Meyer Lemon Curd Tart 18

Passion-Fruit Curd Tart 21

Apple and Quince Tart 23

Fresh Huckleberry and Fig Tart 24

Fresh Apricot and Almond Tart 26

Chocolate Caramel Tart 29

TWO / CAKES 34

Vanilla, Brown Butter,
and Almond Tea Cake 37

Hazelnut Cake 39

Miniature Chocolate, Almond,
and Lime Brown Butter Tea Cakes 41

Goat Cheesecake Enrobed
in Hazelnut Brittle 42

Date Cake with Toffee Sauce 45

Chocolate Bête Noire 47

Spiced Apple and Sour Cream Cake 48

Whipped Brown Butter
and Vanilla Birthday Cake 49

Chocolate Layer Cake
with Milk Chocolate Frosting 52

THREE / COOKIES 55

Crispy, Chewy Chocolate Chip Cookies 57

Double Chocolate and Cherry Cookies 58

Gingersnaps 59

Walnut Cream Cheese
Sandwich Cookies 60

Chocolate Almond Cracks 63

Pignoli Amaretti Cookies 64

Crispy Bittersweet Chocolate Wafers 65

Hazelnut Shortbread 66

Oatmeal Cookies with Golden
Raisins and Milk Chocolate Chips 68

Coconut, Almond, and
Brown Butter Macaroons 70

Hazelnut, Cinnamon, Cardamom,
and Raspberry Sandwich Cookies 71

Walnut, Currant, and
Cinnamon Rugelach 73

Crispy Malted Bitter
Chocolate Meringues 74

Maple-Pecan Meringue Cookies 76

Hazelnut and Orange Macaroons 78

FOUR / CUSTARDS, PUDDINGS, CRÈMES, AND MOUSSES 81

Baked Custard Guidelines 82

Crème Caramels 84

Vanilla/Classic Crème Caramel 86

Espresso Crème Caramel 87

Maple Crème Caramel 88

Prune Armagnac Crème Brûlée 89

Banana Cream with Crunchy Toffee 91

Chocolate Caramel Pot de Crème 93

Creamy Coconut Cardamom
Rice Pudding 94

Chestnut and Amaretti
Cookie Pudding 97

Vanilla Panna Cotta 99

Brioche Pudding with Truffle Honey 101

Honey and Yogurt Panna Cotta 102

Maple–Star Anise Mousse 104

Cinnamon Caramel Mousse 106

Bittersweet Chocolate Mousse 108

Sesame Milk Chocolate Mousse 109

FIVE / SOUFFLÉS 111

Soufflé Guidelines 112

Meyer Lemon Soufflé 114

Goat Cheese and Purple Basil Soufflé 116

Chocolate Soufflé 119

Maple Walnut Soufflé 122

Brandied Dried Fig and Vanilla Soufflé 124

Pumpkin Soufflé 126

SIX / ICE CREAMS, SORBETS, AND FROZEN DESSERTS 129

Ice Cream and Sorbet Guidelines 130

Coconut Cream Cheese Ice Cream 135

Mandarin Ice Cream 136

Banana Malt Ice Cream 137

Espresso Ice Cream 138

Maple-Ginger Ice Cream 139

Port Plum Ice Cream 140

Apple Cider and Caramel Ice Cream 141

Basil Ice Cream 142

Mandarin Orange Sorbet 144

Muscat Grape Sorbet 145

Pineapple-Rosemary Sorbet 146

Dark Chocolate Sorbet 147

Strawberry and Tarragon Sorbet 148

Green Apple and Muscato Sorbet 149

Quince Sorbet 150

Guava Sorbet 152

Candied Kumquat Mascarpone Parfait 153

Cardamom and Honey Pistachio Nougat Glacé 154

Passion-Fruit Soufflé Glacé 155

Lavender and Honey Crème Fraîche Parfait 156

Vanilla Bean and Lemon Verbena Parfait with Summer Raspberries 158

SEVEN / ROASTED FRUITS AND FRUIT SOUPS 161

Granny Smith Apple, Dried Fig, and Dried Cherry Winter Fruit Compote 162

Roasted Medjool Dates Stuffed with Cashews, Currants, and Candied Citrus 165

Bartlett Pears Poached in Muscat Wine 166

Rhubarb Consommé with Summer Berries 167

Strawberry-Rhubarb Crisp 169

Fresh Cherry Vanilla Compote 170

Fresh Fig and Madeira Compote 170

Roasted Glazed Peaches 172

Pineapple Fruit Soup with Mango and Passion Fruit 173

Spiced Plum Compote with Plum Pit Cream 174

Honey-Glazed Roasted Pears 176

Roasted Apple Beignets with Cinnamon Sugar 178

Lemon Verbena Poached Nectarines 181

Stuffed Roasted Fall Apples 182

EIGHT / CHOCOLATES AND CANDIES 185

White Chocolate and Grapefruit Truffles with Hazelnuts 186

White Chocolate, Cardamom, and Pistachio Truffles with Coconut 188

Dark Chocolate, Cinnamon, and Espresso Truffles with Walnuts 190

Five-Spice Chocolate Truffles 191

Almond Honey Caramel Chews 193

Milk Chocolate and Almond Toffees 194

Milk Chocolate Crunch Candies 195

Quince Fruit Jellies 197

Candied Kumquats and Candied Meyer Lemon Zest 198

Guava and Passion-Fruit Jellies 199

Huckleberry Fruit Jellies 200

NINE / EDIBLE GARNISHES AND SNACKS 203

Thin and Delicate Peanut Brittle 204

Fruit Chips 206

Apple and Pear Chips 207

Pineapple Chips 208

Strawberry Chips 209

TEN / SAUCES AND CREAMY ACCOMPANIMENTS 211

Blood Orange Caramel Sauce 212

Cider Caramel Sauce 212

Brandied Crème Fraîche Sauce 213

Rum Caramel Sauce 213

Milk Chocolate Caramel Sauce 214

Toffee Sauce 214

Plum Caramel Sauce 215

Sauternes Sabayon 217

ACKNOWLEDGMENTS 218

SOURCES OF UNUSUAL INGREDIENTS 219

INDEX 220

Introduction

Say the word "Chanterelle" to a food-loving New Yorker, and the first thing he or she will likely think of is not the once-exotic wild mushroom but the beloved restaurant that put SoHo and Tribeca on the culinary map and that has charmed and indulged its patrons for twenty-seven years. Since its opening, New York has been transformed into the food capital of the world, and Chanterelle has become a destination for New Yorkers' celebrations and special evenings. As Chanterelle begins its second quarter-century, David and Karen Waltuck, who opened the restaurant to celebrate David's extraordinary French-American cuisine, continue to cook for and welcome guests every day.

Chanterelle's desserts are the last course, the final salute to a meal at this renowned New York institution. Karen and David's passion for pleasing their customers is a daily challenge for me and my work—as pastry chef, I have to make my desserts match their hospitality and enthusiasm. This book takes the essence of flavor from these sweet concoctions and makes them accessible to cooks and bakers at home, allowing them to bring the special atmosphere of Chanterelle's dining room into their own homes.

I came to Chanterelle in the fall of 1999, the mother of a nine-month-old boy. Having worked in pastry kitchens in Boston, San Francisco, Paris, and New York, I knew full well the extraordinary demands of the job. I wasn't really sure whether it was all going to work out, this mix of pastry and parenthood. But seven years and another kid later, it is a combination I have come to love.

I grew up making cookies for my two big brothers. I liked sweets, but what I really loved was watching my brothers consume and rave about everything I made. Each time I began creaming the butter for my next batch, I thought about the qualities of the cookies my brothers liked best—chewy, with lots of oatmeal, and packed with milk chocolate chunks, raisins, or dried cherries. With each new batch I tried to improve upon the last, to emphasize the characteristics they praised, and then eagerly awaited their comments and cries of adulation.

We all grew up; they moved out; I became interested in my studies. I went to Princeton and studied anthropology, but I found that I could not escape baking for lovers of sweets. I made confections during my summer breaks, and when I finished college

I began working as a baker in restaurants and bakeries.

Over the last fourteen years, I have had many demands placed on me by chefs and restaurateurs. I learned to work hard, to be responsible, to work efficiently and neatly, to develop good technique, and to recognize tastes, textures, and temperatures and their subtle interplay in a dish. In my first few jobs as pastry chef, menu changes were stressful. I struggled to come up with perhaps one new menu selection every month. At Chanterelle, we change the menu, top to bottom, every four weeks. At the beginning of my time there I was somewhat tentative about conceiving and executing four desserts each month. But, over time, as I have fallen in love with the ingredients of the pastry kitchen over and over again, I have become passionate about the process of finding new ways to distill and intensify their flavors. Coming up with new desserts is no longer a burden, but rather has become both deeply satisfying and also somehow essential to how I think about my work.

My desserts are derived from my experiences with food throughout my life. What may seem like a complicated plated dessert is often a dressed-up version of a simple pleasure from my past. I cannot forget the rice pudding I had in India; I love to stroll through orchards at the peak of fall and pick and bite into a crunchy Macoun apple; I cannot get the scent of a ripening guava out of my head; I must watch and smell a golden quince as it cooks and transforms itself into an aromatic compote with a lustrous rose color. These sensual and gastronomic experiences drive my conception of a tart, cake, or crème.

What ultimately turns these passionate memories of tastes and textures into a menu of desserts are the frank realities I am faced with in the kitchen. How much oven space is there? What fruits are in season? Do I have enough molds and plates? What will this month's required chocolate dessert be? Is there a dessert on the menu without nuts for our patrons who are allergic? The constraints I deal with in the professional kitchen mirror those of the home cook, and that friction between creativity and constraint is one of the abiding themes of this book. Home cooks may not have the right pan, the right ingredient, the right oven, or the time to produce a plated dessert composed of multiple preparations, but I believe that the best work comes not from unbounded freedom but from the realistic boundaries we deal with every day. Rather than present "restaurant desserts" as an unreachable pinnacle accompanied by fancy pictures to be admired but not attempted, I guide you through detailed instructions and carefully thought-out methodology so you can find ways to make desserts you'll love to prepare, to serve, and to eat.

Another source of inspiration for this book is my increasing awareness of the role of the pastry chef as chemist and of the sensory tools we use to record data in the pastry kitchen. As a professional baker in a restaurant, I produce recipes on a daily basis. The process of following the same methods and techniques day in and day out forces me to pay attention to very small, subtle changes in my final product. I begin with a hypothesis—to produce a sauce, meringue, or soufflé, for example—my materials, and a procedure. I produce data (the finished sauce, meringue, or soufflé) and answer certain questions based on them. Why, for example, is one meringue less shiny, less satiny than the one made the day before? Why is one financier springier than the other? Why are these apple chips crunchier than yesterday's?

I love this process: every time I begin to make something that I have made before, I reconsider my data and try to make slight improvements. For example, I know how much I browned the butter for my vanilla cake, and I consider how it rose in the oven and felt on my tongue. The cake seemed a bit heavy. So the next time I make it, I will brown my butter a little bit less and note the final consistency of the cake. Making desserts on a daily basis is not about mindless repetition; it is about staying open to the smallest details, to what your five senses are telling you, to the possibility that even though you made it well the day before, it could be better today. I tell every student who comes to intern with me that you have to love the practice as much as the product; you have to view repetition as a source of inspiration and discovery, not of drudgery and boredom.

Alongside my recipes in this book I explain the chemical hows and whys of what is happening. With the help of Kirsten Hubbard, PhD, one of my culinary students and a burgeoning food scientist, I provide clear discussions on, for example, the science behind emulsification, crystallization, or gel formation. However, *The Sweet Life* is first and foremost about the desserts themselves—about great flavors and ideas—and then, only secondarily, I fill in the science to round out the experience.

Some of the recipes in *The Sweet Life* are simple—four ingredients, half an hour. Some are complex, encompassing several distinct preparations. None is a throwaway—I love each of the desserts that I present here. In some recipes, the instructions may seem lengthy, but they are not overwhelmingly complex; rather, they are explicit and detailed in terms of what you need to do and what you need to pay attention to.

I hope you enjoy making my desserts and that you make them often, so that you too can take pleasure in the process, building on past experiences, and seeing new subtleties in each step. I hope you try variations, experimenting with alternative flavors and with serving each dessert alongside different seasonal fruits, ice creams, and sauces. Mostly, of course, I hope you love eating them and sharing them with your family and friends.

A Note About Ingredients, Tools, Terms, and Procedures

Bain-Marie Noted in the "special tools and pots" section of numerous recipes, *bain-marie* is the French cooking term for a metal bowl or container that can sit over or in simmering water to keep the contents of the container or bowl hot—basically, a makeshift double boiler. Fill a pot large enough to hold a medium-sized mixing bowl on top with 1 inch of water and set over low heat. When the water is simmering, set the bowl on top of the pot. If you are using a bain-marie for a sabayon, simmer the water over medium-high heat.

Butter I use high-fat, European-style unsalted butter in all the recipes. Plugra is the most widely available brand, though any butter with more fat and less water content will work. You can substitute regular unsalted stick butter, but I find that the higher fat content of the European-style butters improves the final product.

Cream of Tartar I often call for a pinch of cream of tartar as a way of introducing acid into a recipe, but 1 teaspoon of lemon juice or ½ teaspoon of vinegar can easily be substituted.

Flour I use unbleached, all-purpose flour throughout the book.

Heavy Cream The recipes in this book were tested with 40 percent heavy cream, which is widely available, but you are more likely to find a 36 percent heavy cream in supermarkets, which will work fine.

Ice Bath I often recommend chilling a preparation over an ice bath. Select two medium-sized bowls, one slightly smaller than the other, and preferably metal. Fill one bowl with ice and water and rest the smaller bowl on top. Chill your custard, sorbet, sabayon, or curd in the smaller bowl, stirring every 5 minutes with a rubber spatula, until the mixture is the desired temperature.

Lids Often when you are making caramel, I instruct you to use a lid to cover the pot. You can use anything: a bowl, another pot, a baking pan. The lid doesn't have to "fit" the pot.

Nonstick Silicone Baking Pads Made of laminated sheets of rubberized food-grade silicone, these pads do not react with or flavor foods at temperatures ranging from −30 to 550°F. The pads are cleaned with a dry rag or, if they get greasy, with warm water. They are a bit expensive but well worth the price if you bake regularly, saving on parchment paper, aluminum foil, and extra cleaning materials.

Oven The recipes in this book were tested in a regular, non-convection oven; however, in some cases I recommend using a convection oven when it will improve the final product—cookies and soufflés among them. Whenever you use a convection oven, lower the temperature by 25 degrees and be prepared to test for doneness a few minutes before the time recommended in the recipe.

Pinch A pinch, as in a pinch of salt, is defined as less than ¼ teaspoon. So make it a small pinch, not a big one.

Reducing Maple Syrup When you begin boiling maple syrup to reduce it by half, it will foam up and rise. Once the foam boils off, you will see smaller, darker bubbles closer to the surface of the boiling syrup—it is at this point that you should begin testing the syrup for doneness.

To test the syrup, you can use a thermometer, removing the pot from heat when the syrup reaches 240°F. If you do not have a thermometer, drizzle some syrup on a cool, clean counter and let it cool for a minute. The droplet should scrape off the counter cleanly, though it will still be soft and malleable at this stage.

Room-Temperature Butter I recommend room-temperature butter (between 66° and 70°F) for all recipes that require the creaming of butter and in many recipes where butter is whisked into a finished custard. See the technique tip on creaming butter (page 67) to understand why this temperature range is so important. If room temperature is not specified in the recipe, use chilled butter.

Room-Temperature Eggs Throughout the book, I often call for room-temperature eggs. The easiest way to turn refrigerated eggs into room-temperature eggs is to place them in a bowl of warm water for a few minutes. If room temperature is not specified in the recipe, the temperature of the eggs before combining the ingredients is not crucial. See the sidebar on room-temperature eggs (page 53).

Sugar In all the recipes, I use granulated sugar unless I specify another kind, such as powdered, superfine, raw, or brown.

Testing Sugar at 248°F There are two common methods to determine whether the syrup has reached 248°F (also known as the "hard ball" stage):

Dip a fork in the boiling syrup and allow a few droplets to fall onto a clean, dry counter surface near the syrup. Let it cool for a minute and then examine the consistency. If the syrup is still sticky and gluey, it is not done; allow it to cook for another minute and retest.

If the droplet is rock hard, the temperature is too high. If the droplet is firm but malleable and easily scrapes off the counter with your fingernail, it is at the right temperature.

The second method gives quicker results. Have a little bowl of ice water near the boiling syrup and, as above, dip a fork into the syrup. Let the sugar droplets fall from the fork right into the ice water. Follow the same consistency guidelines I described above to determine if the sugar is at the right temperature.

Using a Blender to Puree Hot Liquid In many of the recipes in this book, particularly the sorbets, I instruct you to puree very hot liquid in a blender. As a safety precaution, place a damp kitchen towel over the top of the blender before you turn it on. Sometimes hot liquid comes flying out of the blender or pours over the sides and this simple precaution prevents burns and major cleanups.

Vanilla Beans Throughout my recipes I call for vanilla beans. Most of the time I indicate that you can substitute vanilla extract, but I prefer vanilla beans if you can find them. Read the section on vanilla on page 159 to understand how much use you can get out of one good vanilla bean.

CHAPTER ONE

Hazelnut Tart Shell

1 cup (5 ounces) hazelnuts

1½ cups plus 2 tablespoons flour

¼ teaspoon baking powder

¼ teaspoon salt

12 tablespoons (6 ounces) butter, at room temperature

½ cup plus 1 tablespoon sugar

2 egg yolks, at room temperature

SPECIAL TOOL AND PANS

Food processor

Stand mixer

8- or 9-inch fluted or straight-sided tart pan

Pie weights or dried beans

YIELD

Two 8- or 9-inch blind-baked tart shells

This tart crust is crispy, light, and full of hazelnut flavor. Use it for the chocolate tart, as I suggest, or with the lemon or passion-fruit tarts.

Grind the hazelnuts and prepare the dry ingredients. In a food processor, combine the hazelnuts and ¼ cup of the flour and grind to a fine powder. In a small bowl, whisk together the hazelnut mixture, the rest of the flour, the baking powder, and the salt.

Cream the butter and incorporate the eggs. *Follow the* TECHNIQUE TIP: *Creaming butter, page 67. See* BEYOND THE BASICS: *Room-temperature eggs, page 53.*

Place the butter in the bowl of the stand mixer with the paddle attachment and beat on medium speed for 1 minute. Add the sugar and beat on medium-high speed until the mixture becomes fluffy and almost white in color, approximately 6 to 8 minutes, stopping the mixer occasionally to scrape down the sides of the bowl. Add the egg yolks, one at a time, and continue to beat until they are fully incorporated and the batter looks smooth and glossy, 1 to 2 minutes.

Add the dry ingredients and finish the dough. Add the dry mixture, all at once, to the butter mixture. Use a rubber spatula and fold the dry mixture into the butter mixture with a few turns before turning on the mixer. Mix the dough at slow speed until thoroughly combined, 1 to 2 minutes. Stop the mixer, scrape down the sides of the bowl with a rubber spatula, and mix on slow speed for another 30 seconds.

Separate the dough into two mounds. Wrap each mound in plastic wrap and press down to form two 1-inch-thick disks. Transfer the dough to the refrigerator and chill for 2 hours or overnight.

Roll and blind-bake the tart dough. *Follow the* TECHNIQUE TIP: *Rolling tart dough, page 17.*

On a cool, dry counter surface, roll the dough into a ⅛-inch-thick circle. Line the tart pan with the dough and freeze the tart shell for ½ hour.

Preheat the oven to 350°F. Remove the shell from the freezer, line it with parchment paper, aluminum foil, or a large coffee filter, and fill it with pie weights or dried beans. Transfer the shell to the oven and bake for 30 minutes. Remove from the oven and let it sit for 10 minutes; take out the liner and weights and place the shell back in the oven. (You can save the beans to use as pie weights again.) Bake until it is golden brown, 10 to 15 minutes.

Storage
The dough, well wrapped, can be refrigerated for up to 4 days or frozen for up to 1 month. The baked shell, well wrapped, will keep for 2 days.

Sweet Tart Shell

This is a versatile, sweet, delicate, but crisp crust. The butter and sugar are creamed together for 8 minutes, which is very unusual. I find that the longer creaming time produces a more tender crust because you introduce a large number of air pockets into the fat. However, because there are so many air pockets that expand during baking, the finished tart shell will tend to be uneven and chip a bit. This can be quite maddening when you are after that perfect-looking tart, with each fluted curve holding its shape flawlessly, but the aerated, crunchy, cookie-like texture that this recipe and technique produce is worth the sacrifice of visual perfection.

Cream the butter and incorporate the eggs.

Follow the TECHNIQUE TIP: *Creaming butter, page 67. See* BEYOND THE BASICS: *Room-temperature eggs, page 53.*

Place the butter in the bowl of the stand mixer with the paddle attachment and beat on medium speed for 1 minute. Add the powdered sugar and lemon zest (if you are using it) and beat on medium-high speed until the mixture becomes fluffy and almost white in color, approximately 6 to 8 minutes, stopping the mixer occasionally to scrape down the sides of the bowl. Add the egg yolks, one at a time, and continue to beat until they are fully incorporated and the batter looks smooth and glossy, 1 to 2 minutes.

Add the dry ingredients and finish the dough.

In a small bowl, whisk together the dry ingredients and add them, all at once, to the butter mixture. Use a rubber spatula and fold the dry mixture into the butter mixture with a few turns before turning on the mixer. Mix the dough at slow speed until thoroughly combined, 1 to 2 minutes. Stop the mixer, scrape down the sides of the bowl with a rubber spatula, and mix on slow speed for another 30 seconds.

Separate the dough into two mounds. Wrap each mound in plastic wrap and press down to form two 1-inch-thick disks. Transfer the dough to the refrigerator and chill for 2 hours or overnight.

Roll and blind-bake the tart dough.

Follow the TECHNIQUE TIP: *Rolling tart dough, page 17.*

On a cool, dry counter surface, roll the dough into a 1/8-inch-thick circle. Line the tart pan with the dough and freeze the tart shell for 1/2 hour.

Preheat the oven to 350°F. Remove the shell from the freezer, line it with parchment paper, aluminum foil, or a large coffee filter, and fill it with pie weights or dried beans. Transfer the shell to the oven and bake for 30 minutes. Remove from the oven and let it sit for 10 minutes; take out the liner and weights and place the shell back in the oven. (You can save the beans to use as pie weights again.) Bake until it is golden brown, 10 to 15 minutes.

Storage

The dough, well wrapped, can be refrigerated for up to 4 days or frozen for up to 1 month. The baked shell, well wrapped, will keep for 2 days.

---

16 tablespoons (8 ounces) butter, at room temperature

1 1/3 cups powdered sugar

Zest of 1 lemon or tangerine (optional)

2 egg yolks, at room temperature

2 cups plus 2 tablespoons flour

1/4 teaspoon salt

SPECIAL TOOLS AND PANS

Stand mixer

8- or 9-inch fluted or straight-sided tart pan

Pie weights or dried beans

YIELD

Two 8- or 9-inch blind-baked tart shells

VARIATION

Vanilla-, Cardamom-, or Cinnamon-Scented Dough:
I suggest lemon or tangerine zest as an option to flavor this dough. You can also add the seeds of a vanilla bean or 1 teaspoon of ground cinnamon or cardamom.

Flaky Tart Shell

2 cups flour

1 teaspoon sugar

½ teaspoon salt

12 tablespoons (6 ounces) butter, chilled

SPECIAL TOOLS AND PANS

11½-inch tart pan, fluted or straight-sided, with a removable bottom

YIELD

One 11½-inch round tart shell

This dough is a cross between the traditional French pâte brisée (savory dough) and an American pie dough. It is wonderfully tender, flaky, and flavorful.

Make the dough.

In a stainless-steel mixing bowl, toss together the flour, sugar, and salt. Cut the cold butter into ¼-inch cubes and add it to the sugar and flour mixture. Using two knives or a pastry cutter, chop and toss the butter until pea-sized and coated with flour. Add 4 to 5 tablespoons of ice water and toss the mixture lightly with a fork. The dough will not come together at this point. It should still seem dry with a few moist clumps.

Empty the contents of the bowl onto a counter and, using the heel of your hand, smear the butter with the dry ingredients to marble the butter into the dough (this technique produces a very flaky, light crust). You might need to repeat this smearing and scraping process one or two times before the dough comes together. Once the dough is moist enough to form a ball, wrap it tightly in plastic wrap and press down to form a flattened disk of dough. Refrigerate the dough for 2 hours or up to 2 days.

Roll out the dough.

Follow the TECHNIQUE TIP: *Rolling tart dough, page 17.*

On a cool, dry counter surface, roll the dough into a 14-inch circle, $1/16$ inch thick. Line the tart pan with the dough and freeze while you prepare the filling.

Storage

The dough, well wrapped, can be refrigerated for up to 2 days or frozen for up to 2 weeks.

TECHNIQUE TIP
Rolling tart dough

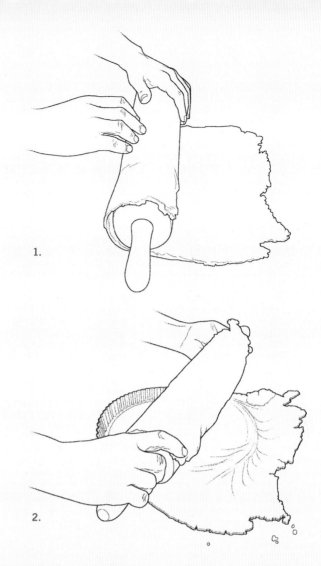

1.

2.

Rolling pins
I prefer to use a heavy rolling pin with two grip pins at either end (on ball bearings) so that the pin rolls independently of the grips. Another choice is a solid dowel, often referred to as a French pin, approximately 1½ inches in diameter, sometimes tapered at either end. This type of rolling pin requires more dexterity in your hands and is used primarily by those who roll out dough every day. It is, however, great for pounding cold butter and softening cold dough.

Rolling surface
My mother had a pastry cloth which I used as a kid. Pastry cloths were popular for two reasons: the heavy canvas material coated with flour is a good insulator and prevented the dough from absorbing the heat of the countertop; and it was neater—you didn't have to sprinkle flour all over your countertop.

As a professional, though, I could not imagine using my mother's cloth—it never seemed clean. At Chanterelle we roll dough directly on our stainless-steel countertops. You can roll directly on any countertop—butcher block, granite, oiled soapstone, Corian, marble, or vinyl-coated pressboard. If your kitchen is particularly hot, a chilled piece of marble maintains the dough beautifully, as does a large piece of wood.

Tools
Have a metal dough scraper, a wide metal spatula, or a thin metal ruler or metal yard stick at your side to release the dough from the rolling surface if it sticks. Lightly flour your rolling surface and your rolling pin and keep an extra cup of flour next to your workspace. Also keep a dry pastry brush available to dust off any excess flour from the dough.

Temperature of the dough
I generally like to roll slightly chilled dough because it is easier to work with when it is fully rolled out. Take your dough out of the refrigerator and let it sit for 5 to 10 minutes.

If it is still too hard to work with, let it warm up for another 15 minutes. If the dough cracks severely as you roll it out, pack it back together and allow it to warm up for another 10 minutes or so. However, avoid letting the dough become so warm that the butter melts—melted butter in tart dough can make your final product greasy and tough.

Rolling the dough
Flatten your circle of dough by banging it with your rolling pin. Once the dough is approximately ½ to ¾ inch thick, begin to roll it out, working from the center outward. Make sure you use enough flour to ensure that the dough does not stick to the rolling surface or the rolling pin. Once you have rolled the dough twice in each direction, run your spatula, ruler, or dough scraper under the dough to loosen and rotate it 90 degrees. Toss some flour under the dough to ensure that it does not stick to your rolling surface. Continue this

process of rolling, rotating, and tossing flour on the underside of the dough until the dough is ⅛ inch thick.

Transferring the dough from the rolling surface to the tart pan
When the dough is rolled out to the size needed, dust off any excess flour with a dry brush. The easiest way to pick up the dough in one piece without cracking or breaking it is to gently rest your rolling pin at one end of the dough and then slowly turn the pin, wrapping the dough around the pin as you turn it (**illustration 1**). Hold the rolling pin over the far rim of your tart shell and unroll the dough toward you, covering the entire tart pan with the sheet of dough (**illustration 2**). Press the dough into the pan. Trim excess dough with your thumb as you press it firmly into all crevices of the shell. If the dough cracks or tears just gently press it back together.

Meyer Lemon Curd Tart

One 8-inch Sweet Tart crust, page 15

6 egg yolks

1 egg

½ cup plus 4 tablespoons sugar

½ cup strained Meyer lemon juice (3 to 4 lemons)

Zest of 1 Meyer lemon

Pinch of salt

8 tablespoons (4 ounces) butter, at room temperature

SPECIAL TOOLS AND PANS

Bain-marie (see page 10)

A whisk, preferably a balloon whisk (the head of the whisk is more rounded than the long variety)

YIELD

One 8-inch tart, serves 8

INGREDIENT

Meyer lemons

Available from November to March, Meyer lemons have a smooth-skinned, deep matte yellow appearance. A cross between a lemon and an orange, the Meyer lemon is slightly sweeter (less acidic) than a regular lemon. The most distinctive feature of this hybrid is the zest, which has a flowery tangerine-like aroma and imparts incredibly round lemony flavor to sweet and savory foods.

Wonderfully creamy and brimming with the flowery, tangerine flavor of Meyer lemons, this lemon curd is an excellent filling for tarts or a delicious condiment for toast and sweet pastries. This curd has a very high proportion of egg yolks, which lends it an intense flavor and a smooth consistency. If you cannot find Meyer lemons you can easily substitute regular lemons. Try adding 1 tablespoon of tangerine zest to make up for the missing Meyer lemon flavor.

Although you only need the zest of 1 lemon in this recipe, do not throw away the precious rinds from the remaining Meyer lemons. Before you slice and juice the lemons, use a peeler to remove the zest. Julienne the zest into thin spaghetti-like strands and candy according to the recipe on page 198. Use the candied zest to garnish the tart or as an added note of flavor on mini fresh berry tarts filled with either lemon or passion-fruit curd.

Prepare and bake the Sweet Tart crust.

Make the lemon curd.
See BEYOND THE BASICS: *The unique consistency of citrus curds, page 20.*

In the bowl of a bain-marie, whisk together the egg yolks, whole egg, and sugar. Add the lemon juice, lemon zest, and salt. Whisk briskly until the mixture has thickened, doubled in volume, and holds the lines of a whisk, 5 to 10 minutes.

Remove the curd from the heat and pass through a fine-mesh strainer into a bowl. Discard the zest. Place the bowl in an ice bath and let cool until warm to the touch. Thoroughly whisk in the butter. At this point you can chill or bake the lemon curd.

Bake the lemon tart.
Preheat the oven to 325°F. Pour the lemon curd into the prepared tart shell. Place the tart on a cookie sheet and bake until the custard sets, 10 to 15 minutes. To test if the custard is set, gently tap the tart ring; if the center does not jiggle, the custard is set. If you have made the curd ahead of time and refrigerated it, the tart will need a few extra minutes in the oven to set.

Serving Suggestions
Serve the tart at room temperature. It is delicious on its own, but whipped cream or crème fraîche and a few raspberries or strawberries make great accompaniments. I also recommend the Spiced Mandarin Ice Cream (page 136), Basil Ice Cream (page 142), Guava Sorbet (page 152), or Pineapple-Rosemary Sorbet (page 146). You can also use the curd as a condiment or as a filling for mini tartlets, topped with fresh berries and candied zest.

Storage
The curd, well sealed and refrigerated, will keep for up to 1 week. The finished tart is best if served the day it is made but will keep, covered and refrigerated, for up to 3 days.

Meyer Lemon Curd Tart

The unique consistency of citrus curds

Mini passion-fruit tartlets with candied kumquats, currants, and berries (above and right)

Lemon curd, as well as all the other curds such as passion-fruit, lime, and berry curds made with lemon juice, has an utterly unique consistency. Unlike most milk- and wine-based custards, citrus curds are dense, creamy, and very tender, and maintain their texture even if spread with a knife. Curd achieves these unique textural properties through the interplay of its three main ingredients: low pH citrus juice, sugar, and egg yolks—the latter two in significantly higher proportions compared to other custards. As we will see in the custard chapter (page 83), which is really an extended riff on the science of egg proteins, custards achieve their creamy consistency through the process of egg proteins forming structures that hold liquid—in other words, forming gels.

Acid changes the chemical processes fairly dramatically by changing how proteins bond and thus gel. The addition of acid to eggs causes three principal simultaneous biochemical changes in the properties of the eggs: **(1)** the ions (positively and negatively charged molecules, of which there are millions upon millions) in solution from the acidic lemon juice break the chemical bonds in individual proteins, causing them to begin to denature or unwind from their ball-like shape; **(2)** additional ions of the same type neutralize the overall charge of the proteins, allowing the not fully denatured proteins to be more likely to interact and bond in solution; and **(3)** acid reduces the likelihood of the formation of disulfide bonds, a strong and rare bond in proteins, but one presumed to be more prevalent in eggs, thereby making acidic protein gels softer, more tender, and less structured. The net result of all three effects is to cause early protein interaction, or bonding, and at the same time to prevent full gelation during and after the addition of heat.

The other two aspects of citrus curds that are unique in comparison with other custards are the high percentage of egg yolks and sugar. The high percentage of egg yolks increases the proportion of egg yolk proteins in the custard, which helps give the curd a thicker, partially gelled tender texture. Also many proteins in egg yolks are lipoproteins; one end of the protein is bonded to an emulsifying fat molecule, one that connects to both water and fat molecules. These emulsifying lipoproteins play a major role in the curd's overall creamy texture as well.

The high percentage of sugar, added to balance the tartness of the citrus juice, has a more complex consequence. To begin with, the high proportion of sugar is dissolved in the added citrus juice, a proportionately small amount of water, which contributes to the finished curd's trademark density. Sugar also acts by interfering in protein-to-protein bonding, preventing full gelation.

One of the beneficial results of the added sugar is that sometimes, while you are cooking a lemon curd, it gets so hot that a bubble or two comes to the surface yet the custard remains smooth and glossy, not lumpy, watery, and broken. This characteristic makes it unlike almost all other custards, where boiling temperatures destroy the gel, ruining the dessert.

There's one thing you need to be careful about, though, in vigorously whisking lemon curd at boiling temperatures. Citrus curd can, if cooked for too long, develop a sandy consistency once it is cooled. This sandiness is due to sugar recrystallization (not, as in other custards, to overcooked eggs). If you whisk the curd over a high temperature for a long period of time, enough of the naturally present water evaporates so that the sugar, as the custard cools, recrystallizes onto itself. This happens because there is simply not enough water remaining for all of the sugar to stay dissolved in it.

Passion-Fruit Curd Tart

Passion-fruit puree or unsweetened juice makes a delicious curd. When I serve little passion-fruit tartlets on a petit four plate, people who are unfamiliar with the fruit often think they are eating the tastiest lemon curd they have ever had. And if you love passion-fruit as I do, this recipe is a guaranteed winner.

Prepare the Sweet Tart crust.

Make the passion-fruit custard.

See BEYOND THE BASICS: *The unique consistency of citrus curds, page 20.*

In the bowl of the bain-marie, whisk together the egg yolks, whole egg, and sugar. Using a paring knife, cut down the center of the vanilla bean and scrape out the tiny black seeds. Add the scraped vanilla bean (or vanilla extract), passion-fruit juice, and salt to the egg mixture. Whisk briskly until the mixture has thickened, doubled in volume, and holds the lines of a whisk, 5 to 10 minutes.

Remove the curd from the heat and pass through a fine-mesh strainer into a bowl. Discard the vanilla bean (or reserve for another time). Place the bowl in an ice bath and let cool until warm to the touch. Thoroughly whisk in the butter.

Bake the passion-fruit tart.

Preheat the oven to 325°F. Pour the passion-fruit curd into the prepared tart shell. Place the tart on a cookie sheet and bake until the custard sets, 10 to 15 minutes. To test if the custard is set, gently tap the tart ring; if the center does not jiggle, the custard is set. If you have made the curd ahead of time and refrigerated it, the tart will need a few extra minutes in the oven to set.

Serving Suggestions

Serve the tart at room temperature. It is delicious on its own, but whipped cream or crème fraîche and a few raspberries or strawberries make great accompaniments. I also recommend the Basil Ice Cream (page 142), Guava Sorbet (page 152), or Pineapple-Rosemary Sorbet (page 146). You can also use the curd as a filling for mini tartlets, topped with fresh berries and candied zest.

Storage

The curd, well sealed and refrigerated, will keep for up to 1 week. The finished tart is best if served the day it is made but will keep, covered and refrigerated, for up to 3 days.

One 8-inch Sweet Tart crust, page 15

6 egg yolks

1 egg

½ cup minus 1 tablespoon sugar

½ vanilla bean or ½ teaspoon vanilla extract

½ cup passion-fruit juice

8 tablespoons (4 ounces) butter, at room temperature

Pinch of salt

SPECIAL TOOLS AND PANS

Bain-marie (see page 10)

A whisk, preferably a balloon whisk (the head of the whisk is more rounded than the long variety)

YIELD

One 8-inch tart, serves 8

Apple and Quince Tart

Apple and Quince Tart

Cubed quince simmered with sugar and butter develops the most round, earthy fruit flavor and a very soft, tender, but shapely texture—it begs to be the center of a warm tart or Charlotte. The wonderful combination of tender apple slices and warm, robust quince in a crisp, light, flaky, savory crust makes this a delicious fall tart.

Prepare and freeze the Flaky Tart crust.

2 hours ahead of time: Cook the quince.
Peel, core, and chop the quince into ⅓-inch pieces. Combine the chopped quince, 4 tablespoons of the butter, and ½ cup of the sugar in a heavy-bottomed medium-sized saucepan and over medium heat. Cover and cook for 20 minutes, stirring every 3 to 5 minutes to make sure that it is not sticking to the bottom. Uncover, turn the heat down to low, and cook until all of the liquid is evaporated and the quince is tender and darkened in color, 40 minutes. Remove the quince from the heat and allow it to cool to room temperature. The quince can be made up to this point and refrigerated for up to 2 days.

Layer the apples and finish the tart.
Follow the TECHNIQUE TIP: *Browning butter, page 51.*

Preheat the oven to 375°F. Adjust the rack to the bottom third of the oven. Peel, core, and quarter the apples. Using a mandoline or very sharp knife, slice the apples as thin as possible and set aside.

Remove the Flaky Tart shell from the freezer. Scrape the cooled quince into the shell and distribute it evenly on the bottom. Begin layering the apples over the quince around the outermost edge of the tart with about ⅕ of the apple hanging over the rim of dough. Each slice should overlap the preceding slice by half. Once you have made a full circle of apples around the outer edge, begin a new circle closer to the center, overlapping the outer circle with about ¼ of the apple slice. Continue layering until you have made a small central circle in the middle of the tart.

In a small frying pan or saucepan, brown the remaining 4 tablespoons of butter. Gently drizzle the browned butter over the apples and sprinkle the remaining ¼ cup of sugar on top.

Bake the tart.
Follow the TECHNIQUE TIP: *Black steel baking pans, page 69.*

Because you are baking a fruit tart in which the crust has not been prebaked, place the tart on a black steel metal cookie sheet or aluminum cookie tray to help conduct heat toward the bottom of the tart. Place the tart in the oven and bake for 70 minutes. Turn the oven down to 350°F and bake until the apples have caramelized, the filling is bubbling, and the crust has browned, 20 minutes. Allow the tart to cool for ½ hour on a wire rack before removing the metal ring.

Serving Suggestions
Serve this tart warm with vanilla ice cream or crème fraîche.

Storage
This tart is best if served the day it is made but will keep overnight, in a cool, dark place, covered but not sealed in plastic wrap.

One recipe of Flaky Tart dough (page 16)

3 large (30 ounces) quince

8 tablespoons (4 ounces) butter

¾ cup sugar

4 medium (1¾ pounds) apples, somewhat tart

SPECIAL TOOLS AND PANS

11½-inch tart pan, fluted or straight-sided, with a removable bottom

Mandoline (optional)

Black steel or aluminum cookie sheet

YIELD

One 11½-inch tart, serves 10 to 12

Fresh Huckleberry and Fig Tart

1 recipe Sweet Tart dough, page 15

7 to 8 ounces puff pastry

2 cups (11 ounces) fresh or frozen huckleberries

8 large (12 ounces) fresh figs

2 tablespoons flour

5 tablespoons sugar

2 tablespoons unseasoned bread crumbs

2 tablespoons (1 ounce) butter

SPECIAL TOOLS AND POTS

11½-inch tart pan, fluted or straight-sided, with a removable bottom

Baking sheet

YIELD

One 11½-inch tart, serves 10 to 12

Wild huckleberries—tart, earthy, and packed with flavor—marry perfectly with figs—light in density, sweet, crunchy, and mellow. This combination, complemented by a sweet, crisp shell and a crunchy puff pastry lattice, makes a truly special dessert. If fresh huckleberries are not available, you can replace them with frozen ones or use raspberries, blackberries, or wild blueberries (though not cultivated ones) which all work beautifully with the figs. If you do not have time to prepare and weave the lattice top, you can skip this step and the tart will still be delicious.

Prepare the Sweet Tart crust.

Follow the TECHNIQUE TIP: *Rolling tart dough, page 17.*

Make the Sweet Tart dough and line the tart pan according to the instructions on page 17. Do not bake. Transfer the unbaked shell to the freezer to chill for at least 20 minutes while you prepare the filling and roll out the puff pastry lattice.

Prepare the puff pastry lattice.

If you cannot find puff pastry in the store, use leftover scraps from the Sweet Tart dough. Make a ball out of the dough scraps and chill. Roll out the scrap dough or the fresh puff pastry into a 12 x 9-inch rectangle, ⅛ inch thick. Transfer the dough to a wax-paper-lined baking sheet and place in the refrigerator to chill for 15 minutes. Remove the chilled dough and, while still on the tray, cut sixteen ½ x 11-inch strips of dough. Place the tray of dough back in the refrigerator to chill until you are ready to weave the top of the tart.

Prepare the filling.

Preheat the oven to 375°F. Position the rack on the bottom shelf of the oven. If you are using frozen huckleberries, defrost by spreading the berries out on paper towels (this will eliminate excess water condensation from the freezer). Cut the hard stems off the tops of the figs and quarter the figs. (If you are using large figs, cut them into ⅛-inch pieces.) Combine the sliced figs and the huckleberries in a stainless-steel mixing bowl. Toss the flour and 3 tablespoons of the sugar over the top of the fruit and gently mix with a metal spoon until incorporated.

Remove the tart shell from the freezer. Sprinkle the bread crumbs in an even layer on the bottom of the tart. Place the fruit mixture over the bread crumbs and gently pack down the fruit. Cut the butter up into 8 pieces and evenly disperse over the fruit.

Weave the lattice topping.

Remove the lattice strips from the refrigerator. Place 8 strips, equally spaced, vertically on the tart. Gently fold every other strip back on itself halfway (**illustration 1**). Lay one strip down horizontally at the fold (**illustration 2**). Unfold the 4 strips over the horizontal piece; fold back the other 4 strips halfway and lay down another horizontal piece at the fold. Repeat this process two more times to complete one half of the lattice (**illustration 3**). Rotate the tart 180 degrees and repeat the weaving process on the other half. Carefully trim away any strips that hang over the side of the tart. With a pastry brush, gently coat the lattice with a thin layer of water and sprinkle the remaining 2 tablespoons of sugar on top. Transfer to the freezer and chill for 10 minutes before baking.

1.

2.

3.

Individual Fresh Huckleberry and Fig Tart

Bake the tart.
Bake the tart for 50 minutes, rotating the pan once during this period. After 50 minutes, turn down the heat to 350°F and bake until the fruit filling is bubbling, the rim of the crust is dark brown, and the lattice has taken on a nice golden to dark brown color, 15 to 30 minutes. Allow the tart to cool for ½ hour on a wire rack before removing the metal ring.

Serving Suggestions
Serve this tart slightly warm with vanilla ice cream. I particularly recommend accompanying this dessert with the Fig Leaf Ice Cream (page 142).

Storage
This tart is best if served the day it is made.

Fresh Apricot and Almond Tart

1 recipe Sweet Tart dough, page 15

8 tablespoons (4 ounces) butter

¼ cup (2 ounces) almond paste

¾ cup sugar

2 eggs

¼ cup flour

¼ teaspoon salt

1 cup crème fraîche

1 cup (approximately 4 ounces) chopped blanched almonds

7 to 8 (1¼ pounds) medium fresh apricots, pitted and sliced

SPECIAL TOOLS AND POTS

11½-inch tart pan, fluted or straight-sided, with a removable bottom

Aluminum foil

YIELD

One 11½-inch tart, serves 10 to 12

VARIATION

Plum and Almond Tart: This tart also works beautifully with fresh plums. Substitute the same amount of plums for apricots.

This tart filling combines three of my favorite ingredients: brown butter, crème fraîche, and almond paste. Together with a few eggs, sugar, and flour, these flavors make a perfect backdrop for summer apricots or plums. Try to use good sweet apricots or plums at the peak of season.

Prepare the Sweet Tart shell.
Prepare the Sweet Tart dough according to the instructions on page 15. Line the tart pan with the dough, place the weights inside, and bake for 30 minutes. Remove from the oven; take out the pie weights and the liner. Wrap a large piece of aluminum foil around the outside of the tart pan so that it comes up the outer sides of the pan and drapes over the browned edge of the shell. Pinch the foil around the edge so that it is covered (this will prevent the rim of the tart from over-browning). Return the tart to the oven and bake until the center of the shell has browned, about 15 to 20 minutes. Remove from the oven and allow it to cool, leaving the outer aluminum foil cover in place.

Make the brown butter and almond custard.
Follow the TECHNIQUE TIP: *Browning butter, page 51.*

In a small frying pan, brown the butter over medium-high heat until it carmelizes and emits a nutty aroma. Remove from heat.

In the bowl of a stand mixer fitted with the paddle attachment, place the almond paste, sugar, and eggs and beat on medium-high speed until the mixture is thoroughly combined. Turn down to a slow speed and add the flour and salt to the almond mixture. Turn the mixture back up to medium speed and slowly drizzle in the brown butter. (The butter will emulsify into the almond cream, leaving the mixture smooth, creamy, and shiny.) Once all the butter has been incorporated, add the crème fraîche and continue mixing on slow speed until thoroughly combined. Scrape down the sides of the bowl and set the custard aside.

Assemble and bake the tart.
Preheat the oven to 350°F. Position the rack in the center of the oven. Cover the bottom of the prebaked tart shell with the chopped almonds and pour the custard on top. Press the sliced apricots into the custard. Bake until the custard puffs a bit and browns, 30 to 40 minutes. Allow the tart to cool for ½ hour on a wire rack before removing it from the metal tart ring.

Serving Suggestions
Serve this tart slightly warm or at room temperature. This tart needs no accompaniment. It is crispy, creamy, tart, and sweet.

Storage
This tart is best if served the day it is made. If you need to plan ahead, the custard and the tart shell can be made and stored separately 2 days in advance.

Chocolate Caramel Tart

Chocolate Caramel Tart

This is a chocolate tart for fans of intense chocolate flavor. Paradoxically, I achieve this flavor by diluting the chocolate with caramel, which actually intensifies and darkens the flavor of the chocolate while adding a silky, smooth texture that chocolate on its own cannot match. So if you don't tell your guests about the caramel, they'll just say that this is the most decadently chocolatey dessert they've ever had. (*See* INGREDIENT: *A little history of chocolate and chocolate labels, page 31*).

I recommend the Hazelnut crust (page 14) for this recipe, but the Sweet Tart crust (page 15) works well also. The filling is the centerpiece of this dessert, so make a crust that you are comfortable with.

Prepare and bake the Sweet Tart or Hazelnut crust.

Make the caramel cream.
See BEYOND THE BASICS: *Cooking caramel successfully, page 107.*

Preheat oven to 325°F. In a medium-sized heavy-bottomed saucepan, combine the sugar, ¼ cup water, and a pinch of cream of tartar or a drop of lemon juice. Cover and bring to a rapid boil over medium-high heat. Boil for 1 minute, uncover, and continue to cook until the sugar caramelizes and becomes a deep, golden brown. Remove the pan from the heat and carefully add the cream (the mixture will bubble and steam furiously). When the bubbling has subsided, return the pan to the heat and whisk the mixture until it comes to a rolling boil. Remove from the heat and let cool for 5 minutes.

Emulsify the chocolate with the caramel cream and the eggs.
In the bowl of a bain-marie, combine the chocolate and butter and stir occasionally with a rubber spatula until melted, about 10 minutes. The subtle texture and flavor of this custard rely on keeping the chocolate mixture from becoming too hot. Test the chocolate mixture with your finger as it melts in the bain-marie; if it hurts your finger, the chocolate is too hot. While the chocolate is melting, combine the egg yolks and whole egg in a metal bowl and whisk

vigorously until they lighten in color a bit, 1 to 2 minutes. Slowly add the caramel cream to the eggs, whisking constantly until completely incorporated. Slowly add the chocolate mixture to the caramel mixture, whisking continuously. The batter should be shiny and smooth, and hold the lines of the whisk.

Bake the tart.
Pour the filling into the prepared tart shell and bake on a cookie tray until the top is shiny and smooth and the center is set, about 30 minutes. To test if the custard is done, gently touch the surface toward the center of the tart. If the custard is still partially liquid and it glazes your finger, bake for an additional 5 minutes. Do not let the filling rise; if it begins to rise, you will end up with a denser tart. Allow the tart to cool for ½ hour on a wire rack before removing it from the metal tart ring.

Serving Suggestions
This tart tastes best served at room temperature or slightly warm. It can be served with a dollop of whipped cream or vanilla ice cream. I also recommend the Espresso Ice Cream (page 138) or the Cinnamon Caramel Mousse (page 106).

Storage
This tart is best if served the day it is made but will keep, covered and refrigerated, for up to 4 days.

---

1 cup sugar

Pinch of cream of tartar

1 cup heavy cream

6 ounces bittersweet to semisweet chocolate (61 to 70 percent cocoa solids)

8 tablespoons (4 ounces) butter

5 egg yolks

1 egg

¼ teaspoon salt

One 9-inch Sweet Tart crust (page 15) or Hazelnut crust (page 14)

SPECIAL TOOLS AND PANS

Bain-marie (see page 10)

9-inch fluted or straight-sided tart pan

YIELD

One 9-inch tart, serves 8 to 10

Cacao pod growing on a cacao tree

A little history of chocolate and chocolate labels

Cacao Trees

The cacao tree grows in tropical climates along the equator all over the world. There are historically three commonly known types of cacao trees: *criollo*, *forastero*, and *trinitario*. The *criollo* trees are a very small percentage of the trees grown in the world; they produce a superior, mellow, rich bean with fruity high notes. This cacao tree is susceptible to numerous diseases and is a challenge to grow. The second type, *forastero*, is a very hardy, reliable tree that produces 90 percent or more of the world's cocoa beans. These beans bear the flavor the average chocolate eater associates with most commercial chocolate. The *trinitario* is a hybrid of the other two, a hardier tree with a rich, fine, fruity-flavored bean. It produces less than 5 percent of the world's cocoa beans. Today, each of these traditionally named types of trees has numerous varieties and strains, some of which have new names or twists on the old.

Harvesting Cacao Beans

A cacao blossom, once successfully pollinated, takes about five to six months to become a mature fruit—a football- to oval-shaped squashlike pod with ridged skin, whose color varies wildly. Workers on the cacao plantations harvest the pods, crack them open, and pull out the sticky white fruit pulp that surrounds the beans. Ideally the farmer will allow the sweet white fruit pulp to ferment in lightly covered vessels until the pulp breaks down and bacteria-producing acid becomes rampant, leading to the death of the beans. Enzymatic reactions continue after the death of the beans, leaving a completely chemically transformed bean, in both flavor and appearance. Unfortunately, cacao pulp is sometimes not fermented at all, and when it is, the fermentation process is often randomly managed and poorly judged. The beans—well fermented, semifermented, and unfermented—are dried using various methods (some better for flavor development than others), including artificial heat, sun, and fire, and then examined for moisture content, bean texture, and color by cocoa-bean brokers who buy, rate, and distribute these dried beans.

Processing Cacao Beans

Once the beans arrive in chocolate factories they are roasted and then crushed by machine. The crushing process fragments the beans and separates the dry husk from the *nibs*, a term used to describe the edible ground pieces of a roasted cacao bean. The nibs are then pulverized into *chocolate liquor*, the chocolate mass derived from the beans, containing both the naturally present *cocoa butter* and the *nonfat cocoa solids*.

At this point, flavoring is added to the chocolate liquor: sugar, vanilla, and powdered milk in the case of milk chocolate. This paste is passed between huge steel rollers that refine the mixture and reduce its particle size. The last process the mixture undergoes is called *conching*, named for a method and machine invented by Rodolphe Lindt. Having developed through the years with the advance of technology, today's conching machine heats, kneads, and agitates the refined chocolate mixture until it is transformed into chocolate— the rich dark, mellow, smooth viscous liquid that we all know and love. During the conching process, chocolate producers adjust the composition with added cocoa butter and lecithin, an emulsifier. The chocolate is then cooled and hardened into bars or small round coins, packaged, and shipped.

Chocolate Products

There are a number of terms used to describe various chocolate products on the market. What follows is a list of these terms, simple definitions, and some clarifications necessary to clear up some marketing misconceptions.

CHOCOLATE NIBS—Nibs are crunchy, earthy, chopped-up bits of roasted cacao beans without any added sweeteners, flavorings, or processes. They are very popular among chefs today to add a crunch to the top of a chocolate dessert, confection, or bonbon or to add a crunchy, bitter chocolate note to a sweeter, creamier preparation.

CHOCOLATE LIQUOR—This is the chocolate mass sometimes referred to as baking chocolate or bitter chocolate, produced by grinding the cocoa nibs.

99 PERCENT CHOCOLATE, UNSWEETENED CHOCOLATE—For some chocolate manufacturers, this chocolate differs from chocolate liquor because it has been conched, which adds a depth of flavor.

NATURAL COCOA POWDER—When chocolate liquor is compressed and squeezed at very high pressure, most of the cocoa butter melts off and you are left with cocoa powder with a light brown or tannish color. Cocoa powder still contains between 10 and 12 percent cocoa butter.

ALKALIZED COCOA POWDER—As a result of the fermentation process or lack of fermentation process, cocoa powder is naturally somewhat to very acidic. Often chocolate manufacturers treat cocoa powder with a mild alkali, such as potassium carbonate, to remove some of its acidic qualities. This process of making the cocoa powder more basic was invented by the Dutch and is often referred to as *Dutch processed cocoa powder*. Alkalization yields a darker, reddish-brown cocoa powder with a less acidic flavor. Some chocolate makers claim that "Dutching" the cocoa removes some of the more subtle flavors in chocolate.

COCOA BUTTER—Cocoa butter is the fat that exists naturally in cocoa beans. The cocoa bean is made up of approximately 54 percent cocoa butter and 46 percent nonfat cocoa solid, depending on the origin of the bean and type of tree. Cocoa butter is extracted during cocoa powder production. In most cases, after the extraction process, cocoa butter is filtered and deodorized to remove any cocoa

Cacao pods on a cacao farm

flavors, producing a uniform cocoa fat product. At room temperature it has a yellowish and opaque color, and it maintains an extremely hard and brittle consistency because it is high in saturated fatty acids. Unlike other saturated fats that are solid at room temperature and contain a broad mix of triglycerides with various melting points, cocoa butter contains a few types of triglycerides that have very similar melting points, just below body temperature. When cocoa butter approaches approximately 96°F it melts precipitously, providing the melt-in-your-mouth sensation of chocolate. Cocoa butter is highly sought after and valued in the cosmetic industry, and chocolate processors, in search of profit, often sacrifice this essential fat and sell it.

BITTERSWEET DARK CHOCOLATE—Bittersweet chocolate and semisweet dark chocolate differ from unsweetened chocolate in that they are always conched and contain varying amounts of sugar and, potentially, added cocoa butter. In the United States chocolate must contain a minimum of 36 percent chocolate liquor to be labeled as bittersweet or semisweet chocolate, and it may also contain small amounts of flavoring and emulsifiers.

CHOCOLATE COUVERTURE—Many European manufacturers make various chocolates that are labeled as *chocolat couverture*, a Swiss

French term often translated to English as "chocolate coating." The use of the word "coating" is misleading for American chocolate consumers. Couverture chocolate has a relatively high proportion of cocoa mass (cocoa solids and cocoa butter) to sugar. As a consequence, this type of chocolate is more easily used for coating and enrobing confections than are chocolates with higher percentages of sugar. For almost all the recipes in this book, I recommend couverture chocolate, with its higher percentage of cocoa solids and lower sugar content, because it has great flavor, a sharp snap as you bite into it, and a wonderful melt-in-your-mouth sensation.

MILK CHOCOLATE—In America, milk chocolate must have a minimum of 10 percent chocolate liquor. Milk solids, sugar, cocoa butter, flavoring, and lecithin are also added to create the flavor we associate with milk chocolate. Some chocolate makers label milk chocolate as they do with bittersweet couverture. Valrhona's Jivara milk chocolate is labeled as 41 percent. This means that the cocoa solids and the added cocoa butter make up 41 percent of the ingredients.

WHITE CHOCOLATE—White chocolate is made with cocoa butter, vanilla, sugar, and milk solids, and sometimes other fats are added as well.

CHOCOLATE COATING OR CONFECTIONARY GLAZE—This substance looks like chocolate but contains a minimum amount of cocoa solids and little to no cocoa butter. Chocolate glaze contains other saturated fats (most commonly palm kernel oil) that mimic the lower-temperature properties of cocoa butter but can be melted at higher temperatures and can set without tempering (see the section on tempering on page 187). Chocolate coating is used by many bakeries, restaurants, and cookie and candy manufacturers because it is easier to work with and cheaper than using couverture chocolate. Chocolate glaze is often called confectionary coating because a

product labeled as "chocolate," even though it may contain cocoa solids, must, in America, contain cocoa butter as its only fat.

Gourmet Chocolate Labels
The boom in high-quality chocolate in the last decade has produced a wealth of terminology, used to label and identify chocolates' origins, types, and styles. It is important to understand these terms in order to distinguish between marketing labels designed to increase a sense of value and terminology that tells you something useful about the quality of the chocolate. You will notice that many of the terms are similar to those used in the wine industry. Chocolate, like wine, comes from a fruit and undergoes fermentation and then multiple ripening processes (drying, roasting, and conching) that further develop its flavor and character.

Today chocolate production has attracted artisan chocolate makers who take an intense interest in how cacao is grown, harvested, fermented, dried, roasted, and processed. They have coined the following terms in hopes of giving the consumer more information about the care and effort behind the choice and origin of a particular cacao bean, its fermentation process, and the formula for a particular bittersweet or semisweet chocolate.

VARIETAL CHOCOLATE describes a particular type of cocoa tree: *criollo, forastero, trinitario*. There are numerous varieties within each of these types of beans. For example, *porcelana* (often touted as a superior varietal) is a type of *criollo* from Venezuela; *arriba*, a type of *forastero*, is prized and commonly grown in Ecuador.

ESTATE CHOCOLATE comes from cocoa beans grown on a single plantation, farm, or estate. The provenance is also very important to artisan chocolate makers because the care taken by workers at a given plantation or farm in growing, harvesting, and fermenting the beans from a specific genetic group of trees can be an integral element in good chocolate. A good example of a famous label that denotes high-quality beans from a small area of cooperative farms is Chuao, a small Venezuelan coastal plantation.

SINGLE-ORIGIN CHOCOLATE comes from cocoa beans grown in a single region; for example, various parts of Venezuela, Hawaii, Ecuador, Ghana, Trinidad, Santo Domingo, Madagascar, and so forth. You see this type of labeling on Pralus and Debauve & Gallais chocolates.

GRAND CRU CHOCOLATE, a term that mimics wine terminology, was coined by the French chocolate maker Valrhona to identify a line of chocolate made from a blend of select cacao beans from specific regions and estates. For example, Grand Cru Guanaja 70% (Valrhona) is made from *criollo* and *trinitario* beans from South America and contains 70 percent cocoa solids. Amedei, an Italian chocolatier, makes a sample box of Grand Cru chocolates, each bar composed of a special blend from particular estates in certain regions. These special blends are chosen and mixed by the resident chocolate maker of a chocolate company.

SIMPLE PERCENTAGES, SUCH AS 72%, 80%, 66%, explain what percentage of the chocolate bar is made up of cocoa mass (nonfat cocoa solids and cocoa butter). The remaining amount— 28 percent, 20 percent, or 34 percent, respectively—refers to the amount of added sugar. Most chocolate makers add a small amount of extra cocoa butter (more than what is naturally present in the chocolate liquor) to their chocolate in order to achieve a desired consistency. The percentages listed on the labels do not tell you how much cocoa butter there is in relation to cocoa solids.

Some companies such as Scharffen Berger simply describe the chocolate as bittersweet or semisweet with the percentage following. Although Scharffen Berger chooses not to label its chocolate Grand Cru, the company blends various types of beans from regions and select growers all along the equator to make chocolate with distinct flavor characteristics that the chocolate maker desires.

ORGANIC CHOCOLATE is a label of uncertain usefulness. In practice, 80 percent of cocoa beans from around the equator are grown organically, that is, without costly pesticides, on small, Third World, economically challenged farms with diverse flora and fauna. Yet most chocolates are not labeled as "organic." How these beans are transported, processed, and overseen ultimately determines their organic status and whether the term can be used in marketing the final product.

Organic certification of cocoa beans— and, thus, chocolate—differs from one international organization to another, each independently and without coordination of the overseas growing, harvesting, and transportation practices in almost thirty nations worldwide. Some organic labels simply verify that cacao is grown and processed without pesticides, while others indicate land sustainability, support for native communities, and job sustainability in the Third World.

Simply put, the term "organic" can indicate such a wide variety of provenances and processes that it does not in any way guarantee that you're getting quality chocolate grown in an environmentally friendly way.

Ultimately, good chocolate begins with well-maintained trees whose beans are harvested, well fermented, and dried with great concentration and care. In the process, these beans undergo multiple ripening processes controlled by expert chocolate makers who not only master the complexities of the numerous machines that roast, chop, blend, compress, and conch, but also continually taste and select cacao beans from around the world. Whether or not the beans are "organic," the care taken in processing is what's most important. The bottom line for you as a consumer, then, is that you should taste what you buy.

What Chocolate Should You Use for Baking?

I bake with good-quality couverture chocolate. Most of the dark chocolate I use has a minimum of 60 percent cocoa solids and a maximum of 72 percent, except when I recommend the addition of unsweetened chocolate, which is generally 99 to 100 percent cocoa solids.

The best way to select a chocolate is to sit down and taste a few bars from different chocolate makers. Decide what flavors and qualities you like or dislike. Scharffen Berger, Valrhona, Pralus, and Cluizel are some of my favorites. Also consider some bars of Lindt, Callebaut, and Guittard.

CAKES

CHAPTER TWO

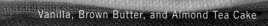
Vanilla, Brown Butter, and Almond Tea Cake

Vanilla, Brown Butter, and Almond Tea Cake

This cake is technically a financier, a dense, chewy, buttery, yet crispy almond flour cake traditionally served as a petit four. My version of this classic dessert adds a technique that utterly transforms it: I infuse the trademark brown butter with a whole vanilla bean; the alchemy of the butter and the vanilla creates an aromatic and flavor powerhouse.

The way I conceive plated desserts at Chanterelle is to take a technique or recipe I am passionate about and enhance it with complementary textures, temperatures, and flavors. For example, one of the best-loved desserts at the restaurant uses this cake. I serve it individually with vanilla custard in the center, with a crispy cookie on the bottom, and garnished with seasonal fruit (see photo on page 163). The combination of the rich, buttery cake, redolent with vanilla, and the warm custard center creates an intense mixture of flavors and consistencies. That said, this cake is perfectly delicious without being dressed up, and if you have any left over from dessert you will eat it for breakfast the rest of the week.

Preheat the oven to 350°F and position the rack in the center of the oven. Butter or oil a 10-inch pan.

Grind the almonds.
Combine the almonds and 1 tablespoon of the flour in a food processor and grind to a fine powder. Set aside.

Brown the butter.
Follow the TECHNIQUE TIP: *Browning butter, page 51.* See BEYOND THE BASICS: *Infusing butter with vanilla, page 38.*

Using a paring knife, cut down the center of the vanilla bean and scrape out the tiny black seeds into a medium-sized saucepan set over medium-high heat. Add the vanilla bean and the butter and cook until the mixture caramelizes and emits a rich nutty vanilla aroma. Remove it from the heat, take out the vanilla bean, dry it, and save it for another use.

Dissolve the sugar in the egg whites.
In the bowl of a bain-marie, whisk together the egg whites and the two sugars until the whites become warm to the touch and the granulated sugar has dissolved. Remove the bowl from the heat.

Add the dry ingredients.
Slowly whisk the remaining ½ cup flour, ground almonds, and salt into the egg whites. The mixture will become thick. Smooth it out with a few turns of the whisk.

Emulsify the brown butter.
Using a ladle, add approximately ¼ cup of the vanilla brown butter to the egg mixture and whisk until incorporated. Repeat this process until you have added all the butter. (This process is very important. If you add the butter too quickly, the mixture will not emulsify and the butter will melt out of the cake when baked, making it greasy and heavy.) The batter can be made up to this point and stored in the refrigerator for up to 4 days.

1 cup (5 ounces) blanched almonds

½ cup plus 1 tablespoon flour

1 vanilla bean

16 tablespoons (8 ounces) butter

7 egg whites (approximately 7 liquid ounces)

1 cup powdered sugar

½ cup granulated sugar

½ teaspoon salt

SPECIAL TOOLS AND PANS

Food processor

10-inch fluted tart pan or round cake pan or springform pan

Bain-marie (see page 10)

YIELD

One 10-inch round tea cake, serves 12

Cinnamon, Star Anise, Cardamom, Pepper, Clove, or Allspice Brown Butter and Almond Cake:
Infuse other flavors into this cake by adding spices such as a cinnamon stick to the browning butter. (Amounts required: cinnamon—3 sticks, cardamom—12 crushed pods, ginger (chopped)—3 ounces.)

Petit Brown Butter Almond Tea Cakes with Fresh Berries:
This cake can also be baked in mini muffin tins or small petit fours tart molds to make individual tea cakes. Fill the molds half full with the cake batter. Press a fresh berry or two to each mini cake and bake until deep golden and slightly springy, 25 minutes.

Bake the tea cake.
Pour the batter into the prepared pan and bake until the cake is a deep golden brown and the center springs back when you touch it or a tester inserted in the middle comes out clean, 50 to 55 minutes. (The cake is very dense, and will not rise more than 2 inches.)

Serving Suggestions
This cake is best served warm. I usually garnish it with powdered sugar and sliced almonds, but any fresh seasonal fruit is a wonderful accompaniment, as are most of the fruit compote recipes in this book.

Storage
The cake can be stored at room temperature, well wrapped, for 1 week.

BEYOND THE BASICS
Infusing butter with vanilla

Many of my recipes call for infusing butter with vanilla or other flavors during the browning process. Through repeated experimentation I have found that browning butter with a vanilla bean brings out a depth of vanilla flavor that cannot be achieved by simply adding vanilla bean seeds to raw batter. There are three main factors in this process:

First, the subtlety and richness of flavor have more to do with the aroma than the actual taste. The tongue can only perceive a limited number of flavors (though depending on whom you ask, it is probably more than the traditional four tastes—sweet, sour, salty, and bitter—that we were taught in school). The nose, however, can detect a vast range of distinct aromas. Butter infusions deepen flavor because butter is chemically composed of short fatty acid chains that, when heated, can unbind and float free, resulting in tiny volatile molecules that are easily picked up by your nose; therefore you perceive the smell as flavor.

Second, the compounds in vanilla beans are more soluble in fats than in water, so the flavors are more readily conveyed to a batter by infusing them in a pure fat than by trying to infuse them into a finished batter, which contains a high percentage of nonfat liquids, mostly water.

Third, butter contains a great number of flavor compounds and precursors that are essentially undeveloped. Heating develops these flavors, increasing the proportion of flavor chemicals to a detectable level. A part of what we perceive as deepened vanilla flavor in browned butter is, in some ways, simply the deepened flavor of the butter. And those flavors happen to meld well with the flavor compounds in vanilla beans.

Hazelnut Cake

This cake, redolent of the rich flavor of hazelnut, light and elegant, but buttery and fully flavored, can be served for brunch or dusted with powdered sugar and offered as an after-dinner treat.

Preheat the oven to 350°F and set the rack in the center of the oven. Grease and flour a 10-inch springform pan or cake pan and line the bottom with parchment paper.

Grind the hazelnuts.
Combine the hazelnuts and cornstarch in a food processor and grind to a fine flour. Set aside.

Cream the butter and incorporate the eggs.
Follow the TECHNIQUE TIP: *Creaming butter, page 67. See* BEYOND THE BASICS: *Room-temperature eggs, page 53.*

Place the butter in the bowl of the stand mixer with the paddle attachment and beat on medium speed for 1 minute. Add the sugar and hazelnut paste and beat on medium-high speed until the mixture becomes fluffy and lighter in color, 6 to 8 minutes, stopping the mixer occasionally to scrape down the sides of the bowl. Add the eggs, one at a time, and continue to beat until they are fully incorporated and the batter looks smooth and glossy, 1 to 2 minutes.

Prepare the dry ingredients.
In a small bowl, whisk together all the remaining dry ingredients and the ground hazelnuts.

Combine the dry ingredients and the crème fraîche.
With the mixer on slow speed, add half the dry ingredients to the butter and beat until the flour is just incorporated. Add all of the crème fraîche and continue mixing on slow speed. Add the rest of the dry ingredients, mixing until the batter is thoroughly combined. Scrape down the sides and bottom of the bowl with a rubber spatula and briefly beat on medium speed for 20 seconds.

Bake the cake.
Scrape the batter into the prepared pan, evening the batter with a rubber spatula. Run a paring knife in a single circular motion through the batter, 1 inch from the edge of the pan. This will help the cake to rise evenly. Bake the cake until a tester inserted in the middle of the cake comes out clean and the center is slightly springy, 50 to 60 minutes. If the center of the cake is still jiggly, bake another 10 minutes. Remove from the oven and allow to cool on a wire rack for 20 minutes. Invert the cake to remove it from the pan, and allow it to cool to room temperature.

Serving Suggestions
Serve this cake warm with a sprinkling of powdered sugar; whipped cream or crème fraîche are also good accompaniments. If you are a lover of gianduja chocolate—the Swiss term for a hazelnut chocolate combination—ice this cake with Milk Chocolate Frosting (page 52). Or go all the way and serve it with Roasted Glazed Peaches (page 172) doused with the peach's roasting liquids, and topped with Sauternes Sabayon (page 217) and Hazelnut Streusel (page 169).

Storage
This cake will keep, wrapped and at room temperature, for 4 days.

1 scant cup (4 ounces) whole hazelnuts

1 tablespoon cornstarch

16 tablespoons (8 ounces) butter, at room temperature

1⅓ cups sugar

2 tablespoons (1 ounce) hazelnut paste or hazelnut butter

3 eggs, at room temperature

½ teaspoon salt

½ teaspoon baking soda

½ teaspoon baking powderr

2 cups minus 2 tablespoons flour

1 cup (8 ounces) crème fraîche or sour cream

SPECIAL TOOLS AND PANS

Food processor

Stand mixer

10-inch springform pan or cake pan

YIELD

One 10-inch round cake, serves 12 to 16

Miniature Chocolate, Almond, and Lime Brown Butter Tea Cakes

Miniature Chocolate, Almond, and Lime Brown Butter Tea Cakes

Lime is an unusual addition to chocolate, but it gives chocolate an exotic tropical undertone that highlights the fruitiness and acidity of high-quality chocolate. This uniquely flavored cake is at its base a financier (brown butter and almond cake) and is perfect for teatime or late afternoon snacks.

Preheat the oven to 375°F. Butter or oil the muffin tins.

Brown the butter.
Follow the TECHNIQUE TIP: *Browning butter, page 51.*

In a small frying pan, brown the butter over medium-high heat until it caramelizes and emits a nutty, butterscotch aroma. Remove from heat.

Melt the chocolate.
In the bowl of a bain-marie, melt the chocolate, stirring frequently. Remove from the heat and allow the water to continue to simmer.

Grind the almonds.
In a food processor, combine the almonds and 1 tablespoon of the flour and grind to a fine powder.

Dissolve the sugar in the egg whites.
In the bowl of a bain-marie, whisk together the egg whites, powdered sugar, lime zest, and honey until the whites become warm to the touch and the granulated sugar has dissolved. Remove the bowl from the heat.

Add the dry ingredients.
Slowly whisk the remaining flour, ground almonds, cocoa powder, and salt into the egg whites. The mixture will become thick. Smooth it out with a few turns of the whisk.

Emulsify the brown butter.
Using a ladle, add approximately ¼ cup of the warm brown butter to the egg mixture and whisk until incorporated. Repeat this process until you have added all the butter. (This process is very important. If you add the butter too quickly, the mixture will not emulsify and the butter will melt out of the cake when baked, making it greasy and heavy.) Once the butter is incorporated, whisk in the melted chocolate. The batter can be made up to this point and stored in the refrigerator for up to 4 days.

Bake the tea cake.
Using a piping bag or a teaspoon, fill the prepared muffin tins ½ full. Bake the cakes until they have risen, cracked, and are springy to the touch, about 15 minutes. For even cooking, rotate your muffin pans from front to back and between each of the baking racks at least once while the muffins are baking.

Serving Suggestions
Serve these tea cakes warm. For a more formal presentation (and to bring out the fruity flavor), I recommend serving them with the Blood Orange Caramel Sauce (page 212) or the Rum Caramel Sauce (page 213).

Storage
These cakes will keep, tightly wrapped and at room temperature, for 1 week.

16 tablespoons (8 ounces) butter

3 ounces bittersweet chocolate (64 to 72 percent cocoa solids)

1 cup (5 ounces) whole blanched almonds

1 cup minus 2 tablespoons flour

9 egg whites

2½ cups plus 2 tablespoons powdered sugar

Zest of 2 limes

2 tablespoons honey

½ cup cocoa powder (natural or Dutch processed)

½ tablespoon salt

SPECIAL TOOLS AND PANS

Bain-marie (see page 10)

Food processor

Mini muffin tins

YIELD

45 to 50 mini muffins

Goat Cheesecake
Enrobed in Hazelnut Brittle

1 egg

1 egg yolk

½ cup sugar

Pinch of salt

10½ ounces fresh goat cheese, at room temperature

½ cup plus 2 tablespoons (5 ounces) crème fraîche

½ recipe Peanut Brittle, substituting hazelnuts (page 204)

SPECIAL TOOLS AND PANS

6-inch round springform pan, or six 4-ounce ramekins or individual aluminum cupcake molds

Thermometer (optional)

Roasting pan or baking pan, at least 8 x 8 x 2 inches

YIELD

One 6-inch round cheesecake or 6 individual cheesecakes

Creamy yet light, with a tangy intensity from the goat cheese and crème fraîche, this cheesecake is a favorite of many of our customers at Chanterelle and is remarkably easy to prepare. The brittle that enrobes the cake is a bit more difficult to make, but the cheesecake works well without it—you can replace the brittle with simple crushed nuts for a crunchy contrast to the creamy cheesecake.

Preheat the oven to 300°F. Butter or oil a 6-inch springform pan or individual ramekins or molds.

Mix the batter.
Combine the eggs, sugar, and salt in a medium bowl and whisk for 1 to 2 minutes. Whisk in the goat cheese until smooth. Add the crème fraîche and whisk for 1 minute. Do not overmix or the cheesecake will have a grainy texture.

Bake the cheesecake.
Spread the batter in the prepared pans or molds. If using a springform pan, wrap a large piece of aluminum foil around the outside, making sure the foil fully encases the pan so that once you set the pan in a deep water bath, none of the water seeps in. Place the foil-wrapped pan in a roasting pan and fill with water so that it comes up 1½ inches along the side of the springform. Bake the cheesecake until the center is set or a thermometer in the center of the cheesecake reads between 150°F and 170°F, approximately 40 minutes. (An air bubble or two might rise to the surface, but the cheesecake will barely expand.)

If you are using individual cheesecakes, you do not need a water bath. Bake the individual cheesecakes for 20 to 24 minutes, rotating the pan halfway through the baking process. If the cheesecakes start to rise, remove them from the oven immediately.

Remove the cheesecake from the oven and allow it to cool. Transfer to the refrigerator and chill for 30 minutes before removing the sides of the springform pan.

Enrobe the cheesecake.
Follow the recipe for Peanut Brittle (page 204), substituting hazelnuts for the almonds. Using both hands, pat the ground Hazelnut Brittle onto the top and the sides of the chilled cheesecake.

Serving Suggestions
This cheesecake works beautifully with the Blood Orange Caramel Sauce (page 212), the Fresh Fig and Madeira Compote (page 170), and the Roasted Medjool Dates Stuffed with Cashews, Currants, and Candied Citrus (page 165).

Storage
The cheesecake will keep, refrigerated, for 4 days.

Goat Cheesecake Enrobed in Hazelnut Brittle

Date Cake with Toffee Sauce

This is my version of the ever-popular sticky toffee pudding, sometimes called sticky date pudding. The sweetness of the dates and toffee is offset by the spices and the coffee, producing a balanced date flavor, especially delicious in the winter months when warm, rich cakes are most comforting.

Preheat the oven to 325°F and adjust the rack to the center of the oven. Butter or spray a baking pan, line the bottom with parchment paper, aluminum foil, or wax paper, then butter or spray it again.

Prepare the date mixture.
With a paring knife or your hands, remove the pits from the dates. In a small mixing bowl, combine the pitted dates, brandy, and espresso powder. Bring 1 cup of water to a boil and pour it over the dates and allow the mixture to sit for 10 minutes to cool. Transfer the date mixture to a food processor and puree until smooth (a few small lumps are okay). Alternatively, puree in a stand mixer with the paddle attachment on medium-low speed for about 10 minutes.

Cream the butter and incorporate the eggs.
Follow the TECHNIQUE TIP: *Creaming butter, page 67. See* BEYOND THE BASICS: *Room-temperature eggs, page 53.*

Place the butter in the bowl of the stand mixer with the paddle attachment and beat on medium speed for 1 minute. Add the sugar and beat on medium-high speed until the mixture becomes fluffy and almost beige in color, 6 to 8 minutes, stopping the mixer occasionally to scrape down the sides of the bowl. Add the eggs, one at a time, mixing the batter slowly for 20 seconds after each addition. This recipe has a high proportion of eggs and not all the eggs will emulsify into the butter. After you add the third egg, the mixture might begin to look curdled. After adding the last egg, mix just enough to distribute the egg in the batter.

Finish the batter.
In a dry bowl, whisk together all the dry ingredients except the baking soda. With the mixer on slow speed, add half of the dry mixture to the butter, scraping down the sides of the bowl. The batter should look less curdled after half the flour is incorporated.

Add the baking soda to the date mixture and stir it with a wooden spoon for 10 seconds. With the mixer on slow speed, add the date mixture to the batter and mix until thoroughly combined. Add the remaining dry ingredients and mix until the batter comes together. Stop the machine and, using a spatula, scrape the bottom of the bowl to bring the batter to the top. Turn the machine back on and mix on slow speed for another 30 seconds.

Bake the cake.
See BEYOND THE BASICS: *Steam—the leavening power of batters with a high percentage of liquids, page 46.*

Scrape the batter into your prepared pan, evening it out with a spatula. Bake until the center of the cake is set or a tester inserted in the middle of the cake comes out clean, 45 minutes to 1 hour. If the center of the cake is still jiggling, continue to bake for 10 minutes. Remove from the oven and allow to cool for at least 40 minutes before inverting it and removing it from the baking pan.

Serving Suggestions
Slice this cake into 2- to 3-inch squares while it is slightly warm and serve it with warm Toffee Sauce (page 214) poured over the top. This cake can be reheated for 10 minutes in a 325°F oven before serving. Vanilla ice cream or whipped cream also provides a nice contrast, both in flavor and temperature, to the dark sweet flavor of this cake. The Coconut Cream Cheese Ice Cream (page 135) is also a wonderful accompaniment.

Storage
This cake will keep, wrapped and at room temperature, for 4 days.

Approximately 11 (9 ounces) large Medjool or moist dates, with pits

2 tablespoons Grand Marnier or plain brandy

2 teaspoons instant espresso powder (preferably Medaglia D'Oro)

12 tablespoons (6 ounces) butter, at room temperature

1 cup light brown sugar

4 eggs, at room temperature

1¾ cups flour

⅛ teaspoon clove

⅛ teaspoon nutmeg

¼ teaspoon cinnamon

½ teaspoon salt

1½ teaspoons baking soda

SPECIAL TOOLS AND POTS
Food processor

Stand mixer

7 × 12-inch rectangular pan or 9-inch square pan

YIELD
One 9-inch square cake, serves 10 to 12

Steam—the leavening power of batters with a high percentage of liquids

Once water is heated to its gaseous state (steam), it occupies vastly more volume than it does as liquid. All baked items are leavened somewhat as liquid turns into steam in the oven. Moist bread dough, in particular, rises well because the water is trapped in well-formed cells with strong gluten walls. Pâte à choux, or cream-puff pastry, depends completely on steam and an intense heat to create those wonderful air pockets bakers and chefs fill with ice cream, mousse, and cheese.

A cake with a high percentage of liquid such as the Steamed Brown Sugar and Date Cake featured here is leavened not only by baking soda's reaction with the acid in the brown sugar, dates, and coffee, but also by the batter's high liquid content.

Baking soda and baking powder

These two chemical leavening agents, when used correctly, produce carbon dioxide, which expands when heated, giving baked goods greater volume and a lighter texture.

Baking soda (sodium bicarbonate) does not act on its own to produce carbon dioxide; it must react with an acidic ingredient such as chocolate, molasses, honey, fermented dairy products, juice, or vinegar or directly with added acids such as cream of tartar.

Baking powder is a complete leavening system waiting to be ignited through exposure to moisture and sometimes heat. It contains both baking soda and acid, which are separated in powder form by a starch like cornstarch. Baking powders can contain different types of acid. Certain acids dissolve and react in the presence of liquid, and certain acids dissolve and react in the presence of heat. Double-acting baking powder is a leavening agent that

contains both types of acids so that carbon dioxide is produced immediately in a moist batter and then again in the oven.

In the Spiced Apple and Sour Cream Cake recipe, you will notice I call for both baking soda and baking powder. The baking powder acts on its own and the baking soda is used to react with and neutralize the acid in the sour cream. The Gingersnap recipe (page 59), on the other hand, calls for only baking soda, which reacts with the acid in the molasses and the brown sugar, which contains molasses.

Chemical leavening agents cannot act alone to inflate baked goods. The baker must first create air pockets by stirring, folding, whipping, and beating the batter in its various stages. Carbon dioxide finds its way into these air pockets and, in the presence of heat, expands in these trapped spaces, leavening baked goods.

Chocolate Bête Noire

Dense and creamy, yet light and elegant, this flourless chocolate cake is remarkably versatile; it serves as the basis of many of my plated chocolate desserts at Chanterelle. The secret to making yours utterly delicious is to use the very best quality chocolate, so find a brand you like to eat and don't be shy about using it in this recipe.

Preheat the oven to 350°F. Grease and sugar an 8-inch springform pan or 8 muffin tins.

Make the sugar syrup.
Using a paring knife, cut down the center of the vanilla bean and scrape out the tiny black seeds into a heavy-bottomed saucepan. Add ½ cup water, the sugar, and the pod to the saucepan and bring to a rolling boil over medium-high heat. Remove the pan from the heat. Allow the syrup to rest for 10 minutes before removing the vanilla bean. Dry the bean and save for another use. (If you are using vanilla extract, you will add it later.)

Prepare the chocolate sauce.
See BEYOND THE BASICS: *Chocolate and water.*

Chop the chocolate into ½-inch pieces and place in a medium-sized bowl. Pour half of the hot vanilla syrup over the chocolate and begin whisking the mixture gently. (The chocolate will seize a bit.) Add the remaining vanilla syrup and continue whisking until you have a shiny, thick chocolate sauce, 2 minutes.

Add the butter and eggs.
Add the eggs and egg yolk, one at a time, to the chocolate sauce, whisking after each addition. Whisk in the salt and the vanilla extract if you have not used a vanilla bean in making the syrup. Add the butter, 1 tablespoon at a time. Continue whisking the batter until all the butter is incorporated. The finished chocolate cake batter should be shiny and somewhat viscous. The batter can be made up to this point and refrigerated for up to 3 days.

Bake the cake.
If the batter has been refrigerated, allow it to come to room temperature. Scrape the batter into the prepared pan, evening the batter with a rubber spatula. Bake the cake until the center of the cake is set and the top has cracked and developed a glossy, thin crust, 45 to 60 minutes (25 to 30 minutes if you are using individual molds). If the center seems a bit jiggly, bake for another 10 minutes. Remove from the oven and allow to cool for 1 hour before serving.

Serving Suggestions
Serve this cake warm with a dollop of whipped cream, crème fraîche, or vanilla ice cream. I also recommend the Cinnamon Caramel Mousse (page 106), Banana Cream (page 91), Espresso Ice Cream (page 138), Fresh Fig and Madeira Compote (page 170), or Rum Caramel Sauce (page 213).

Storage
This cake will keep, wrapped and at room temperature, for 2 days.

½ vanilla bean or 1 teaspoon vanilla extract

¾ cup sugar

9 ounces dark bittersweet chocolate (65 to 70 percent cocoa solids)

3 eggs, at room temperature

1 egg yolk, at room temperature

⅛ teaspoon salt

12 tablespoons (6 ounces) butter, at room temperature

SPECIAL TOOLS AND PANS

8-inch springform pan or 8 muffin tins

YIELD
One 8-inch cake or 8 individual cakes, serves 8

BEYOND THE BASICS
Chocolate and water

Adding water to chocolate is a problem only if you add a small portion. Chocolate is mostly composed of sugar and nonfat cocoa solids, which are largely water-free, suspended in cocoa butter. When you add a small amount of water, these particles immediately absorb the water and clump together, thickening melted chocolate into a seemingly unworkable paste. However, if you continue to add water or any water-based liquid to the chocolate mixture, the cocoa particles and the sugar dissolve, returning the solid mass to a smooth, fluid state.

Spiced Apple and Sour Cream Cake

SAUTÉED APPLES

2 tart apples (approximately 1 pound)

2 tablespoons (1 ounce) butter

2 tablespoons sugar

CAKE

12 tablespoons (6 ounces) butter, at room temperature

1 cup packed light brown sugar

4 egg yolks, at room temperature

1¾ cups flour

½ teaspoon baking powder

¾ teaspoon baking soda

½ teaspoon salt

½ teaspoon allspice

½ teaspoon clove

1 teaspoon cinnamon

¼ teaspoon freshly grated nutmeg

½ cup plus 1 tablespoon (5 ½ ounces) sour cream

¼ cup raw sugar (sometimes called demerara, coarse, or crystal sugar) or granulated sugar

SPECIAL TOOLS AND PANS

Stand mixer

8-inch round springform pan

YIELD

One 8-inch round cake, serves 8 to 10

VARIATION

Spiced Apple Muffins:
This cake also makes wonderful muffins. Evenly divide the batter among a dozen buttered or oiled muffin tins and bake for 30 to 35 minutes.

Sour cream is a classic addition to cake batter; it moistens the crumb and makes the cake tender. This cake captures the essential taste of fall—apples—and, served warm, is great for brunch in the cold days of late autumn.

Preheat the oven to 350°F and position the rack in the center of the oven. Butter or oil an 8-inch springform pan.

Sauté the apples.

Peel, core, and dice the apples into ¼-inch cubes. Place the butter in a sauté pan over medium heat and cook until bubbly. Add the apples and stir for 1 minute with a wooden spoon. Add the sugar and continue to cook for 2 minutes. Turn the heat down and allow the apples to cook, uncovered, until they have softened, 4 to 5 minutes. Remove from the heat and allow to cool. Use only the sautéed apples for the cake; discard any cooking liquid that might have accumulated.

Cream the butter and incorporate the eggs.

Follow the TECHNIQUE TIP: *Creaming butter, page 67. See* BEYOND THE BASICS: *Room-temperature eggs, page 53.*

Place the butter in the bowl of the stand mixer with the paddle attachment and beat on medium speed for 1 minute. Add the sugar and beat on medium-high speed until the mixture becomes fluffy and almost beige in color, 6 to 8 minutes, stopping the mixer occasionally to scrape down the sides of the bowl. Add the egg yolks, one at a time, and continue to beat until they are fully incorporated and the batter looks smooth and glossy, 1 to 2 minutes.

Finish the batter.

See BEYOND THE BASICS: *Baking soda and baking powder, page 46.*

In a separate mixing bowl, toss together all the remaining dry ingredients except the raw sugar. With the mixer set on slow speed, add half the dry ingredients to the butter mixture. Mix until there are no more flour streaks. Add the sour cream all at once and mix on slow speed until the sour cream is incorporated. Stop the mixer and, using a rubber spatula, fold the remaining dry ingredients into the batter. Finish mixing the batter on slow speed until thoroughly combined, 1 minute. Scrape down the sides of the bowl with a rubber spatula and mix for another 30 seconds. The batter should be fairly thick. Using a rubber spatula, fold the sautéed apples into the cake batter.

Bake the cake.

Scrape the batter into the prepared pan and spread the batter evenly. Take a knife and run it in a singular circular motion through the batter 1 inch from the edge of the pan—this will help the cake to rise evenly. Sprinkle the raw sugar over the top and bake until the center of the cake is set or a metal prong inserted in the middle of the cake comes out clean, 60 to 70 minutes. Allow the cake to cool for 10 minutes before removing the sides of the springform pan.

Serving Suggestions

Serve this cake warm either by itself or with a dollop of whipped cream. The Cider Caramel Sauce (page 212) or the Rum Caramel Sauce (page 213) are also wonderful accompaniments.

Storage

This cake will keep, well wrapped and at room temperature, for up to 4 days.

Whipped Brown Butter and Vanilla Birthday Cake

At Chanterelle we are often called on to make custom-ordered birthday cakes and wedding cakes, serving from two to eighty people. We offer our clients a number of options, suggesting any mousse in this book as a cake filling, with any type of berry, and then we provide chocolate ganache or an infinite variety of buttercreams as an icing or garnish. This is my favorite white butter layer cake. It is an adaptation of the all-American yellow cake recipe, using vanilla-infused brown butter instead of regular butter.

2 to 24 hours ahead of time: Brown the butter with the vanilla bean.
Follow the TECHNIQUE TIP: *Browning butter, page 51.*

Run a paring knife down the center of the vanilla bean. Split it open with your fingers and use the knife to scrape out the tiny black seeds into a saucepan. Add the butter and the scraped vanilla bean and turn the heat to medium-high. (If you are using vanilla extract, brown the butter by itself.) Cook the butter with the vanilla bean and seeds until the butter caramelizes and emits a rich nutty vanilla aroma. Remove the vanilla bean, dry, and save for another use. Refrigerate the brown butter until it solidifies, 1 to 2 hours.

Preheat the oven to 350°F and position the rack in the center of the oven. Grease and lightly flour two 9-inch cake pans or 16 muffin tins.

Cream the brown butter and add the eggs.
Follow the TECHNIQUE TIP: *Creaming butter, page 67.*
See BEYOND THE BASICS: *Room-temperature eggs, page 53.*

Place the chilled brown butter in the bowl of the stand mixer with the paddle attachment and beat on medium speed for 1 minute. Add the sugar and beat on medium-high speed. Toward the beginning of the creaming process the mixture will look dry and seem as though it will never come together. Continue creaming, stopping the mixer occasionally to scrape down the sides of the bowl, until the mixture becomes fluffy and almost beige in color, 8 to 12 minutes. Add the whole eggs and yolks, one at a time, and continue to beat until they are fully incorporated and the batter looks smooth and glossy, 1 to 2 minutes. Add the optional vanilla extract.

Assemble the dry ingredients.
In a dry bowl, whisk together all the dry ingredients.

Combine the flour and the milk.
With the mixer set on slow speed, add the dry ingredients to the butter in 3 parts, alternating with the milk. Once you have added the third portion, scrape down the sides of the bowl with a rubber spatula and briefly beat the batter on medium speed until just incorporated, 20 seconds.

Bake the cake.
Scrape the batter into the prepared cake pans, evening out the batter with a rubber spatula. Run a paring knife in a single circular motion through the batter, 1 inch from the edge of the pan. This will help the cake to rise evenly. Bake the cakes until the center is set and a tester inserted in the middle of the cake comes out clean, approximately 40 to 45 minutes. If you are making cupcakes, bake them for 30 minutes.

Allow the cake to cool on a wire rack for about 20 minutes. Run a paring knife around the edge of the pan and invert the cake onto a cooling rack. Allow the cake layers to cool to room temperature.

CAKE

1 vanilla bean or
1 teaspoon vanilla extract

24 tablespoons (12 ounces) butter

1²⁄₃ cups sugar

2 whole eggs,
at room temperature

4 egg yolks,
at room temperature

2 ½ cups plus
2 tablespoons flour

3 teaspoons baking powder

1 teaspoon salt

1 ¼ cups milk,
at room temperature

ICING/FILLING

Double the recipe for Orange Buttercream (page 78)

One 8-ounce container of fresh raspberries

SPECIAL TOOLS AND PANS

Stand mixer

Two 9-inch round cake pans, 1½ inches deep or 16 muffin tins

YIELD

Two 9-inch cake layers or 16 cupcakes

Prepare the buttercream filling.

Fill and ice the cake.
If the individual cake layers domed a bit too much, use a long serrated knife to trim the peaked tops to even out the tops. Place the bottom layer on a decorative serving plate. Cut a 12-inch-long piece of wax paper into 4 equal strips. Place each strip under an edge of the cake to cover the rim of the plate, to prevent the plate from becoming coated with icing **(see illustration)**. Smear a thin layer of icing over the bottom cake layer and then spread the raspberries evenly around on the buttercream. Using an offset spatula, gently smear a layer of buttercream over the raspberries, making sure to smear an equal amount of buttercream around the outer edge of the layer. Place the second cake layer on top. Evenly ice the whole cake with the remaining buttercream. Once you have smoothed out all the rough edges, remove the wax paper strips from underneath the cake to reveal a spotless serving platter.

Serving Suggestions
Serve this cake the day it is made, at room temperature. Any icing will go with this cake, and any fruit or berry can be substituted as well. For an alternative cake filling, make one recipe of the buttercream for the outside of the cake and any of the mousse recipes as a filling. I also recommend the Milk Chocolate Frosting (page 52) and the Cream Cheese Filling (page 60).

Storage
This cake will keep, covered and refrigerated, for 1 week. Allow it to come to room temperature before serving.

TECHNIQUE TIP
Browning butter

Brown butter adds depth of flavor to all sorts of sauces and baked goods.

Brown butter is butter that is boiled until it reaches approximately 250°F, at which point the milk proteins and sugar (lactose) brown through what are called Maillard reactions, producing a complex, nutty, sweet flavor, with a caramel, hazelnut, brown sugar–like aroma.

There are several visual and aromatic clues to watch out for while you are browning butter. As the butter boils, a white foam will accumulate on the surface. In order to control the rate at which the butter browns, I recommend turning the heat down to medium when you see the foam forming.

Observe the butter very carefully. You will begin to notice brown freckles in the creamy white foam. It will then turn a universal beige-brown color and develop a nutty, butterscotch-like perfume. The boiled liquid butter under the foam will change color, from a clear yellow to a clear golden yellow. The best way to see this color change is by scooping up some of the butter with a dry ladle or spoon and then pouring the butter back into the pan, examining the color in the stream of hot butter. Once you have observed this color transformation and you have smelled the wonderful nutty aroma, remove the butter from the heat and set it aside.

If the butter continues to cook and brown further it takes on a golden brown color with an even stronger nutty caramelized flavor. (This deeply flavored butter is desirable for some recipes.) If the butter is heated a bit more it takes on a solid brown color; it then loses its nutty sweetness and becomes somewhat acrid.

Also be aware that the browning milk solids, once caramelized, sink and collect at the bottom of the pan. When you pour off the brown butter you can strain the dark solids out; or, if desired, you can allow some to incorporate into your batter or sauce.

Chocolate Layer Cake
with Milk Chocolate Frosting

CAKE

2 ounces chocolate (61 to 70 percent cocoa solids)

½ cup plus 2 tablespoons cocoa

1 teaspoon vanilla extract

16 tablespoons (8 ounces) butter, at room temperature

1½ cups sugar

3 whole eggs, at room temperature

1 egg yolk, at room temperature

2 cups plus 1 tablespoon flour

3 teaspoons baking powder

½ teaspoon salt

MILK CHOCOLATE FROSTING

10 ounces milk chocolate

½ cup heavy cream

¼ teaspoon salt

¾ cup powdered sugar

16 tablespoons (8 ounces) butter, slightly chilled (around 60°F)

SPECIAL TOOLS AND PANS

Stand mixer

Bain-marie (see page 10)

Two 9 × 2-inch round cake pans or 16 muffin tins

YIELD

Two 9-inch cake layers or 16 cupcakes

This is a classic American chocolate cake: moist, chocolatey, light, yet sumptuously buttery. It is great for birthdays and also wonderful baked as cupcakes.

Preheat the oven to 350°F and position the rack in the center of the oven. Grease and lightly flour two 9-inch cake pans or 16 muffin tins.

Make a chocolate and cocoa syrup.
See BEYOND THE BASICS: *Chocolate and water, page 47.*

Chop the chocolate into ½-inch pieces and combine with the cocoa in a medium-sized bowl. Bring 1 cup of water to a boil and gently whisk half of the hot water into the chopped chocolate. (The chocolate will begin to seize a bit.) Whisk in the remaining hot water and continue whisking until you have a shiny, thick, smooth chocolate syrup, 2 minutes. Add the vanilla extract. Set the syrup aside and allow it to come to room temperature.

Cream the butter and incorporate the eggs.
Follow the TECHNIQUE TIP: *Creaming butter, page 67.*
See BEYOND THE BASICS: *Room-temperature eggs, page 53.*

Place the butter in the bowl of the stand mixer with the paddle attachment and beat on medium speed for 1 minute. Add the sugar and beat on medium-high speed until the mixture becomes fluffy and almost white in color, 6 to 8 minutes, stopping the mixer occasionally to scrape down the sides of the bowl. Add the whole eggs one at a time, and continue to beat until they are fully incorporated. Add the egg yolk and beat until the batter looks smooth and glossy, 30 seconds.

Assemble the dry ingredients.
In a dry bowl, whisk together the dry ingredients.

Combine the flour and the chocolate syrup.
With the mixer on slow speed, add half the dry mixture and beat until the flour is just incorporated. Add all the chocolate syrup and continue mixing on slow speed. Add the second half of the dry ingredients and beat until the

batter is thoroughly combined. Scrape down the sides and bottom of the bowl with a rubber spatula and briefly beat the batter on medium speed for 20 seconds.

Bake the cake.
Scrape the batter into the prepared pans, evening out the batter with a rubber spatula. Run a paring knife in a single circular motion through the batter, 1 inch from the edge of the pan. This will help the cake to rise evenly. Bake the cakes until the center is set and a tester inserted in the middle of the cake comes out clean, approximately 25 to 30 minutes. If you are making cupcakes, bake them for 20 to 25 minutes.

Allow the cakes to cool on a wire rack for about 20 minutes. Run a paring knife around the outer sides of the pan and invert the cakes onto cooling racks. Allow the cake layers to cool to room temperature.

Make the frosting.
In the bowl of a bain-marie, melt the chocolate. Remove the bowl from the heat. Heat the cream in a small saucepan. Add the hot cream to the melted chocolate, whisking continuously, to make a shiny, smooth ganache. Place the bowl of ganache in the refrigerator, scraping the bowl with a rubber spatula every 5 minutes, until the ganache is slightly chilled, around 60°F.

In the bowl of a stand mixer, or with a hand mixer, whisk the slightly chilled ganache together with the salt, powdered sugar, and the slightly chilled butter on medium speed for 4 to 6 minutes. The icing should hold the lines of a whisk, increase in volume, and become a much lighter shade of brown.

Fill and ice the cake.
If the individual cake layers domed a bit too much, use a long serrated knife to trim the

peaked tops to even out the tops. Place the bottom layer on a decorative serving plate. Cut a 12-inch-long piece of wax paper into 4 equal strips. Place each strip under an edge of the cake to cover the rim of the plate, to prevent it from becoming coated with icing **(see illustration, page 50)**. Using an offset spatula, smear a generous layer of icing over the bottom cake layer, making sure to smear an equal amount of icing around the outer edge of the layer. Place the second cake layer on top. Evenly ice the whole cake with the remaining icing. Once you have smoothed out all the rough edges, remove the wax paper strips from underneath the cake to reveal a spotless serving platter beneath your finished cake.

Serving Suggestions

Serve this cake at room temperature with a glass of milk or a cup of tea. It needs no accompaniment. I also recommend using the Cinnamon Caramel Mousse (page 106)—Karen Waltuck's favorite—and the Sesame Milk Chocolate Mousse (page 109) as delicious, lighter alternatives to the ganache filling.

Storage

This cake will keep, covered and at room temperature, for 4 days. If it is very hot in your kitchen, store the cake, covered, in the refrigerator but serve it at room temperature.

BEYOND THE BASICS
Room-temperature eggs

In most of my recipes I call for room-temperature eggs. There are two reasons for this.

First, room-temperature eggs potentially have more denatured proteins, which are more likely to interconnect with their neighboring proteins to form egg gels. These gels make a stronger batter.

Second, the emulsifiers in egg yolks, such as lecithin, are more effective in the cake or cookie batter at room temperature. Eggs are generally added to a batter after the butter has been whipped and aerated with sugar. Warm or room-temperature eggs, as opposed to cold eggs, are more likely to incorporate into the whipped butter, yielding a shiny, smooth mixture.

Emulsifiers are similar to fats and oils in molecular structure but are nonetheless defined differently. Lecithin, and all of the important emulsifiers in yolks, are phospholipids—they have two fatty acids attached to glycerol, and instead of a third fatty acid (as fats and oils have) they have a phosphate group. This phosphate group, unlike

fatty acids (which are attracted to other fatty acids), is attracted to water. Emulsifiers such as lecithin function in cake batters by binding to both fat-based and water-based ingredients, mixing these otherwise unmixable molecules.

Emulsifiers encourage fat globules to mix with water-based ingredients (as opposed to conglomerating together, which fat tends to do—which is why your salad dressing always separates) and intersperse more evenly in a batter. Warm, agitated fat globules are smaller than cold ones, which in turn makes them easier to intersperse in a batter. If the liquid substance of egg yolks adds subtle heat to a batter as opposed to cooling a batter, the batter will have smaller fat globules, and emulsifiers will be better able to do their job— binding the otherwise unmixable fat globules and water in the batter together. The result is a shinier, stronger, more emulsified batter. (Get the batter too hot, though, and emulsifiers don't work at all.)

COOKIES

CHAPTER THREE

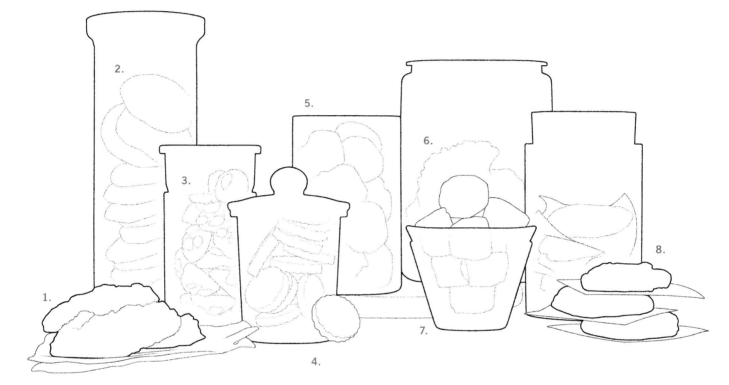

1. **Oatmeal Cookies with Golden Raisins and Milk Chocolate Chips**

2. **Gingersnaps**

3. **Pignoli Amaretti Cookies**

4. **Hazelnut Shortbread**

5. **Chocolate Almond Cracks**

6. **Oatmeal Cookies with Golden Raisins and Milk Chocolate Chips**

7. **Walnut, Currant, and Cinnamon Rugelach**

8. **Double Chocolate and Cherry Cookies**

Crispy, Chewy Chocolate Chip Cookies

There are hundreds upon hundreds of chocolate chip cookie recipes in the world, but this is my favorite. Super-flat, chewy, and moist, with just the outer edge caramelized to butterscotchy perfection, these cookies take my childhood experiments with Tollhouse and bring them to a heavenly new level.

Preheat the oven to 350°F. Spray cookie sheets with oil or line with aluminum foil, parchment, or silicone pads, or use nonstick pans.

Cream the butter and incorporate the eggs.
Follow the TECHNIQUE TIP: *Creaming butter, page 67. See* BEYOND THE BASICS: *Room-temperature eggs, page 53.*

Place the butter in the bowl of the stand mixer with the paddle attachment and beat on medium speed for 1 minute. Add the sugar and beat on medium-high speed until the mixture becomes fluffy and lighter in color, 6 to 8 minutes, stopping the mixer occasionally to scrape down the sides of the bowl. Add the egg and egg white and continue to beat until they are fully incorporated and the batter looks smooth and glossy, 1 to 2 minutes.

Assemble the dry ingredients and finish the dough.
In a dry bowl, whisk together the baking soda, salt, and flour. Add the dry mixture, all at once, to the butter mixture. Using a rubber spatula, fold together for a few turns. With the mixer on slow speed, mix the dough until thoroughly combined, 1 minute. Add the chocolate chips, vanilla, and walnuts, if you are using them. Scrape down the sides of the bowl with a rubber spatula and mix for another 30 seconds. The batter can be made up to this point and refrigerated, well wrapped, for up to 4 days.

Bake the cookies.
Using 2 teaspoons, scoop the dough into mounds arranged 2 inches apart on the prepared cookie sheets. Bake the cookies until they are a light golden brown with darker coloring at the edges, 12 to 15 minutes. For a crunchier, darker, more caramelized cookie, bake a little longer. For even browning, rotate the sheets from front to back and between each of the baking racks at least once while the cookies are baking.

Serving Suggestions
Serve these cookies warm, 20 minutes after you take them out of the oven.

Storage
These cookies will keep, sealed in a container, for 3 days.

16 tablespoons (8 ounces) butter, at room temperature

1½ cups light brown sugar

1 egg, at room temperature

1 egg white, at room temperature

1 teaspoon baking soda

¼ teaspoon salt

1¾ cups flour

8 ounces semisweet chocolate chips (or chocolate with 61 to 66 percent cocoa solids, chopped)

½ teaspoon vanilla extract

1½ cups (6 ounces) chopped walnuts (optional)

SPECIAL TOOLS AND PANS

Stand mixer

Cookie sheets

YIELD

4 dozen cookies

BEYOND THE BASICS
A little extra baking soda

Some cookie recipes call for more baking soda than seems necessary. Extra baking soda has a few effects that can enhance a good cookie. Once baking soda reacts with an acidic ingredient such as brown sugar, it produces carbon dioxide, salt, and water. Cookies with a little extra baking soda have that extra punch of salt that brings out flavor.

More important, with added alkalinity (baking soda), browning reactions are stronger, producing a cookie that is crispy on the outside and a bit underbaked and chewy on the inside. This contrast is the most sought-after quality in a chocolate chip cookie. The cookies also spread more because alkalinity weakens proteins in wheat and dairy products.

Some bakeries use an excessive amount of baking soda, yielding a large, flat, amazingly chewy, butterscotch-like, crispy cookie but with an overwhelmingly soapy, off flavor.

Double Chocolate and Cherry Cookies

½ cup plus 1 tablespoon flour

¼ teaspoon baking soda

½ teaspoon salt

¼ teaspoon cream of tartar

5 ounces bittersweet chocolate (62 to 70 percent cocoa solids)

4 ounces unsweetened chocolate (98 to 100 percent cocoa solids)

8 tablespoons (4 ounces) butter

4 eggs, at room temperature

1½ cups sugar

½ tablespoon freshly ground coffee

4 ounces semisweet chocolate chips (or chocolate with 54 to 64 percent cocoa solids, chopped)

¾ cup (4½ ounces) dried cherries, chopped

SPECIAL TOOLS AND PANS

Stand mixer

Bain-marie (see page 10)

Cookie sheets

YIELD

Approximately 30 large cookies

This is one of Rick Katz's amazing recipes (see the Classic Crème Caramel recipe on page 86 for another of my favorites). Katz is a truly brilliant and passionate pastry chef for whom I worked early in my career. I make this recipe almost exactly as Rick taught it to me; this delectable recipe appeared in Julia Child's *Baking with Julia*, and I know that the chocolate cookie lovers in your life will be thrilled with the results.

Assemble the dry ingredients.
In a mixing bowl, whisk together the flour, baking soda, salt, and cream of tartar and set aside.

Prepare the chocolate.
In the bowl of a bain-marie, combine the bittersweet chocolate, unsweetened chocolate, and butter and melt, stirring frequently. Remove from the heat and allow to cool for 10 minutes.

Whip the eggs.
Place the eggs in the bowl of a stand mixer with the whisk attachment and beat on medium speed. Add the sugar and continue beating until the eggs triple in volume and hold the lines of the whisk, approximately 10 minutes. Add the coffee and beat for 1 minute more.

Combine the ingredients.
With the mixer at slow speed, add the melted chocolate to the egg mixture and beat until incorporated. Add the dry ingredients, chopped chocolate, and chopped dried cherries and beat until just incorporated. Do not overmix. Remove the bowl from the mixer and finish mixing by hand with a rubber spatula. The batter will be very runny. Cover the bowl and refrigerate for at least 2 hours or for up to 2 days.

Bake the cookies.
Preheat the oven to 350°F ½ hour before baking the cookies. Spray cookie sheets with oil and line with aluminum foil, parchment, or silicone pads, or use nonstick pans.

Using 2 tablespoons, scoop the batter into large mounds arranged 2 inches apart on the prepared cookie sheets. Bake the cookies for 12 to 15 minutes. If you want to make small cookies, use 2 teaspoons for scooping the batter and bake for 8 to 10 minutes. The cookies will puff in the oven and fall once removed from the oven. Allow the cookies to cool on the sheets.

Serving Suggestions
Enjoy these cookies with a glass of milk or a cup of coffee or tea.

Storage
These cookies will keep, well wrapped and at room temperature, for 5 days.

Gingersnaps

Even after all these years of preparing multicomponent desserts at restaurants, what I really love is a good cookie, crispy on the outside, chewy in the middle, and bursting with flavor. This is one of my favorites. Use freshly ground spices if possible.

Cream the butter and incorporate the eggs.
Follow the TECHNIQUE TIP: *Creaming butter, page 67. See* BEYOND THE BASICS: *Room-temperature eggs, page 53.*

Place the butter in the bowl of the stand mixer with the paddle attachment and beat on medium speed for 1 minute. Add the light brown sugar and beat on medium-high speed until the mixture becomes fluffy and lighter in color, 6 to 8 minutes, stopping the mixer occasionally to scrape down the sides of the bowl. Add the eggs, one at a time, and continue to beat until they are fully incorporated and the batter looks smooth and glossy, 1 to 2 minutes.

Add the dry ingredients and molasses.
See BEYOND THE BASICS: *A little extra baking soda, page 57.*

In a dry bowl, whisk together the dry ingredients. Add the dry mixture, all at once, to the butter mixture. Using a rubber spatula, fold together for a few turns. With the mixer on slow speed, mix the dough until thoroughly combined, 1 minute.

Add the molasses and mix until incorporated. Cover the dough in plastic wrap and refrigerate it for at least 2 hours.

Bake the cookies.
Preheat the oven to 350°F ½ hour before baking the cookies. Spray cookie sheets with oil and line with aluminum foil, parchment, or silicone pads, or use nonstick pans.

Place the raw sugar in a small bowl. Pinch off 1½-inch pieces of batter and roll into balls. Roll each ball in the sugar to coat. Arrange the cookies on the prepared sheet 2 inches apart and press your thumb in the center of each cookie to flatten it a bit. Bake until the cookies spread, crack a bit, and take on a dark golden brown color, 10 to 15 minutes. For even browning, rotate your cookie sheets from front to back and between each of the baking racks at least once while the cookies are baking.

Serving Suggestions
Serve these cookies with Maple-Ginger Ice Cream (page 139).

Storage
These cookies will keep, sealed in a container, for 3 days.

---

18 tablespoons (9 ounces) butter, at room temperature

1 ¼ cups packed light brown sugar

2 eggs, at room temperature

½ teaspoon salt

2 teaspoons baking soda

2 ¼ cups flour

2 teaspoons powdered ginger

1 ½ teaspoons ground cloves

1 ½ teaspoons ground cinnamon

¼ cup molasses

1 cup raw sugar (sometimes called demerara, coarse, or crystal sugar) or granulated sugar, for dusting

SPECIAL TOOLS AND PANS

Stand mixer

Cookie sheets

YIELD

4 dozen cookies

Walnut Cream Cheese Sandwich Cookies

WALNUT COOKIE DOUGH

1 cup (approximately 4 ounces) walnuts

2 ½ cups flour

½ teaspoon salt

16 tablespoons (8 ounces) butter, at room temperature

¾ cup sugar

1 egg, at room temperature

CREAM CHEESE FILLING

4 ounces cream cheese, at room temperature

4 tablespoons (2 ounces) butter, at room temperature

½ cup powdered sugar, plus ¼ cup for dusting

Pinch of salt

SPECIAL TOOLS AND PANS

Food processor

Stand mixer

1½-inch cookie cutter (round, round and fluted, or square or triangular)

Small hole puncher to create ½-inch hole (½-inch round pastry tip, wide straw, apple corer, or tiny cookie cutter), optional

Pastry bag (optional)

Sugar sifter or mesh strainer

Cookie sheets

YIELD

4 dozen sandwich cookies

Crunchy, delicate, and redolent of walnuts, with a creamy, tangy center, these cookies are incredibly satisfying. They play on dessert classics such as carrot cake with walnuts and cream cheese icing or cinnamon-raisin bagels with walnut cream cheese or even cheese strudels with walnuts and honey.

Grind the walnuts and assemble the dry ingredients.

Combine the walnuts and 1 tablespoon of the flour in a food processor and grind to a fine powder. In a dry bowl, whisk together the walnut powder, remaining flour, and salt and set aside.

Cream the butter and incorporate the egg.

Follow the TECHNIQUE TIP: *Creaming butter, page 67. See* BEYOND THE BASICS: *Room-temperature eggs, page 53.*

Place the butter in the bowl of the stand mixer with the paddle attachment and beat on medium speed for 1 minute. Add the sugar and beat on medium-high speed until the mixture becomes fluffy and lighter in color, 6 to 8 minutes, stopping the mixer occasionally to scrape down the sides of the bowl. Add the egg and continue to beat until it is fully incorporated and the batter looks smooth and glossy, 1 to 2 minutes.

Finish the dough.

Add the dry mixture, all at once, to the butter mixture. Using a rubber spatula, fold together for a few turns. With the mixer on slow speed, mix the dough until thoroughly combined, 1 to 2 minutes. Scrape down sides of bowl with a rubber spatula and mix for another 30 seconds.

Using a rubber spatula, scrape the dough onto a piece of plastic wrap. Wrap the dough tightly and press it into a 1-inch-thick rectangle. Refrigerate the dough for 2 hours or overnight.

Shape the cookies.

Preheat the oven to 350°F. Spray cookie sheets with oil and line with aluminum foil, parchment, or silicone pads, or use nonstick pans.

Quick Method for Shaping

If you do not have time to roll out the cookies, here is a shortcut that will still produce delicious wafers, but the cookies will not have uniform shape and finesse. Using a sharp knife and a cutting board, cut as many 1½ x 3-inch-long bars of the chilled dough as you can. Cut each bar into ⅛- to ¼-inch-thick slices and place the cookies ½ inch apart on the prepared cookie sheets.

Shaping by Rolling and Cutting

Follow the TECHNIQUE TIP: *Rolling tart dough, page 17.*

Roll the chilled dough out to ⅛ inch thick. Using your cookie cutter of choice, punch out cookies as close together on the dough as you can. Place the cookies ½ inch apart on the prepared cookie sheets. Make sure you have an even number of cookies. With your hole punch, make a small hole in the center of half of the cookies. (This is purely decorative; if you wish, you can skip this step.) Shape any remaining scraps of dough into a ball, wrap in plastic wrap, press it down into a disk, and refrigerate for at least 20 minutes before rolling it out again.

If you have room in your refrigerator, chill the cookies on the cookie sheets for 15 minutes before baking. If not, you can bake each tray as soon as it is filled with shaped cookies.

Bake the walnut cookies.

Bake the cookies until golden brown and you smell the wonderful aroma of toasted walnuts with butter, 12 to 15 minutes. For even browning, rotate your cookie sheets from front to back and between each of the baking racks at least once while the cookies are baking. Allow the cookies to cool on the sheets.

Hazelnut, Cinnamon, Cardamom, and Raspberry Sandwich Cookies
Walnut Cream Cheese Sandwich Cookies

Make the cream cheese filling.

Using a stand mixer fitted with the whisk attachment (or a hand mixer), whisk together the cream cheese, butter, powdered sugar, and salt until the filling has increased in volume, lightened in color, and formed stiff peaks, 4 to 5 minutes.

Fill and sandwich the cookies.

Using a piping bag or a tiny teaspoon, dot the cookies without holes (or half of the cookies) with the cream cheese filling. Cover with the remaining cookies to make a sandwich. Place ¼ cup powdered sugar in a strainer or sifter and sift the sugar over the finished cookies.

Serving Suggestions

Serve these cookies as an afternoon snack with a cup of tea.

Storage

Because of the moisture in the filling, these cookies loose their crunchiness after 1 day. They are best eaten up to 4 hours after sandwiching. You can bake the cookies and store them in an airtight container for up to 4 days ahead, then fill them the day you plan to serve them.

HINT
The effect of moisture on Chocolate Almond Cracks

Sometimes, while shaping these cookies, your hands will become completely coated in sticky chocolate batter. If you need to wash your hands in order to do something else or just to reorganize, make sure you dry them very well before continuing to shape the cookies. If these cookies are rolled in moist hands the sugar coating will dissolve, resulting in a cookie that still tastes great but does not have the exciting appearance of a white mound with jagged black lines peering through.

The cracked appearance of these cookies can also be affected by other foods baking in the oven simultaneously. The moisture produced from other foods melts some of the sugar on the exterior of the cookies, so be sure to bake these cookies by themselves.

Chocolate Almond Cracks

These cookies have a dramatic, mouth-watering appearance—moist on the inside and slightly crisp on the exterior, domed and powdery white, with jagged cracks where dark chocolate pokes through and teases the eye. The cookies, with their dark chocolate flavor rounded out with almonds and Amaretto, are terrific to make around the holidays.

Grind the almonds and assemble the dry ingredients.
Combine the almonds and 1 tablespoon of the flour in a food processor and grind to a fine powder. In a dry bowl, whisk together the almond powder, remaining flour, and baking powder and set aside.

Prepare the chocolate.
In the bowl of a bain-marie, melt the chocolate and butter, stirring with a rubber spatula every 2 minutes. Remove from the heat and set aside.

Whisk the sugar and the eggs.
Place the sugar and eggs in the bowl of a stand mixer with the whisk attachment and beat on medium speed for about 2 minutes. Add the amaretto and the salt.

Combine the wet and the dry ingredients.
With the mixer on slow speed, add the melted chocolate to the egg mixture, whisking them together until the batter is thoroughly combined, shiny, and holds the lines of a whisk. Add the dry ingredients and whisk just until the ingredients come together smoothly. Cover the batter in plastic wrap and refrigerate for at least 2 hours or up to 2 days.

Shape the cookies.
Preheat the oven to 350°F ½ hour before baking the cookies. Spray cookie sheets with oil and line with aluminum foil, parchment, or silicone pads, or use nonstick pans.

Place the granulated sugar and powdered sugar in separate bowls. Pinch off 1-inch pieces of batter and roll into balls. Roll a few balls at a time in the granulated sugar to coat. Then, with clean, dry hands, drop the sugar-coated cookies in the powdered sugar and roll them around until they are completely coated. Arrange the cookies on your prepared cookie sheets 1 inch apart.

Bake the cookies.
Bake the cookies until they rise, dome, and crack and are slightly firm when tapped, 11 to 14 minutes. If you continue to bake these cookies after they have finished rising, the result will be a drier cookie. If you underbake the cookies they will flatten out as they cool, but they will still be delicious.

Serving Suggestions
Serve these cookies with a glass of milk or a cup of coffee or tea.

Storage
These cookies will keep, sealed in a container, for 4 days.

1 cup (5 ounces) blanched almonds

½ cup flour

½ teaspoon baking powder

7 ounces bittersweet chocolate (61 to 66 percent cocoa solids)

4 tablespoons (2 ounces) butter

⅓ cup sugar

3 eggs, at room temperature

2 teaspoon Amaretto

Pinch of salt

½ cup granulated sugar, for dusting

½ cup powdered sugar, for dusting

SPECIAL TOOLS AND PANS

Food processor

Bain-marie (see page 10)

Cookie sheets

YIELD

4 dozen cookies

Pignoli Amaretti Cookies

2 large egg whites

½ cup plus 4 tablespoons sugar

Pinch of salt

Scant 1 cup (8 ounces) almond paste

½ cup (2½ ounces) pignoli nuts

SPECIAL TOOLS AND PANS

Stand mixer

Pastry bag with a ½-inch (#6) round tip (optional)

Cookie sheets

YIELD

3 dozen cookies

INGREDIENT
Almond paste

Almond paste can be found in most supermarkets, by mail order, or at online baking supply sites. If you cannot find almond paste, you can try to mimic it. Using a food processor or coffee grinder, grind a heaping cup (6 ounces) of blanched almonds with ½ cup confectionary sugar, 2 tablespoons light corn syrup, and ½ teaspoon almond extract. Once you have ground the nuts into a paste, knead the mixture a bit with a mortar and pestle. You should end up with approximately 8 ounces of almond paste.

Susan Punturieri, who was my sous-chef for six years at Chanterelle, introduced me to these marzipan-flavored Italian macaroon cookies. Other than the fact that they are delicious—intensely chewy on the inside and crispy and full of pignoli nuts on the outside—these are great cookies for two reasons: they are simple to prepare, and they will keep for about a week.

Preheat the oven to 350°F and position the rack in the center of the oven. Spray cookie sheets with oil and line with aluminum foil, parchment, or silicone pads, or use nonstick pans.

Combine the ingredients.
In the bowl of a stand mixer, whisk together the egg whites, granulated sugar, and salt by hand for 1 minute. Add the almond paste and, using the stand mixer fitted with the paddle attachment, beat the mixture on medium speed until it is thoroughly combined, 3 to 5 minutes. If the almond paste is dry and not incorporating well, continue beating until you have a smooth paste.

Pipe or shape the cookies.
Using a pastry bag fitted with a ½-inch tip, squeeze out large chocolate-kiss-shaped mounds, arranged 1 inch apart on your prepared cookie sheets. You should end up with around 36 mounds. (If you do not have a piping bag, use 2 teaspoons, one to scoop and the other to smooth out a mound of dough. Alternatively you can chill the dough for 1 hour and then roll balls of dough between your hands.) Press at least 6 to 8 pignoli nuts into the top of each cookie.

Bake the cookies.
Bake the cookies until golden brown and you smell the wonderful aroma of toasted almonds, 18 to 20 minutes. If you are among those who prefer these cookies to be dark and crunchy throughout, bake them for 5 minutes more. If you are making these cookies for the Chestnut and Amaretti Cookie Pudding (page 97), bake them for the extra 5 minutes. For even browning, rotate your cookie sheet once or even twice while the cookies are baking.

Serving Suggestions
These cookies go well with a shot of brandy, a cup of coffee, or on a cookie platter. I use them to flavor my Chestnut and Amaretti Cookie Pudding (page 97).

Storage
The chewy version of this recipe will keep, sealed in a container, for 4 days. The crunchier, darker version will keep, sealed in a container, for 1 week.

Crispy Bittersweet Chocolate Wafers

Thin, crispy, and light, these chocolatey cookies are my most beloved garnish for a chocolate dessert. Once half baked, these cookies can be cut into any size or shape. They make a wonderful Napoleon, layered between Sesame Milk Chocolate Mousse (page 109) or Cinnamon Caramel Mousse (page 106).

In the process of cutting these wafers into perfect round circles, you will be left with many oddly shaped crispy chocolate wafer scraps. Save these scraps and grind them up to use in any crumb crust recipe.

Preheat the oven to 350°F. Line two 16 x 13-inch cookie sheets with parchment or with nonstick baking pads.

Prepare the dry ingredients.
In a dry bowl, whisk together the flour, baking soda, and salt. Set aside.

Prepare the chocolate.
In the bowl of a bain-marie, melt the chocolate and butter, stirring frequently. Remove from the heat and set aside.

Whip the sugar with the egg.
In a medium bowl, whisk together the sugar, corn syrup, and egg by hand for 30 seconds. Whisk in the melted chocolate.

Finish the batter.
Add the dry mixture, all at once, to the chocolate mixture. Slowly whisk the mixture until the batter is lump-free and thoroughly combined.

Spread the batter onto the cookie sheets.
Divide the batter between the 2 prepared cookie sheets and, using an offset spatula, spread out as much as possible. Cover the cookie batter with another sheet of parchment or wax paper. The batter will now be sandwiched between 2 layers of paper. Using your hands, press the paper to spread the batter between the sheets until it covers the entire cookie sheet. Once the batter is evenly distributed over the whole pan, quickly peel off the top layer of parchment. Repeat the process on the second tray.

Bake and shape the wafers.
Place both trays in the oven and bake until the sheets no longer appear shiny and wet and resemble the top of a chocolate cake, 12 minutes. Remove one sheet and, holding the pan steady with one hand, use a cookie cutter to punch and shape your cookies without removing them from the cookie sheet. Or use a knife to cut the cookies into triangles, rectangles, or squares. You must work quickly because these cookies will crack and break as they cool. If the cookies get too cool, place the tray back in the oven for a minute. Once you have cut and shaped all the cookies on a tray, put it back in the oven for 6 to 10 minutes or until you smell the chocolate caramelizing while you repeat the shaping process with the second tray.

Allow the cookies to cool on the trays. Once the cookies have cooled they should be light and crispy. If they are still soft, you can return them to the oven and bake for an additional 3 to 5 minutes.

Serving Suggestions
Serve these cookies with milk. They are also a perfect accompaniment to any of the mousse recipes. They also make the best crumb crust for the Banana Cream Pie (page 91) with Chocolate Crumb Crust.

Storage
These cookies will keep, well sealed and stored in a cool place, for 1 week.

1 cup flour

½ teaspoon baking soda

¼ teaspoon salt

8 tablespoons (4 ounces) butter

6 ounces dark chocolate (61 to 70 percent cocoa solids)

⅓ cup sugar

¼ cup light corn syrup

1 egg, at room temperature

SPECIAL TOOLS AND PANS

Bain-marie (see page 10)

Cookie sheets (16 x 13 inches)

Offset spatula

3-inch round, square, or triangular cookie cutter, optional

YIELD

Sixty 3-inch round wafers

VARIATION

Chocolate Crumb Crust:
Preheat the oven to 350°F. Grind one baking sheet of the cookies in a food processor. You should have approximately 2 cups of crumbs. Melt 5 tablespoons of butter. In a bowl, using a fork, toss the crumbs with the melted butter and 2 tablespoons of sugar. Press the crumbs into a 9-inch pie dish. Cover the crumbs with a piece of aluminum foil and fill the pie shell with pie weights or dry beans. Bake the crust for 25 minutes. Allow the crust to cool then remove the weights and the aluminum lining.

Hazelnut Shortbread

¾ cup (3.25 ounces) filberts (skinned hazelnuts)

⅓ cup cornstarch

2 ⅓ cups flour

½ teaspoon salt

16 tablespoons (8 ounces) butter, at room temperature

¾ cup sugar

SPECIAL TOOLS AND PANS

Food processor

Stand mixer

Cookie sheets

Cookie cutter (optional)

Decorative wooden rolling pin (optional)

YIELD

About 50 small cookies

This shortbread has a distinctly nutty flavor with melt-in-your-mouth crispiness. The cookies have a very small proportion of sugar and no eggs or leavening agents—they rely on incredibly well-creamed butter for lightness. When they come out of the oven, they have risen and increased in size dramatically

At Chanterelle we make the shortbread look extra fancy by using "Chittara" wooden rolling pins from Italy that are meant for rolling and cutting spaghetti out of pasta dough. We roll the grooved rolling pin in multiple directions over the top of the rolled shortbread dough to form little grooved diamonds on the tops of the cookies. We then cut the cookies into rectangles, and they retain this pattern when they bake. There are a number of grooved and patterned wooden rolling pins made to decorate children's Play-Doh that you can use on the top of this dough.

Grind the hazelnuts and assemble the dry ingredients.
Combine the hazelnuts and 1 tablespoon of the cornstarch in a food processor and grind to a fine powder. In a dry bowl, whisk together the hazelnut powder, remaining cornstarch, flour, and salt, and set aside.

Cream the butter.
Follow the TECHNIQUE TIP: *Creaming butter, page 67.*

Place the butter in the bowl of the stand mixer with the paddle attachment and beat on medium speed for 1 minute. Add the sugar and beat on medium-high speed until the mixture becomes fluffy and almost white, 8 to 10 minutes, stopping the mixer occasionally to scrape down the sides of the bowl. This dough has no added leavening agents. It is extremely important to cream the butter well and incorporate as many air pockets as possible into the fat structure.

Finish the dough.
Add the dry ingredients, all at once, to the butter mixture. Using a rubber spatula, fold together for a few turns. With the mixer on slow speed, mix the dough until thoroughly combined, 1 minute.

Using a rubber spatula, scrape the dough onto a piece of plastic wrap. Wrap the dough tightly and press it into a 1-inch-thick rectangle. Refrigerate for at least 2 hours.

Shape the cookies.
Preheat the oven to 350°F. Spray cookie sheets with oil and line with aluminum foil, parchment, or silicone pads, or use nonstick pans.

Quick Method for Shaping
Using a sharp knife and a cutting board, cut the chilled dough into 1 ½ x 3-inch bars. Cut each bar into 8 or 9 even slices. You should aim for a raw cookie that is 1 ½ x 1 x ⅓ inch thick. Place the cookies 1 inch apart on the prepared cookie sheets.

Shaping by Rolling and Cutting
Follow the TECHNIQUE TIP: *Rolling tart dough, page 17.*

Roll out the dough to ⅓ inch thick. Using a knife and ruler, cut the cookies into perfect rectangles. You may also use a small 1 ½-inch cookie cutter to punch out shaped cookies. Place the cookies 1 inch apart on the prepared cookie sheets. Refrigerate any remaining dough scraps for 20 minutes before rerolling them.

Bake the cookies.

Bake the cookies until golden brown and you can smell the wonderful aroma of toasted hazelnuts with butter, 12 to 15 minutes. For even browning, rotate your cookie sheets from front to back and between each of the baking racks at least once while the cookies are baking. Allow the cookies to cool on the sheets.

Serving Suggestions

These cookies go well with almost all the recipes in this book.

Storage

These cookies will keep, sealed in a container, for 1 week.

Creaming butter

When you cream butter well, you introduce thousands of air pockets into your dough or cake batter, leavening it and yielding a delicate, seemingly light baked product. Leavening agents like baking powder act on the air bubbles already created in the creaming process.

There are numerous opinions about what temperature butter should be before you work with it. Most chefs agree that creaming slightly melted butter or warm butter yields a product with low volume and a greasy, tough, heavy texture. The question arises: To what extent should your butter be chilled to avoid its melting in the creaming process?

In all my recipes with creamed butter and sugar I recommend that you start with room-temperature butter (66°F to 70°F). Room-temperature butter should yield to the pressure of your fingers without being slippery or overly soft. Butter properly whipped and creamed in this temperature range stores the maximum amount of air bubbles in your cake or cookie batter.

The agents that force air into the butter are your beater or whisk and sugar crystals. There are certain visual signs that signal the extent to which air has been incorporated into your creaming butter. Well-creamed butter increases in volume and dramatically lightens

in color—if you are using white sugar, the color of your butter will change from yellow to almost white after creaming.

There are also visual clues to look out for if you are worried that your butter is becoming too warm. The butter becomes very shiny and glossy—properly whipped butter is matte white. Overly warm butter no longer gains in volume or lightens in color. If this happens, place the mixing bowl in the refrigerator for 5 minutes. Also make sure that none of the remaining ingredients yet to be added is warm, in order to prevent further melting.

Oatmeal Cookies with Golden Raisins and Milk Chocolate Chips

1 ¼ cups flour

1 teaspoon baking soda

½ teaspoon salt

16 tablespoons (8 ounces) butter, at room temperature

1 cup sugar

1 cup dark brown sugar

2 eggs plus 1 egg white, at room temperature

3 cups raw oatmeal

8 ounces milk chocolate, chopped into ¼-inch pieces

1 cup (5 ½ ounces) golden raisins

SPECIAL TOOLS AND PANS

Stand mixer

Cookie sheets

YIELD

40 large round cookies

VARIATION

Dried Cherry or Dried Pear and Chocolate Chip Oatmeal Cookies: Substitute dried cherries or diced dried pears for the raisins and dark chocolate for the milk chocolate.

Chewy, caramelized, crispy, and packed with oats, these cookies draw oohs and aahs whenever I make them for my family or for the staff at Chanterelle. They are quite large and flat with a crisp outer edge and a chewy, buttery center.

Make sure you do not use quick-cooking oats—they have a high water content and less flavor. Since the dough can be made in advance, I always bring some with me when I take my kids to visit friends out at the beach or upstate. If I show up without it, I get pouts of disappointment.

Preheat the oven to 350°F. Spray cookie sheets with oil and line with aluminum foil, parchment, or silicone pads, or use nonstick pans.

Prepare the dry ingredients.
In a dry bowl, whisk together the flour, baking soda, and salt. Set aside.

Cream the butter and incorporate the eggs.
Follow the TECHNIQUE TIP: *Creaming butter, page 67. See* BEYOND THE BASICS: *Room-temperature eggs, page 53.*

Place the butter in the bowl of the stand mixer with the paddle attachment and beat on medium speed for 1 minute. Add the sugar, and beat on medium-high speed until the mixture becomes fluffy and lighter in color, approximately 5 minutes. Add the dark brown sugar and continue creaming for 3 to 4 minutes, stopping the mixer occasionally to scrape down the sides of the bowl. Turn the mixer down to slow speed. Add the eggs and egg white, one at a time, and continue to beat until they are fully incorporated and the batter looks smooth and glossy, 1 to 2 minutes.

Finish the dough.
Add the dry mixture, all at once, to the butter mixture. Using a rubber spatula, fold together for a few turns. With the mixer on slow speed, mix the dough until thoroughly combined, 1 minute. Add the chopped milk chocolate and the golden raisins. Scrape down the sides of the bowl with a rubber spatula and mix for another 30 seconds. The dough can be made up to this point and refrigerated, well wrapped, for up to 3 days.

Shape the cookies.
Using 2 teaspoons, scoop the dough into mounds and place 2 inches apart on your prepared cookie sheets. Flatten each mound with the back of a spoon or two fingertips.

Bake the cookies.
Bake the cookies until they spread, rise, and turn a light golden brown, 12 to 15 minutes. For even browning, rotate your cookie sheets from front to back and between each of the baking racks at least once while the cookies are baking. Remove from the oven and let cool on the sheets. Once cooled they will be crispy on the outside and chewy, moist, and buttery in the middle. If you continue to bake the cookies they will color more and your result will be a crunchy, caramelized, and intensely flavorful cookie.

Serving Suggestions
These cookies are delicious all on their own.

Storage
These cookies are best served the day they are baked but will keep, sealed and at room temperature, for 4 days.

TECHNIQUE TIP
Black steel baking pans

During an internship in France about nine years ago, I discovered black steel baking pans. In the pastry kitchen where I worked we used only these heavy, relatively thin black steel pans. We never lined the pans with parchment paper and, as with cast iron, never washed the pans with soap and water. After each use, we simply wiped the pan down with a rag and allowed it to cool.

Beyond the obvious benefits—less need for materials (parchment, water, and soap) and less labor (no scrubbing, washing, and drying)—these pans seemed to give baked goods a quick jolt of heat, imparting a crisp, golden exterior while maintaining a chewy moist interior.

I find that these pans improve the texture and color of many of my cookies, especially oatmeal cookies, chocolate chip cookies, and the gingersnaps.

Steel is a tough alloy of iron and carbon. Black steel or blue steel pans are a special form of carbonized steel that undergoes an annealing process, which causes them to be more durable and less reactive to acidic food and oxygen.

Like cast iron pans, these black steel pans have high heat capacity and relatively low thermal conductivity. But because of the black steel manufacturing process, these cookie sheets are significantly thinner than cast iron, so you get the benefits of cast iron without its limitations, specifically its thickness, weight, reactivity, and slowness to heat up.

In the oven, heat is transmitted to the food in two different ways: heat is transferred from the pan to the food by conduction and from the heating element to the food by radiation. Darker materials absorb and transmit more radiative heat than do lighter materials; therefore, a dark pan will transmit more heat to the food than a light-colored one, even if the dark and light pans are made of the same material. This makes black steel pans particularly appropriate for the hot, quick cooking required for cookie baking.

Coconut, Almond, and Brown Butter Macaroons

½ vanilla bean or
½ teaspoon vanilla extract

6 tablespoons (3 ounces) butter

¼ cup (2 ounces) almond paste
(see page 64)

4 egg whites

1 cup sugar

¼ teaspoon salt

3 cups shredded unsweethood
coconut

2 tablespoons flour

SPECIAL TOOLS AND PANS

Stand mixer

Cookie sheets

YIELD

35 cookies

VARIATION

Flourless Macaroons:
To make these cookies without flour (in order to make them kosher for Passover), replace the flour with potato starch.

My staff and I have tried dozens of recipes in search of a re-creation of our idealized memories of childhood macaroons. We wanted a cookie that was moist and chewy on the inside and crispy on the outside. This one best matches our nostalgic imaginations. What makes these coconut macaroons particularly tasty is the addition of almond paste and brown butter.

Preheat the oven to 350°F. Spray cookie sheets with oil and line with aluminum foil, parchment, or silicone pads, or use nonstick pans.

Brown the butter with the vanilla bean.
Follow the TECHNIQUE TIP: *Browning butter, page 51.*

Run a paring knife down the center of the vanilla bean. Split it open with your fingers and use the knife to scrape out the tiny black seeds into a saucepan. Add the butter and the scraped vanilla bean and turn the heat to medium-high. (If you are using vanilla extract, brown the butter by itself.) Cook the butter with the vanilla bean and seeds until the butter caramelizes and emits a rich nutty vanilla aroma. Remove the vanilla bean, dry, and save for another use.

Mix the batter.
In the bowl of a stand mixer fitted with the paddle attachment, combine the almond paste, 1 egg white, and sugar. Beat on medium speed until the mixture is thoroughly combined. Add the remaining 3 egg whites, salt, and coconut and continue to beat for 1 minute. Add the vanilla extract if you are using it. Turn the mixer to slow speed. Add the flour and beat until just incorporated. Drizzle the browned butter down the side of the bowl and beat until it is completely incorporated and the dough is shiny.

Using a rubber spatula, scrape the dough onto a piece of plastic wrap. Wrap the dough and chill for 1 hour. The dough will keep, chilled and wrapped, for up to 2 days.

Shape and bake the macaroons.
Pinch off 1-inch chunks of the chilled dough and roll into balls. Place on the prepared cookie sheet, 1 inch apart, and press your thumb in the center of each cookie to flatten it a bit. Bake the cookies until they spread and rise, and are light brown on the tops, 15 to 20 minutes. For even browning, rotate your cookie sheet once or even twice while the cookies are baking. Remove them from the oven and allow to cool on the sheets. Once cooled they should be crispy on the outside and chewy in the middle.

Serving Suggestions
Serve these cookies with a cup of tea or coffee.

Storage
These cookies will keep, well wrapped at room temperature, for 4 days.

Hazelnut, Cinnamon, Cardamom, and Raspberry Sandwich Cookies

This recipe is a riff on the classic Linzer cookie, jazzed up with cardamom, my favorite spice. I prefer to use raspberry jam with seeds, as the seeds add another textural dimension. The dough for this recipe does not call for too much sugar, because of the sweetness of the jam and the final dusting of powdered sugar, so do not be surprised if the dough doesn't seem sweet enough when you taste it.

Grind the hazelnuts and assemble the dry ingredients.

Combine the hazelnuts, ½ cup of the flour, and salt in a food processor and grind to a fine powder. In a dry bowl, whisk together the hazelnut powder, remaining flour, cinnamon, cardamom, and baking powder, and set aside.

Cream the butter and incorporate the eggs.
Follow the TECHNIQUE TIP: Creaming butter, page 67. See BEYOND THE BASICS: Room-temperature eggs, page 53.

Place the butter in the bowl of the stand mixer with the paddle attachment and beat on medium speed for 1 minute. Add the sugar and beat on medium-high speed until the mixture becomes fluffy and almost white in color, 6 to 8 minutes, stopping the mixer occasionally to scrape down the sides of the bowl. Add the egg and continue to beat until fully incorporated and the batter looks smooth and glossy, 1 to 2 minutes.

Add the dry ingredients and finish the dough.
Add the dry mixture, all at once, to the butter mixture. Using a rubber spatula, fold together for a few turns. With the mixer on slow speed, mix the dough until thoroughly combined, 1 to 2 minutes. Scrape down the sides of the bowl with a rubber spatula and mix for another 30 seconds.

Using a rubber spatula, scrape the dough onto a piece of plastic wrap. Wrap the dough tightly and press it down to form a flat rectangle, 1 inch thick. Refrigerate the dough at least 2 hours or overnight.

Preheat the oven to 350°F. Spray cookie sheets with oil and line with aluminum foil, parchment, or silicone pads, or use nonstick pans.

Roll and shape the cookies.

Quick Method for Shaping
If you do not have time to roll out the cookies, here is a shortcut that will still produce delicious wafers, but the cookies will not have uniform shape and finesse. Using a sharp knife and a cutting board, cut as many 1½ x 3-inch-long bars of the chilled dough as you can. Cut each bar into ⅛- to ¹⁄₁₆-inch-thick slices and place the cookies ½ inch apart on the prepared cookie sheets.

Shaping by Rolling and Cutting
Follow the TECHNIQUE TIP: Rolling tart dough, page 17.

Roll the chilled dough out to ¹⁄₁₆ inch thick. Using your cookie cutter of choice, punch out cookies as close together on the dough as you can. Place the cookies 1 inch apart on the prepared cookie sheets. Make sure you have an even number of cookies. With your hole punch, make a small hole in the center of half of the cookies. (This is purely decorative; if you wish, you can skip this step.) Shape any remaining scraps of dough into a ball, wrap in plastic wrap, press it down into a disk, and refrigerate for at least 20 minutes before rolling it out again.

If you have room in your refrigerator, chill the cookies on the cookie sheets for 15 minutes before baking. If not, you can bake each tray as soon as it is filled with shaped cookies.

1 heaping cup (approximately 5 ounces) hazelnuts

2 ½ cups flour

¼ teaspoon salt

1 teaspoon cinnamon

½ teaspoon ground cardamom

¼ teaspoon baking powder

16 tablespoons (8 ounces) butter, at room temperature

¾ cup sugar

1 egg, at room temperature

½ cup raspberry jam

¼ cup powdered sugar, for dusting

SPECIAL TOOLS AND PANS

Coffee grinder or food processor for grinding nuts

Stand mixer

Small 1½-inch cookie cutter (round, round and fluted, or square or triangular), optional

Small hole puncher to make ½-inch hole (½-inch round pastry tip, straw, apple corer, or tiny cookie cutter), optional

Sifter or mesh strainer

Cookie sheets

YIELD

5 dozen sandwich cookies

Bake the cookies.

Bake the cookies until golden brown and you can smell the wonderful aroma of toasted hazelnuts with butter, 12 to 15 minutes. For even browning, rotate the cookie sheets once or even twice while the cookies are baking. Remove the cookies from the oven and allow them to cool on the sheets.

Fill and sandwich the cookies.

Using a piping bag or a tiny teaspoon, dot the cookies without holes (or half of the cookies) with the raspberry jam. Cover with the remaining cookies to make a sandwich. Place the powdered sugar in a strainer or sifter and sift the sugar over the finished cookies.

Serving Suggestions

Serve these cookies with a cup of tea or coffee.

Storage

Because of the moisture in the filling, these cookies loose their crunchiness after 1 day. They are best eaten up to 4 hours after sandwiching. You can bake the cookies and store them in an airtight container for up to 4 days ahead, then fill them the day you plan to serve them.

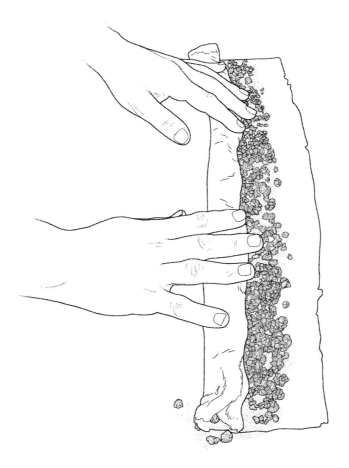

Walnut, Currant, and Cinnamon Rugelach

The dough for this rugelach is magical—I am not really sure why this works. Creaming together the butter and cream cheese in equal parts and then adding the flour produces a dough that bakes like puff pastry without even a tenth of the effort. It doesn't bake up as crispy as puff pastry, but its appealingly sour flavor and soft, multilayered texture are irresistible.

The logs keep in the freezer quite well, so you can make a double batch if you like and keep some on hand for quick baking.

Make the dough.
Using a stand mixer fitted with the paddle attachment or a hand mixer, combine the butter and cream cheese and beat on medium speed until the mixture is light, fluffy, and has increased in volume, 5 to 8 minutes. On slow speed, add the dry ingredients and beat until the dough is thoroughly combined. Set the mixer on medium speed and beat the dough for 15 seconds.

Using a rubber spatula, scrape the dough onto a piece of plastic wrap. Wrap the dough tightly and press it down until it is 1 inch thick. Refrigerate the dough at least 2 hours or overnight.

Make the filling.
In a bowl, using a fork, toss together the chopped walnuts, cinnamon, currants, and ¼ cup of the sugar.

Roll out the dough.
On a floured surface, roll out the chilled dough into a rough rectangle approximately 13 x 16 inches. Using a pizza cutter or paring knife, trim the dough into 2 rectangles measuring 6 ½ x 16 inches.

Fill and shape the dough.
In a small bowl, whisk the egg. Lay out each rectangle with the 16-inch side directly in front of you on the counter. Brush off any excess flour. Brush the egg wash over the entire surface of the dough. Evenly coat both rectangles of dough with the walnut filling, leaving a 1-inch-wide strip of dough on the edge farther away from you. Starting with the dough edge closer to you, tightly roll the dough away from you, tucking the filling under the dough as you roll **(see illustration, opposite)**. When you reach the strip of dough without topping, apply a little pressure to seal, and roll the log so that the seam is on the bottom, against the counter. Gently slide the logs of dough onto a cookie sheet, cover them with plastic wrap, and refrigerate for at least 30 minutes and up to 1 hour. Refrigerate the remaining egg wash. The logs can be stored in the refrigerator for 24 hours or in the freezer for 1 week.

Bake the rugelach.
Preheat the oven to 350°F ½ hour before baking. Spray cookie sheets with oil and line with aluminum foil, parchment, or silicone pads, or use nonstick pans.

Glaze the chilled logs with the reserved egg and sprinkle with the remaining ¼ cup of sugar. Slice each log into 1-inch cross sections; you should get between 16 and 18 slices from each log. Place the cookies 1 inch apart on the prepared cookie sheets. Bake until puffed and dark golden brown, 15 to 18 minutes. Rotate the pans from front to back and in between shelves about halfway through the baking time. Allow the cookies to cool for 15 minutes before removing from the cookie sheets.

Serving Suggestions
Serve these cookies for brunch or as dessert with coffee or tea.

Storage
These cookies will keep, well wrapped, for 4 days.

DOUGH

8 tablespoons (4 ounces) butter, at room temperature

4 ounces cream cheese, at room temperature

1 cup flour, plus more for rolling dough

¼ teaspoon salt

1 teaspoon sugar

FILLING

1 cup (4 ounces) finely chopped walnuts

½ teaspoon cinnamon

½ cup (2 ounces) currants

½ cup sugar

1 egg, for egg wash

SPECIAL TOOLS AND PANS

Stand mixer

Cookie sheets

YIELD

32 to 36 rugelach

Crispy Malted Bitter Chocolate Meringues

4 ounces unsweetened chocolate

1 ¼ cups granulated sugar

7 egg whites (approximately
1 cup), at room temperature

¼ teaspoon cream of tartar
(or ½ teaspoon lemon juice)

½ cup confectionary sugar

¼ cup barley malt syrup or
ice cream shop malt syrup

SPECIAL TOOLS AND PANS

Stand mixer

Piping bag, fitted with a ⁹⁄₁₆-inch-
diameter round tip (#7), optional

Cookie sheets

YIELD
70 piped mini domes or
30 large hand-shaped cookies

VARIATION

**Milk Chocolate–Coated
Malted Meringues:** *See* BEYOND
THE BASICS: *Tempered chocolate,
page 187.* Temper 8 ounces
of milk chocolate according
to the instructions on page 195.
Using a fork with long tines
or a chocolate dipping two-
pronged tool, dip each
meringue one at a time in the
bowl of tempered chocolate,
flipping it over and coating
evenly. Remove the meringue
with the fork, letting the excess
chocolate drip off. Place the
dipped meringues on a sheet
of parchment paper and allow
the chocolate coating to set.

Crispy meringues, sweetened with the dark, round flavor of malt and accented with shaved bitter chocolate, make a perfect sweet ending for a meal. These cookies are a dressed-up, flavorful version of those addictive milk chocolate–coated maltballs that I ate as a kid. The milk chocolate coating is optional. The meringues are light and delicious on their own.

Make sure you make these cookies on a cool, dry day. Meringues are packed with sugar, which absorbs humidity. If you do follow the optional step and dip these cookies in tempered milk chocolate, they will keep for weeks, stored in a cool, dry place. The cocoa butter in the chocolate acts as a humidity barrier, preserving the crisp, aerated meringue.

Preheat the oven to 225°F. Line cookie sheets with parchment or use nonstick pans.

Prepare the chocolate and sugar mixture.
Chop the unsweetened chocolate very fine by hand and combine it with ¼ cup of the granulated sugar.

Make the meringue.
See BEYOND THE BASICS: *A French meringue and egg white foams, page 75.*

In a stand mixer fitted with the whisk attachment, whisk the egg whites on medium-high speed until frothy and no longer liquid. Add the cream of tartar and whisk for another 2 minutes. Add the remaining 1 cup sugar, 1 tablespoon at a time, whisking on medium-high speed for 1 to 1 ½ minutes after each addition. The whites will continually increase in volume, shine, and whiteness (at least 15 minutes of whisking is required). Add the confectionary sugar in 3 additions, whisking for 30 seconds after each addition. Add the barley malt syrup and whisk on slow speed for 1 minute.

Fold in the chocolate.
Remove the bowl from the mixer and, using a spatula, fold in the chocolate and sugar mixture. To fold in ingredients, place the spatula in the center of the bowl, scrape the bottom, and bring the bottom over the top. Rotate the bowl

45 degrees and repeat this motion. Continue folding the mixture until the chocolate is evenly distributed throughout the meringue.

Shape the meringues.

SIMPLE, FREE-FORM MERINGUES
For a lovely, free-form meringue, use the tip of a rubber spatula to scoop up about 3 tablespoons of meringue and quickly flick it onto the cookie sheet, allowing 1 inch between meringues.

PIPED MERINGUES
For a more finished, uniform-looking meringue, scrape half of the meringue into a pastry bag fitted with a ⁹⁄₁₆-inch-diameter round tip and the top folded back in a 4-inch cuff. Unfold the cuff and twist the top of the bag closed, pushing and squeezing the meringue down toward the tip. Hold the bag upright, about 1 inch above the parchment paper, and gently squeeze, raising the bag as you squeeze a small dome of meringue 1 inch in diameter and 1 ½ inches high onto the cookie sheet, allowing 1 inch between the meringues.

Bake the meringues.
Follow the TECHNIQUE TIP: *Making and baking a French meringue, page 75.*

Bake the meringues for 45 minutes, rotating the pans multiple times. If the meringues are rapidly coloring, turn off the oven. After 45 minutes, turn down the oven to 200°F and bake for another 1½ hours, continuing to rotate the trays. Turn off the oven and allow the meringues to remain in the oven for 1 hour. Remove the meringues from the oven and allow them to cool completely. They should be hard and crisp once they have cooled.

Serving Suggestions
Serve these sweet crispy confections as an afternoon snack.

Storage
Keep these meringues sealed at room temperature in a dry environment.

BEYOND THE BASICS
A French meringue and egg white foams

Egg whites, in their fresh translucent state, consist largely of proteins suspended in liquid (mostly water). In the process of making a French meringue or any egg white foam, some proteins are coaxed (denatured) out of their yarn-ball shape through agitation, exposure to warmer temperatures, and added acid, and stretched into strands that eventually link together (a process called coagulation) and absorb water, forming a scaffolding that traps air pockets.

If this scaffolding of proteins is overagitated, more and more proteins coagulate, leaving no room to hold liquid. Water leaches out of the gel and the foam begins to collapse. You can see this if you notice small beads of egg whites forming around the edges of your bowl. If egg whites are whipped further after these early signs they become chunky, uneven, wet, and very difficult to incorporate into mousses, soufflés, or cake batters.

Sugar gets in the way of protein strands and prevents early coagulation. In a French meringue the continued addition of sugar allows the egg whites to be beaten for a very long period of time, encouraging the incorporation of more and more air into the protein strands holding liquid. In addition, sugar dissolves in water, making the liquid in an egg white foam more viscous and enabling a stronger foam to exist, which can last longer.

TECHNIQUE TIP
Making and baking a French meringue

Use room-temperature egg whites when making a meringue. Make sure the egg whites are fully frothed before you add your cream of tartar or acid. Whip the acid into the egg whites for at least 1 minute until the whites foam and hold the lines of a whisk for 20 seconds. Begin adding your sugar slowly, 1 tablespoon at a time. If you see egg whites beading or curdling on the side of the bowl, slow the machine down and add the sugar 2 tablespoons at a time

A French meringue is done when all the sugar is incorporated and the egg white foam is shiny, smooth (not grainy), opaque white and has gained around 10 times its volume. Stop the machine, detach the whisk, and try moving the whisk around in the meringue with your hand. The meringue should feel stiff and dense.

Bake the meringues in a low oven (200°F to 225°F) for approximately 2 hours, depending on the size and thickness of the meringues. Through baking you are slowly drawing the moisture out of the egg white foam, leaving sugar to help stabilize it. This moisture must evaporate and escape the oven for the meringues to dry out and hold their shape. Gas ovens are vented. If you are using an electric oven, leave the door slightly ajar as you bake and dry out your meringues.

Do not allow your meringues to brown— browning is a sign that the oven is too hot. If you notice your meringues expanding 5 minutes after you have placed them in the oven, turn the heat down. You do not want to heat the air trapped in the egg white foam so much that it expands and causes the protein webs to collapse, leaving your meringue cookies shrunk and shriveled.

Too high an oven temperature also causes proteins to squeeze out the water bound in the foam faster than the rate at which the water would evaporate. These water beads can caramelize on the outside of the meringue, leaving a yellow-brown dotted coloring on the outside of the finished meringue cookies.

Maple-Pecan Meringue Cookies

1 cup (4 ounces) pecans

2 tablespoons cornstarch

1 cup sugar

7 egg whites (approximately
1 cup), at room temperature

¼ teaspoon cream of tartar
(or ½ teaspoon lemon juice)

1¼ cups maple syrup

SPECIAL TOOLS AND PANS

Stand mixer

Piping bag, fitted with a ⁹⁄₁₆-inch-
diameter round tip (#7), optional

Food processor

Candy thermometer (optional)

Cookie sheets

Medium-sized heavy-bottomed
saucepan with at least 4-inch
sides

YIELD

70 cookies

These cookies are ethereal and light, richly flavored with concentrated maple syrup and ground toasted pecans. At Chanterelle we spread this meringue batter thinly over an entire cookie pan and cut it into rectangular wafers while it is still hot, then layer the cookies between Maple–Star Anise Mousse (page 104) and serve alongside Maple Crème Caramel (page 88) and Maple-Ginger Ice Cream (page 139), creating a trio of maple desserts. You may also want to simply enjoy the flavor of these cookies as an afternoon snack or as a sweet ending to a dinner.

These meringues should not be made on a hot, humid day. The sugar in the meringue will absorb the humidity and cause the cookie to become soft and sticky.

Preheat the oven to 225°F. Line cookie sheets with parchment or use nonstick pans.

Grind the pecans.

Combine the pecans and cornstarch in a food processor and grind to a fine powder. In a bowl, combine the pecan powder and ½ cup of the sugar. Set aside.

Make the meringue.

See BEYOND THE BASICS: *A French meringue and egg white foams, page 75.*

In a stand mixer fitted with the whisk attachment, whisk the egg whites on medium-high speed until frothy and no longer liquid. Add the cream of tartar and whisk for another 2 minutes. Add remaining ½ cup of the sugar, 1 tablespoon at a time, whisking on medium-high speed for 1 to 1½ minutes after each addition.

Simultaneously, boil the maple syrup in a heavy-bottomed saucepan over medium-high heat until the syrup registers 240°F on a candy thermometer. If you do not have a thermometer, test the syrup after it has boiled, foamed, and reduced somewhat. Drop a fork tong of syrup on the counter—if it dries in a mound, scrapes off the counter cleanly with your fingernail, and is somewhat pliable and gummy between two fingers, it is ready.

Once the syrup is ready, you should have finished adding the sugar to the egg white foam. It should have risen and gained whiteness and shine. With the mixer on medium-high speed, slowly pour the hot maple syrup down the inside of the bowl. The meringue will gain in volume, take on a beige appearance, and become more shiny and opaque. Continue whisking the meringue until it gains 10 times its volume and is shiny and stiff, at least 5 minutes.

Fold in the nuts and the remaining sugar.

Remove the bowl of maple meringue from the mixer and, using a rubber spatula, fold in the nut mixture. To fold in ingredients, place the spatula in the center of the bowl, scrape the bottom, and bring the bottom over the top. Rotate the bowl 45 degrees and repeat this motion. Continue folding the mixture together until the nut mixture is evenly distributed in the meringue.

Shape the meringues.

Simple, Free-form Meringues

For a lovely, free-form meringue, use the tip of a rubber spatula to scoop up about 3 tablespoons of meringue and quickly flick it onto the cookie sheet, allowing 1 inch between meringues.

Piped Meringues

For a more finished, uniform-looking meringue, scrape half of the meringue into a pastry bag fitted with a 9/16-inch-diameter round tip and the top folded back in a 4-inch cuff. Unfold the cuff and twist the top of the bag closed, pushing and squeezing the meringue down toward the tip. Hold the bag upright, about 1 inch above the parchment paper, and gently squeeze, raising the bag as you squeeze a small dome of meringue 1 inch in diameter and 1 ½ inches high onto the cookie sheet, allowing 1 inch between the meringues. Refill the bag with the remaining meringue and continue to pipe the cookies.

Bake the meringues.
Follow the TECHNIQUE TIP: *Making and baking a French meringue, page 75.*

Bake the meringues for 1 hour, rotating the pans multiple times. If the meringues are rapidly coloring, turn off the oven. After 1 hour, turn down the oven to 200°F and bake for another 1 ½ hours, continuing to rotate the trays. Turn off the oven and allow the meringues to remain in the oven for 1 hour. Remove the meringues from the oven and allow them to cool completely. They should be hard and crisp once they have cooled.

Serving Suggestions
Serve these cookies with a bowl of whipped cream or by themselves as an after-dinner snack.

Storage
These cookies will keep, in an airtight container, for 1 week.

Hazelnut and Orange Macaroons

HAZELNUT MACAROON

About 2 cups (10 ounces) filberts (skinned hazelnuts)

1 (16-ounce) box confectionary sugar

½ teaspoon salt

8 egg whites (1 cup), at room temperature

⅓ cup sugar

Pinch of cream of tartar

ORANGE BUTTERCREAM

3 egg yolks

½ cup plus 2 tablespoons sugar

Zest of 1 orange or tangerine

16 tablespoons (8 ounces) butter, at room temperature

2 tablespoons Grand Marnier

SPECIAL TOOLS AND PANS

Nut grinder or food processor

4 cookie sheets

Stand mixer

Piping bag, fitted with a ⁶/₁₆- to ⁸/₁₆-inch-diameter tip (#4 to #6)

Candy thermometer (optional)

YIELD

Approximately sixty 1½-inch round sandwich cookies

This is a different kind of cookie from the ones we generally call macaroons here in America. These are French macaroons, two light, crispy hazelnut, almond, or pistachio meringues sandwiched together around a filling. See the variations below for delicious filling alternatives.

Grind and sift the dry ingredients.
Combine the hazelnuts and 1 cup of the confectionary sugar in a nut grinder or food processor and grind to a fine powder, stopping the machine once or twice to scrape down the corners and sides and toss the nuts around. In a dry bowl, whisk the ground nuts with the remaining confectionary sugar and salt. Set aside.

Make the meringue.
See BEYOND THE BASICS: *A French meringue and egg white foams, page 75.*

In a stand mixer fitted with the whisk attachment, whisk the egg whites on medium-high speed until they begin to foam. Add the cream of tartar and whisk until the whites are completely foamy and begin to hold the line of the whisk. Add the sugar, 2 teaspoons at a time. As you add the sugar, the whites will become shiny and gain volume. Turn the mixer to slow speed, add the remaining sugar, and beat until the meringue is shiny and smooth with soft peaks.

Fold the dry ingredients into the meringue.
Scrape the meringue into the dry ingredients and gently fold together until the dry ingredients have been absorbed by the meringue and the mixture is smooth and creamy. If the batter seems a bit stiff—it holds the point of a spatula if you quickly remove it—continue folding until it has a more fluid texture. Do not work it so much that the batter becomes runny.

Pipe the cookies.
Line 4 cookie sheets with parchment. Scrape half of the batter into a pastry bag with the top folded back in a 4-inch cuff, and fitted with a round tip (#4 to #6). Unfold the cuff and twist the top of the bag closed, pushing and squeezing the batter down toward the tip. Hold the bag upright,

about 1 inch above the cookie sheet, and gently squeeze out small mounds 1¼ inches in diameter, which will settle into 1½-inch circles. Give the bag a gentle squeeze and then quickly pull the tip up so you control how much comes out and how the cookie ultimately takes shape. Squeeze out 6 rows of 7 cookies per cookie sheet. Allow the cookies to sit at room temperature for 1 to 2 hours, to dry out the tops. Do not bake until you can gently touch the top of a piped cookie without any residue remaining on your finger.

Make an orange buttercream.
In the bowl of a stand mixer with the whisk attachment (or a medium-sized stainless-steel bowl on a wet rag to hold the bowl in place), combine the yolks and 2 tablespoons of the sugar and whisk for 30 seconds.

Simultaneously, in a small saucepan, combine the orange zest, remaining ½ cup of sugar, and 3 tablespoons of water. Cook over high heat until the mixture reaches 248°F on a candy thermometer. To test the syrup without a thermometer, dip a fork into the syrup and drizzle a bit on the counter. The sugar droplet should cool into a pliable ball that scrapes cleanly off the counter.

Drizzle the orange syrup down the side of the bowl into the egg yolks, whisking them briskly to blend. Continue whisking the egg yolk mixture until the yolks have tripled in volume, hold the lines of the whisk, and have cooled. Add the butter and Grand Marnier and whisk until the buttercream is fluffy and creamy with stiff, shiny, pointy peaks.

Preheat the oven to 350°F. Set two racks in the oven, one at the very top and one on the bottom.

Bake the macaroons.

Once the macaroons have dried properly, place one cookie sheet in the oven on the top shelf for 8 minutes. Open the oven door, rotate the cookie sheet, and place it on the bottom shelf. Place the second cookie sheet in the oven on the top shelf and bake for another 8 minutes. After baking first on the top shelf and then on the bottom, the cookies should be ready. Remove the sheet on the bottom shelf from the oven and repeat this baking process until all four cookie sheets have been baked. The macaroons should have puffed evenly, become shiny, and fallen slightly. They almost look like half a hamburger bun.

Fill and sandwich the macaroons.

Once the cookies have cooled, flip half of the cookies over. Scrape the buttercream into a pastry bag with the top folded back in a 4-inch cuff, and fitted with a $\frac{1}{3}$-inch-diameter round tip. Unfold the cuff and twist the top of the bag closed, pushing and squeezing the buttercream down toward the tip. Hold the bag upright, about 1 inch above each inverted cookie, and gently squeeze out a small mound of buttercream, about the size of a nickel, onto the upturned cookies. Do not cover the whole cookie; there should be a clear rim of cookie around the mound of buttercream. Top each cookie with a second macaroon, gently pressing down so the buttercream spreads to the edges of the sandwich.

Serving Suggestions

Serve these cookies with a cup or coffee or tea.

Storage

These cookies will keep, stored in a container, in the freezer for 1 month.

Hazelnut and Orange Macaroons

VARIATIONS

Almond Macaroons:

Substitute almonds for hazelnuts and use any flavor of buttercream.

Vanilla Buttercream:

To make a vanilla buttercream, omit the orange zest and slice and scrape a vanilla bean into the boiling syrup. The Grand Marnier (or other alcohol) is optional.

Chocolate Buttercream:

Melt 2 ounces of chocolate, allow it to cool, and whisk it into the finished buttercream.

CUSTARDS, PUDDINGS, CRÈMES, AND MOUSSES

CHAPTER FOUR

Baked Custard Guidelines

Baked custards are divine, sumptuous desserts. The magical texture found in an excellent crème caramel, crème brûlée, panna cotta, or any other baked custard derives from the cooking process. You need a good recipe, but, truthfully, custard recipes do not vary that much. You need to know how to cook a custard properly and determine whether it is done at just the right moment.

Custard-Baking Tips

The most important step in cooking custards is to make sure the custard cooks slowly and evenly at a controllable rate. A water bath, an aluminum foil cover with vent holes, a low baking temperature, and a fanless oven aid in the cooking process. Another common recommendation for custard baking is to line your baking pan with a towel so that there is no direct contact between the baking dish and the ramekins holding the custard. If you feel that your oven does not maintain its temperature very well or has hot spots, I would recommend this added precaution.

Because the bottom or the top oven shelves often cook more rapidly and unevenly, I suggest baking your custards on the middle shelf. Approximately two-thirds into the cooking time, open the oven and make sure your water bath is not boiling. If the water has begun to boil, lift off one corner of the aluminum foil or rotate the baking sheet (which is functioning as a cover for the baking pan) 90 degrees so there is more room for steam to escape.

Testing for Doneness

When your timer goes off after the designated cooking period has elapsed, open the oven, carefully remove the aluminum foil cover, and tap the baking pan holding all the custards. The top of the custards should be set. The center part of the custard should not shimmy separately from the outer ring of custard. If you touch the top of the custard very gently with your index finger you should feel a very slight firmness in the center— the custard in the center should not be a liquid that glazes the tip of your finger. You might also notice two or three dots in the center. These are very tiny air bubbles that indicate that the custard is set.

Another way to test the custard is to stick a paring knife straight down to the bottom of a custard, not quite in the center, but away from the sides. If you are testing a custard with a layer of caramel on the bottom of the mold, then it should rise up though the custard in a clear stream of caramel liquid, indicating that the custard is set. If you cannot see a clear stream of caramel, only runny custard, then the clear caramel on the bottom is being prevented from rising to the top because of the viscosity of the uncooked custard. If there is no caramel bottom in the custard recipe then when you pull out the knife it should not be glazed with a viscous layer of uncooked custard. Additionally a candy thermometer gently inserted into the custard should read between 170°F and 175°F.

If your custards are not done, cover them, close the oven, and bake for another 8 minutes. If when you check them for the second time they seem as if they have made no progress, then put them back in the oven and check in 20 minutes. Every time you open the oven, you allow the heat to escape, so constant checking can lead to zero cooking.

If your custards are set like Jell-O and they have many dots on the top (which are tiny air bubbles) then they are a few minutes overdone. They are still edible but they might have a slight but detectable eggy flavor and a dense texture after they have been chilled. If they are slightly overdone, they will still be delicious, but they should be eaten sooner—the longer they sit in the refrigerator, the more dense they will become. If your custards have begun to rise, then they are completely overcooked; you have no choice but to discard them.

Slow-baked egg-based custards

The secret to delicious, perfectly textured custards is the cooking process. The most delicate yet sliceable custard is the one with the most water bound by the least structure. You accomplish this by gently heating the custard and removing it from the heat the moment the custard solidifies.

Eggs contain numerous proteins. A protein is a long chain of amino acids; amino acids are chemically active molecules that, in food, come in a number of different types. Under normal conditions, the amino acid chains in proteins fold back upon themselves, because the various amino acids bond to each other. As a result, rather than being shaped in long strands, proteins have overall "ball" (or sometimes "rod") shapes. Once the egg proteins in custards are denatured—detangled and unwound—in the presence of heat, they are ready to form numerous types of bonds, some stronger than others. This mass of crisscrossing, linking proteins is able to hold water, and when it does, it is called a gel.

A perfect baked custard, with a requisite amount of egg protein in the recipe, is a gel of egg yolk proteins in which enough of the thousands of amino acid chains have unwound through slow and gradual exposure to heat while simultaneously bonding both to liquid and to other proteins surrounding liquid, their multiple patterns forming a tenuous network, or soft gel, one that has a delicate and unctuous feel in the mouth.

Aside from the heating process, proteins can denature though exposure to acid, salt, high pH ingredients, pressure, and agitation. While many egg-based preparations form gels through multiple denaturing processes, creamy baked custards undergo only one denaturing process—heat—which is why temperature control is so crucial when baking custards. Early gradual heat is the only means for the proteins to unwind. For every second that heat continues to intensify after the fragile gel is formed, proteins continue to bond, with more speed and ever-increasing tightness and density, firming the custard. Eventually with sustained heat the bonds will become so tight that they begin to squeeze out the trapped water. This process, called "syneresis," allows the gel to simultaneously toughen and "weep" fluid, completely ruining the custard.

Crème Caramels

There are a million crème caramel and crème brûlée recipes in the world. Yet making them remains something of a mystery to most home cooks. Indeed, the recipes, for the most part, are nearly identical: a little more cream in one, a little less egg yolk in the other, but the ingredients and proportions follow very clear patterns. So what makes these restaurant dessert favorites such a challenge at home?

To answer that, I have to tell you about how I became a professional pastry cook. In my first year out of college, I worked at Biba, Lidia Shire's extraordinary, pathbreaking, and sadly now departed fusion restaurant in Boston. After I had worked for her for a year as a line cook, she introduced me to her former pastry chef, Rick Katz, who at the time owned a small bakery in Newton called Bentonwood. Rick made the most amazing crème caramels I had ever tasted, and I took a job working for him in no small part because I wanted to learn how to make them. I still use Rick's recipe to this day, though in the recipes that follow I give some variations on the theme by adding maple syrup to one and espresso to another.

Rick taught me that the secret was not in the ingredients and their proportions (though these are no doubt important); the secret was in the technique. How you mix the ingredients, how you chill them, but most important, how you bake them, was the holy grail of Rick's pastry kitchen. His crème caramels are not the only recipes of his that still find their way into my repertoire. In every one of his recipes, it's his subtle but powerful technique that underlies the excellence of his work.

A note about timing: If you want to spread out your work and you are well organized, make the raw custard and store it in the refrigerator for a day or two before baking. Also bear in mind that these custards should sit in the refrigerator after baking for at least 12 hours before you serve them, and they can remain in the refrigerator after baking for up to 4 days before serving. At a minimum you need to leave 14 hours from the time you begin to make the custard until you serve the custard. You can, however, start your custard up to 5 days in advance of serving. (*See* TECHNIQUE TIP: *Caramel sauce—a liquid or a solid? page 98.*)

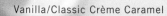

Vanilla/Classic Crème Caramel

Vanilla/Classic Crème Caramel

CARAMEL MOLDS

²/₃ cup sugar

Pinch of cream of tartar

CUSTARD

1 vanilla bean or
1 teaspoon vanilla extract

2 cups plus 2 tablespoons heavy cream

1 cup whole milk

½ cup sugar

5 egg yolks

1 egg

Pinch of salt

SPECIAL TOOLS AND PANS

12 x 9-inch metal baking pan with 2-inch sides

Eight 4-ounce ramekins or 4-ounce aluminum cupcake tins

Fine-mesh strainer

See Baked Custard Guidelines (page 82).

YIELD

Eight 4-ounce custards

Preheat the oven to 325°F (if you have a convection oven, make sure the fan is switched off).

Prepare the caramel molds.
See BEYOND THE BASICS: *Cooking caramel successfully, page 107.*

In a heavy-bottomed medium-sized saucepan combine the sugar, cream of tartar, and 3 tablespoons water. Cover and bring to a boil over medium-high heat. After 1 minute of rapid boiling uncover the pan. Cook until the sugar caramelizes and turns a light golden brown, approximately 5 minutes. Remove the pan from the heat (the sugar will continue to cook). When the caramel is a deep golden brown, pour just enough caramel to lightly coat the bottom of each ramekin.

Make the custard base.
Run a paring knife down the center of the vanilla bean. Split it open with your fingers and use the knife to scrape out the tiny black seeds into a heavy-bottomed saucepan. (If you are using vanilla extract, add it to the custard as directed below.) Add the cream, milk, ¼ cup of the sugar, and vanilla pod and bring to just barely a simmer over medium heat. Remove from the heat, cover, and allow the vanilla to steep in the cream for at least 15 minutes.

In a medium-sized bowl, whisk together the egg yolks, egg, remaining sugar, and salt. Using a ladle, slowly whisk some of the hot cream into the egg mixture to warm it. Gradually pour the warmed egg mixture into the remaining hot cream, whisking constantly as you pour. Strain the custard to remove the vanilla bean. Rinse, dry, and save the vanilla bean for another use. Stir in the vanilla extract, if using. You can bake the custard right away or chill it over an ice bath, cover, and refrigerate for up to 3 days.

Prepare the crème caramel for baking.
Place the caramel-bottomed ramekins in a baking dish. Using a ladle, fill each ramekin with exactly the same amount of custard, filling ⁴/₅ of the way up the inside of the mold. Add enough hot tap water to the baking dish to reach ²/₃ of the way up the outside of the ramekins. Cover the baking dish with a cookie tray or aluminum foil. If you use aluminum foil, punch a few air holes in it with a paring knife to prevent the custards from steaming and overcooking.

Bake the crème caramel.
Follow the TECHNIQUE TIP: *Caramel sauce—a liquid or a solid? page 98.*

Gently place the dish in the oven, being careful not to splash water onto the custards. Bake until the custards are set and have a uniform jiggle, 40 to 45 minutes. (If you use a chilled custard base, bake for 60 to 70 minutes.) Carefully remove the baking dish from the oven and allow the custards to cool uncovered. As soon as the custard cups are not too hot to touch, remove them from the water bath, cover, and chill in the refrigerator for at least 12 hours.

Unmold the crème caramel.
Remove the custards from the refrigerator. Fill a small bowl (just large enough to hold one ramekin) with 2 inches of very hot water. Set a ramekin in the bowl for 30 seconds. Dip a paring knife in the hot water and run it around the edge of the custard, hugging the side of the mold as much as possible. Turn the mold upside down over a serving plate and allow the custard to invert slowly with the caramel sauce pouring out around the sides. If the custard is stuck, run the hot knife around the sides a second time. If you are using disposable aluminum custard cups, invert each cup, then gently, with the tip of a paring knife, puncture the bottom of the mold and allow some air to enter. The custard should slide right out.

Serving Suggestions
This crème caramel stands alone. But as always, cold and creamy goes wonderfully with hot and crunchy—and if not hot, at least crunchy. Gingersnaps (page 59), Hazelnut Shortbread (page 66), or Crispy Bittersweet Chocolate Wafers (page 65) are a perfect complement. A simple sugar cookie or a store-bought cigarette wafer also works well.

Storage
These custards will keep, refrigerated, for 5 days.

Espresso Crème Caramel

Preheat the oven to 325°F (if you have a convection oven, make sure the fan is switched off).

Prepare the caramel molds.
See BEYOND THE BASICS: *Cooking caramel successfully, page 107.*

In a heavy-bottomed medium-sized saucepan combine the sugar, cream of tartar, and 3 tablespoons water. Cover and bring to a boil over medium-high heat. After 1 minute of rapid boiling uncover the pan. Cook until the sugar caramelizes and turns a light golden brown, approximately 5 minutes. Remove the pan from the heat (the sugar will continue to cook). When the caramel is a deep golden brown, pour just enough caramel to lightly coat the bottom of each ramekin.

Make the crème caramel.
In a heavy-bottomed saucepan combine the sugar, cream of tartar, and ¼ cup of water. Cover and bring to a boil over medium-high heat. Once the sugar caramelizes, turning a deep golden brown, remove the pan from the heat, stand back, and slowly add the cream. The mixture will bubble and steam furiously. Begin whisking the caramel cream once the bubbling has subsided. Add the milk and espresso. Whisk until all of the caramel is dissolved and the liquid is hot, but do not let it boil. Remove from the heat.

In a bowl, combine the egg yolks, egg, espresso powder, and salt and whisk for 1 minute. Slowly, one ladle at a time, whisk the hot coffee cream into the eggs. Strain the custard through a fine-mesh strainer. You can bake the custard immediately or chill it over an ice bath, cover, and refrigerate for up to 3 days.

Prepare the crème caramel for baking.
Place the caramel-bottomed ramekins in a baking dish. Using a ladle, fill each ramekin with exactly the same amount of custard, filling ⅘ of the way up the inside of the mold. Add enough hot tap water to the baking dish to reach ⅔ of the way up the outside of the ramekins. Cover the baking dish with a cookie tray or aluminum foil. If you use aluminum foil, punch a few air holes in it with a paring knife to prevent the custards from steaming and overcooking.

Bake the crème caramel.
Follow the TECHNIQUE TIP: *Caramel sauce— a liquid or a solid? page 98.*

Gently place the dish in the oven, being careful not to splash water onto the custards. Bake until the custards are set and have a uniform jiggle, 40 to 45 minutes. (If you use a chilled custard base, bake for 60 to 70 minutes.) Carefully remove the baking dish from the oven and allow the custards to cool uncovered. As soon as the custard cups are not too hot to touch, remove them from the water bath, cover, and chill in the refrigerator for at least 12 hours.

Unmold the crème caramel.
Remove the custards from the refrigerator. Fill a small bowl (just large enough to hold one ramekin) with 2 inches of very hot water. Set a ramekin in the bowl for 30 seconds. Dip a paring knife in the hot water and run it around the edge of the custard, hugging the side of the mold as much as possible. Turn the mold upside down over a serving plate and allow the custard to invert slowly with the caramel sauce pouring out around the sides. If the custard is stuck, run the hot knife around the sides a second time. If you are using disposable aluminum custard cups, invert each cup, then gently, with the tip of a paring knife, puncture the bottom of the mold and allow some air to enter. The custard should slide right out.

Serving Suggestions
This crème caramel stands alone. But as always, cold and creamy goes wonderfully with hot and crunchy—and if not hot, at least crunchy. Walnut Cream Cheese Sandwich Cookies (page 60) are my first choice. A simple sugar cookie or a store-bought cigarette wafer also works well.

Storage
These custards will keep, refrigerated, for 5 days.

CARAMEL MOLDS
⅔ cup sugar

Pinch of cream of tartar

ESPRESSO CUSTARD
1 cup sugar

Pinch of cream of tartar

2 cups heavy cream

½ cup whole milk

½ cup freshly pressed, strong espresso

5 egg yolks

1 egg

1 tablespoon instant espresso powder (I use Medaglia D'Oro)

Pinch of salt

SPECIAL TOOLS AND PANS
Fine-mesh strainer

Eight 4- to 5-ounce ramekins or 4-ounce aluminum cupcake tins

12 x 9-inch metal baking pan with 2-inch sides

See Baked Custard Guidelines (page 82).

YIELD
Eight 4-ounce custards

Maple Crème Caramel

CARAMEL MOLDS

²/₃ cup sugar

Pinch of cream of tartar

CUSTARD

¾ cup plus 1 tablespoon maple syrup

2 cups heavy cream

1 cup whole milk

Pinch of salt

5 egg yolks

1 egg

1 tablespoon sugar

SPECIAL TOOLS AND PANS

Eight 4-ounce ramekins or 4-ounce aluminum cupcake tins

12 x 9-inch metal baking pan with 2-inch sides

Fine-mesh strainer

Digital thermometer or candy thermometer (optional)

See Baked Custard Guidelines (page 82).

YIELD

Eight 4-ounce custards

Preheat the oven to 325°F (if you have a convection oven, make sure the fan is switched off).

Prepare the caramel molds. *See* BEYOND THE BASICS: *Cooking caramel successfully, page 107.*

In a heavy-bottomed medium-sized saucepan combine the sugar, cream of tartar, and 3 tablespoons water. Cover and bring to a boil over medium-high heat. After 1 minute of rapid boiling uncover the pan. Cook until the sugar caramelizes and turns a light golden brown, approximately 5 minutes. Remove the pan from the heat (the sugar will continue to cook). When the caramel is a deep golden brown, pour just enough caramel to lightly coat the bottom of each ramekin.

Reduce the maple syrup.
Boil the maple syrup in a heavy-bottomed saucepan over medium-high heat until the syrup registers 240°F on a candy thermometer. If you do not have a thermometer, test the syrup after it has boiled, foamed, and reduced somewhat. Drop a fork tong of syrup on the counter—if it dries in a mound, scrapes off the counter cleanly with your fingernail, and is somewhat pliable and gummy between two fingers, it is ready.

Make the crème caramel.
Add the cream to the reduced maple syrup, and then add the milk and salt. Bring the mixture to just under a boil and remove the pan from the heat. In a bowl, whisk the egg yolks, whole egg, and the sugar together for about 1 minute. Slowly, one ladle at a time, whisk the hot maple cream into the eggs. When you are done, strain the custard through a fine-mesh strainer. You can bake the custard immediately or chill it over an ice bath and refrigerate for up to 3 days.

Prepare the crème caramel for baking.
Place the caramel-bottomed ramekins in a baking dish. Using a ladle, fill each ramekin with exactly the same amount of custard, filling ⁴/₅ of the way up the inside of the mold. Add enough hot tap water to the baking dish to reach ²/₃ of the way up the outside of the ramekins. Cover the baking dish with a cookie tray or aluminum foil. If you

use aluminum foil, punch a few air holes in it with a paring knife.

Bake the crème caramel.
Follow the TECHNIQUE TIP: *Caramel sauce— a liquid or a solid? page 98.*

Gently place the dish in the oven, being careful not to splash water onto the custards. Bake until the custards are set and have a uniform jiggle, 40 to 45 minutes. (If you use a chilled custard base, bake for 60 to 70 minutes.) Carefully remove the baking dish from the oven and allow the custards to cool uncovered. As soon as the custard cups are not too hot to touch, remove them from the water bath, cover, and chill in the refrigerator for at least 12 hours.

Unmold the crème caramel.
Remove the custards from the refrigerator. Fill a small bowl (just large enough to hold one ramekin) with 2 inches of very hot water. Set a ramekin in the bowl for 30 seconds. Dip a paring knife in the hot water and run it around the edge of the custard, hugging the side of the mold as much as possible. Turn the mold upside down over a serving plate and allow the custard to invert slowly with the caramel sauce pouring out around the sides. If the custard is stuck, run the hot knife around the sides a second time. If you are using disposable aluminum custard cups, invert each cup, then gently, with the tip of a paring knife, puncture the bottom of the mold and allow some air to enter. The custard should slide right out.

Serving Suggestions
This crème caramel stands alone. But as always, cold and creamy goes wonderfully with hot and crunchy—and if not hot, at least crunchy. Warm, crispy financier cookies are my first choice. A simple sugar cookie or a store-bought cigarette wafer also works well.

Storage
These custards will keep, refrigerated, for 5 days.

Prune Armagnac Crème Brûlée

Prunes macerated in Armagnac, a French brandy, set off against a cold and creamy backdrop, are one of the classic flavor combinations of the pastry kitchen. This classic dessert has three layers of flavor and texture: the burnt sugar on top, the rich vanilla custard in the middle, and the compote of prunes and Armagnac on the bottom.

12 to 24 hours ahead of time: Chop and macerate the prunes.

Cut each prune in half and then each half into 4 pieces. Place the chopped prunes in a small bowl and drizzle the Armagnac over the prunes. Cover and allow to macerate overnight.

Preheat the oven to 325°F (if you have a convection oven, make sure the fan is switched off).

Prepare the caramel molds.

Divide the chopped, macerated prunes evenly among the 8 ramekins. Use your fingers to pack the prunes down in a tight cluster in the center of the ramekin. *See* BEYOND THE BASICS: *Cooking caramel successfully, page 107.*

In a heavy-bottomed medium-sized saucepan combine the sugar, cream of tartar, and 3 tablespoons water. Cover and bring to a boil over medium-high heat. After 1 minute of rapid boiling uncover the pan. Cook until the sugar caramelizes and turns a light golden brown, approximately 5 minutes. Remove the pan from the heat (the sugar will continue to cook). When the caramel is a deep golden brown, drizzle it over the macerated prunes in the bottom of each ramekin, using just enough caramel to glue down the prunes (see photo, page 90).

Make the vanilla custard base.

Run a paring knife down the center of the vanilla bean. Split it open with your fingers and use the knife to scrape out the tiny black seeds into a heavy-bottomed saucepan. (If you are using vanilla extract, add it to the custard as directed below.) Add the cream, ¼ cup of the sugar, and vanilla pod and bring to just barely a simmer over medium heat. Remove from the heat, cover, and allow the vanilla to steep in the cream for at least 15 minutes.

In a medium-sized bowl, whisk together the egg yolks, remaining sugar, and salt. Using a ladle, slowly whisk some of the hot cream into the egg mixture to warm it. Gradually pour the warmed egg mixture into the remaining hot cream, whisking constantly as you pour. Strain the custard to remove the vanilla bean. Rinse, dry, and save the vanilla bean for another use. Stir in the vanilla extract, if using. You can bake the custard right away or chill it over an ice bath, cover, and refrigerate for up to 3 days.

Prepare the crème caramel for baking.

Place the caramel-bottomed ramekins in a baking dish. Using a ladle, fill each ramekin with exactly the same amount of custard, filling ⅘ of the way up the inside of the mold. Add enough hot tap water to the baking dish to reach ⅔ of the way up the outside of the ramekins. Cover the baking dish with a cookie tray or aluminum foil. If you use aluminum foil, punch a few air holes in it with a paring knife to prevent the custards from steaming and overcooking.

Bake the crème caramel.

Follow the TECHNIQUE TIP: *Caramel sauce— a liquid or a solid? page 98.*

Gently place the dish in the oven, being careful not to splash water onto the custards. Bake until the custards are set and have a uniform jiggle, 40 to 45 minutes. (If you use a chilled custard base, bake for 60 to 70 minutes.) Carefully remove the baking dish from the oven and allow the custard to cool uncovered. As soon as the custard cups are not too hot to touch, remove them from the water bath, cover, and chill in the refrigerator for at least 12 hours.

MACERATED PRUNES

8 (3 ounces) pitted prunes

4 tablespoons Armagnac or brandy

CARAMEL MOLDS

½ cup sugar

Pinch of cream of tartar

CRÈME BRÛLÉE CUSTARD

1 vanilla bean

4 cups heavy cream

¾ cup sugar

8 egg yolks

¼ teaspoon salt

BRÛLÉE

¾ cup sugar

SPECIAL TOOLS AND PANS

Eight 4-ounce ceramic ramekins or 4-ounce aluminum cupcake tins

Propane or butane blowtorch

12 x 9-inch metal baking pan with at least 3-inch sides to hold the ramekins

See Baked Custard Guidelines (page 82).

YIELD

Eight 4-ounce custards

Prune Armagnac Crème Brûlée

Brûlée.

Remove the custards from the refrigerator ½ hour before you plan to brûlée them. If there seem to be many water droplets on the tops of your custards, drape a paper towel over the top of each to remove the moisture. Evenly coat the tops of the chilled custards with approximately ½ cup sugar. Clean off any sugar that sticks to the rims of the ramekins. Ignite your torch and adjust the flame to medium-low. Melt the sugar by moving the flame back and forth across the custard, maintaining a distance of 2 inches between the tip of the flame and the sugar. The sugar will melt, bubble, and then turn a golden caramel. Dust the caramelized tops with another thin layer of sugar, and repeat the brûléing process. Allow the caramelized sugar to cool for 3 to 5 minutes before serving. Do not brûlée the custards more than 20 minutes in advance of serving.

Serving Suggestions

These custards are delicious on their own.

Storage

These custards will keep, refrigerated, for 5 days.

BEYOND THE BASICS
Starch in cooked custards

Starches—including sugar, flour, cornstarch, potato starch, rice, tapioca, arrowroot, and even chocolate and cocoa—are especially effective at slowing (and sometimes preventing) protein coagulation because they both dilute the concentration of proteins and add large molecules that physically block gel formation. A custard containing starch, therefore, can be agitated and heated to boiling temperatures, thickening the custard dramatically but never causing it to overcook, curdle, and separate into hard bits of cooked eggs and liquid. When you heat starch it swells, absorbing liquid and forming a gel. Custards containing flour and egg yolks must be boiled because egg yolks contain an enzyme called amylase, which, if it is not deactivated by intense heat (boiling), disintegrates starch-based gels over time, causing the custard to become increasingly liquidy as it sits in the refrigerator.

Banana Cream
with Crunchy Toffee

Down-home banana pudding is one of the things many of us crave. Alas, when we find one on a menu or at a bakery we are inevitably disappointed either by the cloying texture of starch-thickened custard or by the artificial banana flavoring, of which there are many. The solution? If you really want good banana pudding, make it yourself.

At Chanterelle, I use this custard to fill tiny cream puffs, served as an after-dinner treat; sometimes banana cream serves as the filling for a mini petit four tart. But, most of all, it's comforting and delicious.

Steep the banana in milk.
Slice the bananas into ½-inch cross sections. Run a paring knife down the center of the vanilla bean. Split it open with your fingers and use the knife to scrape out the tiny black seeds into a heavy-bottomed medium saucepan. Add the vanilla pod, half the sugar, milk, and bananas to the saucepan and bring the mixture to a simmer over medium heat. Remove from the heat, cover, and allow the bananas and the vanilla to steep 10 minutes.

In a mixing bowl, combine the egg yolks, egg, and remaining sugar, malt syrup if you're using it, and salt and briskly whisk for 2 minutes. Add the flour and the cornstarch, whisking briskly and continuously until the mixture is smooth and no signs of the flour remain.

Using a ladle, slowly whisk some of the hot liquid into the egg mixture to warm it. Gradually pour the warmed egg mixture into the hot milk mixture, whisking constantly as you pour.

Cook the custard.
Cook the custard over medium heat, whisking vigorously and making sure to scrape the bottom of the pan every 10 strokes of the whisk. The custard will thicken significantly. Once bubbles rise to the top of the custard, cook for 30 seconds longer and remove from the heat. Pass the custard through a fine-mesh strainer into a stainless-steel bowl. Rinse and dry the vanilla bean and save it for another use. Allow the custard to cool for 5 minutes, stirring occasionally to allow the heat to escape. Whisk in the butter, transfer to the refrigerator, and chill for 30 minutes.

Lighten the custard with cream.
In a chilled stainless-steel bowl, whip the cream until it holds soft peaks. Scrape the whipped cream into the bowl with the banana custard. Fold the two mixtures together: place the spatula in the center of the bowl, scrape the bottom, and bring the bottom over the top. Rotate the bowl 45 degrees and continue folding until the cream is fully incorporated.

At this point you can portion this banana cream into parfait glasses or bowls or you can chill it in a quart container.

Serving Suggestions
Serve this banana cream with crunchy toffee sprinkled on top. You can also use this as a cream topping for the Chocolate Bête Noire (page 47) or the Chocolate Caramel Tart (page 29).

Storage
The banana cream will keep, refrigerated, for 2 days.

2 large or 3 small ripe bananas (14 ounces)

1 vanilla bean

¾ cup sugar

2 cups milk

6 egg yolks

1 egg

2 tablespoons barley malt syrup (optional)

¼ teaspoon salt

3 tablespoons flour

3 tablespoons cornstarch

7 tablespoons (3 ½ ounces) butter, at room temperature

1 cup cream

½ recipe of Almond Toffee (page 194), ground in a food processor

SPECIAL TOOLS AND PANS

6 to 8 parfait cups or decorative serving dishes (optional)

Fine-mesh strainer

YIELD

4 cups, serves 6 to 8

VARIATION

Banana Cream Pie: Make the Chocolate Crumb Crust (page 65) and fill the baked crust with the banana cream. Top off the pie with 1½ cups of whipped cream and a sprinkling of Almond Toffee (page 194).

Chocolate Caramel Pot de Crème

Chocolate Caramel Pot de Crème

This is a slight variation on a classic baked chocolate custard. As with many of the recipes in this book, caramel is an underlying layer of flavor that hides out beneath the chocolate. This recipe is truly wonderful if you do two things: buy and use good-quality chocolate, and achieve an incredible creamy consistency in your custard by baking it for the correct amount of time in a slow, continuous, balanced heat source.

Preheat the oven to 325°F (if you have a convection oven, make sure the fan is switched off).

Make the caramel cream.
See BEYOND THE BASICS: *Cooking caramel successfully, page 107.*

In a heavy-bottomed medium-sized saucepan combine the sugar, cream of tartar, and ¼ cup water. Cover and bring to a boil over medium-high heat. After 1 minute of rapid boiling uncover the pan. Cook until the sugar caramelizes and turns a light golden brown, approximately 5 minutes. Remove the pan from the heat (the sugar will continue to cook). When the caramel is a deep golden brown, stand back and carefully add the cream. The caramel will erupt with bubbles and steam. Place the pan back on the stove over medium heat and whisk the cream until the caramel is completely dissolved and smooth. Add the milk and continue cooking for 1 minute. Set the caramel cream aside.

Temper the caramel cream, the eggs, and the chocolate.
Meanwhile, melt the chocolate in the bowl of a bain-marie, stirring occasionally with a rubber spatula. Once the chocolate is melted, remove it from the heat. In a metal bowl, vigorously whisk the egg yolks and salt until they lighten in color a bit, 1 minute. Slowly, 1 cup at a time, add the caramel cream to the egg yolks, whisking constantly. Then slowly whisk the caramel and egg mixture, one ladle at a time, into the bowl with the melted chocolate. After each addition of the caramel and egg mixture, the chocolate should appear shiny and hold the lines of a whisk.

After adding about half of the caramel cream, the chocolate custard will become thinner, like hot chocolate. You can bake the chocolate and caramel custard immediately or chill it over an ice bath and refrigerate it for up to 2 days.

Prepare the custard for baking.
Place the ramekins in a baking dish. Using a ladle, fill each ramekin with exactly the same amount of custard, filling ⅘ of the way up the inside of the mold. Add enough hot tap water to the baking dish to reach ⅔ of the way up the outside of the ramekins. Cover the baking dish with a cookie tray or foil. If you use aluminum foil, punch a few air holes in it with a paring knife to prevent the custards from steaming and overcooking.

Bake the custard.
Gently place the dish in the oven, being careful not to splash water onto the custards. Bake until the custards are set and have a uniform jiggle, 40 to 45 minutes. (If you use a chilled custard base, bake for 60 to 70 minutes.) Carefully remove the baking dish from the oven and allow the custards to cool uncovered. As soon as the custard cups are not too hot to touch, remove them from the water bath, cover, and chill in the refrigerator for at least 12 hours.

Serving Suggestions
These custards should be served slightly chilled in the ramekins. Remove them from the refrigerator 1 hour before serving. Garnish them with a dollop of whipped cream and some crunchy cocoa nibs or Ground-up Almond Toffee (page 194).

Storage
These custards will keep, refrigerated, for 5 days.

---

1 cup sugar

Pinch of cream of tartar

2 cups heavy cream

1 cup plus 3 tablespoons whole milk

5 ounces bittersweet chocolate (66 to 70 percent cocoa solids)

7 egg yolks

¼ teaspoon salt

SPECIAL TOOLS AND PANS

12 x 9-inch metal baking pan with 3-inch sides

Eight 4-ounce ramekins or dishes or 4-ounce disposable aluminum cupcake cups

Bain-marie (see page 10)

See Baked Custard Guidelines (page 82).

YIELD

Eight 4-ounce pots of cream

Creamy Coconut Cardamom Rice Pudding

RICE

½ cup plus 2 tablespoons jasmine rice or basmati rice

¼ cup sugar

1 (13 ½-fluid-ounce) can coconut milk

1 cup whole milk

¼ teaspoon salt

CUSTARD

16 cardamom pods

½ cup plus 2 tablespoons sugar

1 cup whole milk

2 cups heavy cream

5 egg yolks

1 egg

1 teaspoon vanilla extract

SPECIAL TOOLS AND PANS

Fine-mesh strainer

YIELD

6 cups, serves 8 to 12

VARIATIONS

Tangerine and Lemon Verbena Rice Pudding: One of my other favorite flavor combinations is lemon verbena and tangerine. Leave out the vanilla and the cardamom, and add 2 tablespoons dried lemon verbena tea leaves or 6 fresh leaves and the zest of one tangerine. Cook the custard with the zest and the leaves, and then strain them out when the custard is done.

(Continued on page 96)

I spent some time in India as a college student, and the quintessential Indian rice pudding, suffused with coconut and cardamom pods, was a comfort and a pleasure throughout my travels. Ever since I started making desserts for a living, I've played around with these flavors—sometimes adding pistachios, almonds, or honey; sometimes using them in truffles, frozen confections, or custards—but this is, in the end, my favorite version, and a staple on the menu at Chanterelle. I've adapted the classic Indian recipe by thickening the coconut rice with a crème anglaise, combining French custard technique with these irresistible flavors.

Cook the rice.

Preheat the oven to 325°F. Place the rice in a strainer and rinse with cold water. Place the rice in a heavy-bottomed medium-sized saucepan with 2 cups cold water. Bring the rice to a boil and immediately remove the pan from the heat. Strain the rice and discard the starchy water. Place the blanched rice back in the pan and add the sugar, coconut milk, milk, and salt. Bring to a boil, remove from the heat, and cover the pan with aluminum foil or the lid. Place the pan in the oven and bake until the rice expands, and absorbs all the liquids, 30 minutes. (If the pan is not oven-proof, transfer the rice and liquid to a metal or glass baking dish and cover with aluminum foil.) If there is still runny milk in the pan, continue to bake, covered, for another 5 to 10 minutes. When the rice is done, remove it from the oven, leave it covered, and set it aside.

Make the custard.

Follow the TECHNIQUE TIP: *Cooking a stirred custard and testing for doneness, page 96.*

While the rice is baking, make the custard. Using the bottom of a small frying pan, crush the cardamom pods to split them open. In a heavy saucepan combine the cardamom pods and seeds, ½ cup of the sugar, milk, and cream and bring to a simmer over medium heat. Remove from the heat and allow the cardamom to steep for 10 minutes.

In a mixing bowl, combine the egg yolks, egg, and remaining 2 tablespoons of sugar and briskly whisk for 1 minute. Using a ladle, slowly whisk some of the hot cream into the egg mixture to warm it. Gradually pour the warmed egg mixture into the hot cream, whisking the cream constantly as you pour.

Cook the custard over medium heat, stirring continuously and scraping the bottom with a rubber spatula or wooden spoon, until the custard thickens enough to coat the back of a spoon. Remove from the heat and strain the custard to remove the cracked cardamom pods and seeds.

Combine the custard and the rice.

Scoop the rice into a large mixing bowl. Pour the hot custard over the rice and, using a whisk, slowly whisk until all of the rice granules are dispersed evenly and the mixture is thoroughly combined. Add the vanilla extract. Allow the rice pudding to cool completely.

Serving Suggestions

Serve this pudding by itself—it is wonderfully satisfying.

Storage

This pudding will keep, refrigerated, for 3 days.

Creamy Coconut Cardamom Rice Pudding

Cooking a stirred custard and testing for doneness

Rice Pudding Brûlée:
In a small coastal town in northern Spain, I had an amazing lemony anise version of this pudding served in a flat gratin dish and brûléed on top. If you would like to serve this rice pudding like crème brûlée, use a 6-ounce ladle to portion the hot rice pudding into 8 gratin or crème brûlée dishes. Tap the dishes on the counter until the rice pudding settles and flattens out. Chill the pudding for 1 hour. Coat the top of the custards with granulated sugar and brûlée. (*See the Prune Armagnac Crème Brûlée recipe, page 89.*)

Stirred custards can be tricky. Overheating can produce a custard in which the eggs curdle and the custard is potentially unusable. If your custard is overcooked it will become more liquidy with noticeable small bits of cooked scrambled eggs.

See BEYOND THE BASICS: *Slow-baked egg-based custards (page 83)* to understand how proteins denature through exposure to heat to form gels. In stirred custards, proteins are denatured not only through heat but also through agitation, either whisking or stirring. Agitation denatures proteins but it also helps to prevent proteins from early coagulation in two ways: by dispersing heat, so that too much heat isn't transferred too fast; and by breaking up tightly bound proteins.

In the presence of the right amount of heat and agitation, egg proteins unwind and reconnect, binding water, forming a gel, and gently thickening the custard. You must continuously stir custard to encourage even, consistent heating. Don't turn the temperature up so high that the egg proteins link together so quickly and tightly that they immediately curdle. It is important to pay attention to visual and sensual clues that indicate that the proteins have linked, thickened the custard, and no longer need to be heated or stirred.

To note the change in viscosity of a custard, dip a rubber spatula into the cooking custard and lift it 6 inches over the pan. Watch how the custard remaining on the spatula dribbles back into the pan: a thickened custard falls in teardrops, not in a runny, thin stream like uncooked milk. Run a finger along a custard-coated wooden spoon; if the custard holds the line of your finger for a few seconds, remove the custard from the heat. You can also use a thermometer and remove the custard when it reaches between 170°F and 175°F.

Rescuing a curdled custard
If you do happen to curdle your custard, there is a pretty good solution to the problem. While the custard is still hot, using a blender, food processor, or stick blender, puree the curdled custard for a minute or two. The blender breaks up all the coagulated proteins and leaves them in their strandlike state suspended in liquid, making the custard smooth again. Your final result will not be as thick as a gently cooked custard, but it will have some body and it should remain creamy, not grainy, on your tongue. In some cases these proteins will link loosely with other proteins, holding some liquid and the air created through blending.

Chestnut and Amaretti Cookie Pudding

Like many of the desserts I make, this one is based on a memory. On our honeymoon my husband and I traveled through Italy, spending a memorable week in Piedmont. Though justifiably famous for its extraordinary red wines—Barolo and Barbaresco—as well as for the white truffles that scent the entire region, the cuisine of the area is also unique and wonderful. One night we had what was called a *budino di castagne*, or "chestnut pudding," and it was clear to me that it had been thickened with either soaked cake or cookies. Much transmuted, this recipe is my version of that night's dessert.

Preheat the oven to 325°F (if you have a convection oven, make sure the fan is switched off). Set the rack in the middle of the oven.

Prepare the caramel molds.
See BEYOND THE BASICS: *Cooking caramel successfully, page 107.*

In a heavy-bottomed medium-sized saucepan combine the sugar, cream of tartar, and ¼ cup water. Cover and bring to a boil over medium-high heat. After 1 minute of rapid boiling uncover the pan. Cook until the sugar caramelizes and turns a light golden brown, approximately 5 minutes. Remove the pan from the heat (the sugar will continue to cook). When the caramel is a deep golden brown, pour just enough caramel to lightly coat the bottom of each ramekin.

Cook the chestnuts.
Place the chestnuts, milk, 2 tablespoons of the sugar, and the salt in a saucepan and cook over medium heat until the mixture comes to a boil. Turn down the heat to low, cover, and simmer until the chestnuts are soft and falling apart, 12 minutes, scraping the bottom every 2 to 3 minutes.

Infuse the custard.
Add the cream and the amaretti cookies to the cooked chestnut cream and bring the mixture to just under a boil, scraping the bottom with a rubber spatula every 3 minutes. Remove it from the heat and allow the amaretti cookies to infuse the chestnut cream and soften for 10 minutes.

Transfer the mixture to a blender or food processor and puree until smooth.

Combine the chestnut-amaretti cream with the eggs.
Place the eggs and egg yolks in a bowl with the remaining ½ cup of sugar and briskly whisk for 1 to 2 minutes. Using a ladle, slowly add the hot chestnut mixture to the eggs, whisking after every addition. Strain the custard through a wire mesh strainer into a bowl (it does not need to be a fine-mesh strainer). Stir the amaretto into the finished, strained custard.

Bake the custard.
Follow the TECHNIQUE TIP: *Caramel sauce— a liquid or a solid? page 98.*

Place the caramel-bottomed ramekins in a baking dish. Using a ladle, fill each ramekin with exactly the same amount of custard, filling ⁴/₅ of the way up the inside of the mold. Add enough hot tap water to the baking dish to reach ½ of the way up the outside of the ramekins. Gently place the dish in the oven, being careful not to splash water onto the custards. Bake, uncovered, until the custards are set and have a uniform jiggle, 50 minutes. Remove from the oven and allow the custards to cool for 1 hour.

Cool and unmold the custard.
The custards should be served warm. You can serve these custards once they have cooled a bit or you can refrigerate them for up to 2 days and reheat them at 320°F for 10 minutes before

CARAMEL MOLDS
1 cup sugar

Pinch of cream of tartar

CUSTARD
½ pound frozen, canned, or Cryovacked blanched chestnuts

1 ⅓ cups whole milk

½ cup plus 2 tablespoons sugar

½ teaspoon salt

2 cups heavy cream

Approximately 20 (1-inch round) Pignoli Amaretti Cookies, recipe page 64, or store-bought amaretti cookies (5 ounces)

2 eggs

5 egg yolks

1 tablespoon Amaretto

SPECIAL TOOLS AND PANS
12 x 9-inch metal baking pan with 3-inch sides

Nine 4-ounce ramekins or 4-ounce disposable cupcake cups

Blender, food processor, or stick blender

See Baked Custard Guidelines (page 82).

YIELD
Ten 4-ounce custards

serving. If you allow the custards to sit in the refrigerator for a few hours at the very least, more of the hard caramel at the bottom of the molds will liquefy and pour out over your warm custards when you serve them. (*See* TECHNIQUE TIP: *Caramel sauce—a liquid or a solid? below.*)

To unmold the custards, take a paring knife and run it around the edge of the custard, hugging the side of the mold as much as possible. Have a kitchen towel nearby in case the custard molds are too hot to handle. Turn the mold over the serving plate and allow the custard to invert slowly with the caramel sauce pouring out around the sides.

Serving Suggestions

These custards stand beautifully on their own, but a crisp cookie or wafer is always a nice crunchy accompaniment to this dessert. At Chanterelle I surround the custard with perfectly diced Bartlett Pears Poached in Muscat Wine (page 166) and a corkscrew-shaped piece of Thin and Delicate Peanut Brittle (substituting almonds) (page 204).

Storage

These custards keep, refrigerated, for 3 days.

TECHNIQUE TIP
Caramel sauce—
a liquid or a solid?

The major complaint I hear from people making crème caramels or puddings with a caramel layer on the bottom is that the caramel remains in a solid state—a hard disk of caramel at the top of their crème caramel. Sugar is hygroscopic, which means that it absorbs surrounding liquids readily. The longer sugar sits in a chilled or humid environment, the more liquid it absorbs. The caramel at the bottom of the custard needs at least 12 hours in the refrigerator to give it enough time to absorb some of the liquid surrounding it, converting it from a hard candy to a delicious, ambrosial liquid caramel.

Vanilla Panna Cotta

On our honeymoon in Italy, in a small city called Cuneo, at a restaurant called Osteria della Chiocciola, my husband and I had one of the best desserts of our journey, a panna cotta that tasted like the essence of cream. Though set, the custard seemed not to have the jiggly texture of gelatin, and when I asked in broken Italian how they made it, they described a cooked custard made with egg whites, milk, cream, and sugar. I was determined to make my own, though I have never quite figured out how to achieve the creamy flavor solely with egg whites and no gelatin. This version uses as little gelatin as possible, just enough to bind the thickened egg white custard.

Bloom the gelatin.
In a small bowl, sprinkle the gelatin over 5 teaspoons of water and set aside for 10 minutes. The gelatin will soak up all the water and expand into a gummy paste.

Infuse the cream.
Run a paring knife down the center of the vanilla bean. Split it open with your fingers and use the knife to scrape out the tiny black seeds into a heavy-bottomed saucepan. Bring the cream, the milk, ¼ cup of the sugar, and the vanilla pod and seeds (or vanilla extract, if you are using it) to a simmer. Remove from the heat, cover, and let the mixture steep for at least 15 minutes.

Make the egg white custard.
Follow the TECHNIQUE TIP: *Cooking a stirred custard and testing for doneness, page 96.*

In a small bowl whisk together the remaining ¼ cup sugar, salt, and egg whites. Slowly, using a ladle, whisk some of the hot milk into the egg white mixture to warm it. Gradually pour the warmed egg white mixture into the hot milk, whisking constantly as you pour.

Cook the custard over medium heat, stirring continuously and scraping the bottom with a rubber spatula or wooden spoon, until the custard thickens enough to coat the back of the spoon. Remove from the heat and add

about ½ cup of the cooked custard to the gelatin and whisk until the gelatin dissolves. Add this small amount of custard back to the remaining custard and whisk the two together. Strain the custard through a fine-mesh strainer. Chill the custard over an ice bath until it comes to room temperature. Remove the vanilla bean with a fork. Rinse it, dry it, and save it for another use.

Pour the custard into the molds.
Pour the custard into the molds and refrigerate for at least 6 hours to allow the gelatin to set. At the restaurant we dip the 2-ounce plastic ketchup cups in hot water to release the custard from the sides of the plastic, unmolding them onto dessert plates. It is also nice to set the custard into small decorative dishes.

Serving Suggestions
Serve these custards with fresh passion-fruit, macerated strawberries, raspberries, or blackberries. Peaches, nectarines, and apricots are also wonderful. Any thin crispy cookie adds a nice crunch to this luxurious, refreshing, creamy vanilla custard.

Storage
The custards keep, refrigerated, for 3 days.

1¼ teaspoons unflavored gelatin

1 vanilla bean or
1 teaspoon vanilla extract

1½ cups heavy cream

1½ cups whole milk

½ cup sugar

Pinch of salt

4 egg whites

SPECIAL TOOLS AND PANS

Six 4-ounce dishes or twelve 2-ounce plastic ketchup cups

Fine-mesh strainer

Ice bath

YIELD
Six 4-ounce custards

VARIATION

Herb-infused or Spiced Panna Cotta: You can infuse the cream with any number of spices or herbs. Use 4 fresh lemon verbena leaves, a stalk of lemon grass, 3 fresh bay leaves, a small bunch of fresh basil, 1 tablespoon of any good citrus zest, 3 sticks of cinnamon, 4 star anise, 1 tablespoon of aniseed, 12 cardamom pods (crushed), or ½ cup of toasted coconut to infuse the hot milk and cream. Allow the flavors to steep for at least 15 minutes before cooking the custard.

Brioche Pudding with Truffle Honey

Brioche Pudding with Truffle Honey

This is the most basic form of bread pudding, made with a rich custard and a good brioche-like bread, and baked in a slow oven. What makes this dessert superb is the light glaze of white truffle–marinated honey drizzled on the top right before serving. This honey is probably not available at your local gourmet grocery—even if you live in a big city—so if you want to make this simple but showstopping dessert, try looking for truffle honey online at one of the many sites dedicated to high-quality ingredients. It is worth every bit of effort to acquire this exotic ambrosia; the flavor of truffle honey is unique and exciting, and this is the best way I know to enjoy it. Once you buy it, truffle honey keeps for 2 months at the most, so use it lavishly; it is one of life's great pleasures and luxuries.

Preheat the oven to 350°F. Butter a 12 x 8-inch baking dish.

Toast the brioche.
Trim off the hard brown crusts and cut each slice into about 6 rectangles measuring 1¼ x 1½ inches. Place the bread on a cookie sheet and drizzle with the melted butter. Bake until the bread turns a golden brown. Remove from the oven and turn the oven down to 300°F.

Make the custard.
In a saucepan, combine the cream and milk over medium heat and bring almost to a boil. Meanwhile, in a medium-sized bowl, whisk together the sugar, egg yolks, eggs, and salt. Slowly, using a ladle, whisk some of the hot milk and cream into the egg mixture to warm it. Gradually pour the warmed egg mixture into the hot milk and cream, whisking constantly as you pour. Do not cook the custard; set it aside.

Bake the pudding.
Place the toasted bread pieces in the prepared baking dish. Pour the warm custard over the bread. Bake the pudding until the chunks sticking out turn crispy and brown and the center is set and has a slight spring when touched, 30 minutes. Scoop a portion of the pudding onto a plate and drizzle approximately 1½ tablespoons truffle honey over each serving.

Serving Suggestions
Serve this dessert warm. The Honey-Glazed Roasted Pears (page 176) are also delicious with the truffle honey drizzled over the top.

Storage
This pudding will keep, refrigerated, for 4 days.

8 slices (approximately 11 ounces) of brioche, cut ½ inch thick (you may also use challah or any buttery bread)

2 tablespoons (1 ounce) butter, melted

1½ cups heavy cream

1½ cups whole milk

⅔ cup sugar

3 egg yolks

2 eggs

¼ teaspoon salt

¾ cup truffle honey, for drizzling

SPECIAL TOOLS AND PANS

12 x 8-inch baking dish with 2-inch sides

Baking sheet

YIELD

12 x 8-inch baked pudding, serves 8 to 12

Honey and Yogurt Panna Cotta

32-ounce container of plain
whole milk yogurt

1 cup (8 ounces) crème fraîche

¼ cup honey

1 tablespoon unflavored gelatin

⅔ cup whole milk

⅔ cup cream

¾ cup sugar

Pinch of salt

3 egg whites

SPECIAL TOOLS AND PANS

Unmolded: Twelve 3- to 5-ounce
ramekins or eighteen 2-ounce
disposable ketchup or salad
dressing cups

Molded: 10 to 12 small bowls
or glasses or a large decorative
serving dish that can hold
36 ounces of custard

18-inch-square piece of
cheesecloth or a thin dish towel

Fine-mesh strainer

YIELD

One 36-ounce custard,
or twelve 3-ounce portions

My favorite Greek dessert, even more than the decadently honey-and-nut-filled pastries like baklava, is fresh strained yogurt topped with a layer of flavorful honey. This dessert takes these quintessential flavors of Greece and brings them across the Mediterranean to make a classic Italian treat even more sublime.

8 to 24 hours ahead of time: Strain the yogurt.
Drape a piece of cheesecloth or thin towel inside a strainer or colander. Place the colander over a bowl so that the strainer is suspended and does not touch the bottom of the bowl. Scrape the yogurt into the cheesecloth. Wrap the edges of the cloth around the yogurt and refrigerate it for at least 8 hours and up to 24 hours. The yogurt will lose half its volume and a greenish water will collect at the bottom of the bowl.

Combine the yogurt, crème fraîche, and honey.
With a rubber spatula, scrape the strained yogurt into a stainless-steel bowl. Add the crème fraîche and honey and whisk until the ingredients come together. Set aside at room temperature.

Bloom the gelatin.
In a small bowl sprinkle the gelatin over 2 ½ tablespoons of water and set aside for 10 minutes. The gelatin will soak up all the water and expand into a gummy paste.

Make the egg white custard.
Follow the TECHNIQUE TIP: *Cooking a stirred custard and testing for doneness, page 96.*

In a small heavy saucepan, combine the milk, cream, and ½ cup of the sugar and bring the mixture to a simmer.

In a small bowl whisk together the remaining ¼ cup sugar, salt, and egg whites. Slowly, using a ladle, whisk some of the hot milk into the egg white mixture to warm it. Gradually pour the warmed egg white mixture into the hot milk, whisking constantly as you pour.

Cook the custard over medium heat, stirring continuously and scraping the bottom with a rubber spatula or wooden spoon, until the custard thickens enough to coat the back of the

spoon. Remove from the heat and add about ½ cup of the cooked custard to the the gelatin and whisk until the gelatin dissolves. Add this small amount of custard back to the remaining custard and whisk the two together. Strain the custard through a fine-mesh strainer. Chill the custard over an ice bath until it comes to room temperature.

Once the custard has cooled off, whisk in the yogurt and crème fraîche until thoroughly combined and smooth.

Pour the custard into the molds.
Pour the custard into your desired molds or dishes and tap them on the counter so that the custard settles and flattens on top. Refrigerate the custards for at least 2 hours or for up to 2 days before serving.

Unmold the custard.
If you set the custard in a serving dish or dishes, disregard these directions. Remove the custards from the refrigerator. Dip a paring knife in hot water and run it around the edge of the custard, hugging the side of the mold as much as possible. Turn the mold upside down over a serving plate and allow the custard to invert slowly.

Serving Suggestions
These custards can be served with a crisp wafer or cookie or some fresh seasonal fruit (raspberries, blueberries, figs, melon, peaches, pineapple, or strawberries). Many of the fruit preparations in this book work beautifully also. My favorite is the Rhubarb Consommé (page 167).

Honey and Yogurt Panna Cotta in Rhubarb Consommé with Tropical Fruits

Maple–Star Anise Mousse

6 egg yolks

Pinch of salt

1 tablespoon unflavored gelatin

1 cup plus 2 tablespoons maple syrup

4 whole star anise

2 cups heavy cream

SPECIAL TOOLS AND PANS

Stand mixer

Medium-sized heavy-bottomed saucepan with at least 4-inch sides

Digital candy thermometer (optional)

YIELD

4 cups, serves 6

Maple syrup infused with star anise creates a flavor that is clearly more than the sum of its parts. This mousse has a light, creamy, buttery, licorice-like flavor that barely registers maple as its principal sweetener. Serve it in glasses with some crushed pecans or walnuts as a terrific dessert, or use it as a filling for a torte or carrot cake.

Begin the mousse.

In the bowl of a stand mixer, whisk together the egg yolks and salt on medium speed. In a small bowl, sprinkle the gelatin over ¼ cup of cold water and let this mixture sit while you reduce the maple syrup.

Reduce the maple syrup.

Combine the maple syrup and star anise in a heavy-bottomed saucepan over medium-high heat and boil until the syrup registers 240°F on a candy thermometer. If you do not have a thermometer, test the syrup after it has boiled, foamed, and reduced somewhat. Drop a fork tong of syrup on the counter—if it dries in a mound, scrapes off the counter cleanly with your fingernail, and is somewhat pliable and gummy between two fingers, it is ready.

Add the maple syrup to the egg yolks.

Remove the star anise with a fork and discard. With the mixer on medium-high speed, slowly pour the hot maple syrup down the side of the bowl into the yolks. Using a rubber spatula, scrape the gelatin into the empty pan in which you cooked the maple syrup, and let it melt into a syrupy liquid. Pour the gelatin into the egg yolk mixture and whisk at medium-high speed until it triples in volume and cools to room temperature.

Finish the mousse.

Remove the bowl with the mousse base from the mixer. In a separate bowl, whip the heavy cream until it has soft peaks. Scrape the whipped cream on top of the mousse base. Fold the two together with a spatula or bowl scraper: place your spatula in the center of the bowl, scrape the bottom, and bring the bottom over the top. Rotate the bowl 45 degrees and continue folding until all the whipped cream is incorporated.

If you want to serve the mousse in a casual manner, let it chill and gel in a large bowl or plastic container for at least 2 hours before dolloping it out onto individual plates. Alternatively, for a more finished look, pour the mousse into 6 to 8 small serving dishes and let it set in the refrigerator, covered, for at least 2 hours before serving.

Serving Suggestions

Serve this mousse with a crunchy cookie or some chopped hazelnuts, pecans, or walnuts.

Storage

This mousse keeps, refrigerated, for 3 days.

Clockwise from the top: Bittersweet Chocolate Mousse,
Sesame Milk Chocolate Mousse, Maple–Star Anise Mousse

Cinnamon Caramel Mousse

6 egg yolks

Pinch of salt

1 tablespoon unflavored gelatin

1 cup sugar

Pinch of cream of tartar

3 cinnamon sticks

2 cups heavy cream

SPECIAL TOOLS AND PANS

Stand mixer

YIELD

5 cups, serves 6 to 8

Like most pastry chefs, I use a set of core recipes that provide the building blocks for many of my seemingly elaborate preparations. One of the secrets to success, whether at home or in the restaurant kitchen, is to know just how many ways a single recipe can be used in different plated desserts, rather than inventing new recipes for each dessert.

This simple, delicious mousse is one of my most basic and central recipes. It can be served on its own, alongside a crisp wafer-like cookie or Thin and Delicate Peanut Brittle (page 204). I use this mousse in a variety of "Napoleons"—layered between apple or pear chips or infused with star anise and cinnamon and sandwiched in tempered chocolate. With a little extra gelatin, this mousse becomes a cake filling; frozen, it becomes a parfait. And this is just the start: once you're comfortable with the recipe, you can use it, as I do, as a cornerstone of your pastry kitchen.

VARIATION

Star Anise Caramel Mousse, Cardamom Caramel Mousse, Clove Caramel Mousse: Add 4 star anise, or 10 cardamom pods, or 10 cloves to the sugar syrup before it comes to a rapid boil and let the spices boil in the syrup and infuse the caramel. Strain the hot caramel syrup to remove the bits of hard spice before adding it to the yolks. Another way to intensify these flavors is to infuse the hot cream with the spices. Strain the spices and chill the cream before whipping it and incorporating it into the mousse base mixture.

Begin the mousse.
In the bowl of a stand mixer, whisk together the egg yolks and salt on medium speed. In a small bowl, sprinkle the gelatin over ¼ cup of cold water and let this mixture sit while you prepare the caramel.

Make the caramel syrup.
See BEYOND THE BASICS: *Cooking caramel successfully, page 107.*

Combine the sugar, cream of tartar, cinnamon sticks, and ¼ cup water in a heavy-bottomed saucepan. Cover and bring to a rapid boil over medium-high heat. Once boiling, uncover the pan and cook the sugar until deep golden brown. Turn off the heat and very carefully pour ¼ cup water into the hot caramel. Stand back—the caramel will hiss and bubble and spurt.

Add the caramel to the yolks.
Once you have added the water, the caramel syrup will come back to a rolling boil from the residual heat. Remove the cinnamon sticks with a fork and discard. When the caramel syrup stops boiling, slowly pour it into the egg yolks with the mixer running on high speed. With a rubber spatula scrape the gelatin into the empty saucepan in which you cooked the caramel and let it melt into a syrupy liquid. Pour the gelatin into the egg yolk mixture and whisk at medium-high speed until it triples in volume and cools to room temperature.

Finish the mousse.
Remove the bowl with the mousse base from the mixer. In a separate bowl, whip the heavy cream until it has soft peaks. Scrape the whipped cream on top of the mousse base. Fold the two together with a spatula or bowl scraper: place your spatula in the center of the bowl, scrape the bottom, and bring the bottom over the top. Rotate the bowl 45 degrees and continue folding until all the whipped cream is incorporated.

If you want to serve the mousse in a casual manner, let it chill and gel in a large bowl or plastic container for at least 2 hours before dolloping it out onto individual plates. Alternatively, for a more finished look, pour the mousse into 6 to 8 small serving dishes and let it set in the refrigerator, covered, for at least 2 hours before serving.

Serving Suggestions

Serve this mousse with the Thin and Delicate Peanut Brittle (page 204) or any crunchy thin cookie. You can also serve it in classic mousse style, in a bowl or cup with some whipped cream, shaved bittersweet chocolate (use a peeler and peel the edge of a cold block of good bittersweet chocolate), and a sprinkle of ground cinnamon.

Cooking caramel successfully

There are two common problems cooks encounter when making caramel: crystallization and burnt caramel.

Crystallization

Boiling sugar can sometimes crystallize and never make it to a caramelized state. Crystallized sugar appears suddenly in your pan as a blurry, hard white mass that looks like rock candy. There are a couple of strategies to prevent sugar from crystallizing:

1. Change the composition of the sugar syrup. Once the water boils away, plain sugar syrups are almost 100 percent sucrose (table sugar). Pure substances of any kind can crystallize easily. On the other hand, impure substances—those with more than one type of molecule—don't crystallize readily. To reduce the chance that your caramel will crystallize, you can add other sugar molecules such as glucose or fructose, to reduce the syrup's purity. Sugar syrups containing glucose or fructose are called "inverted."

• Invert the sugar syrup directly, with liquid sugars, like corn syrup, which is mostly glucose, or honey, which contains a lot of fructose.

• Add an acidic ingredient such as cream of tartar or lemon juice (which I recommend in my recipes), which breaks sucrose down into component molecules—fructose and glucose—when heated.

2. Do not allow other crystals or particles to grow in your syrup. Any tiny particle, or "seed," in a boiling syrup can spark crystallization. Seeds can be anything, from dust to air bubbles to sugar crystals themselves. For example, a bit of syrup can splash up the side of the pan, dry there, and then fall back again as a seed. To discourage the growth of "seeds" in your caramel:

• Cover the pan. When syrup boils rapidly in a covered pan, steam washes down the sides, dissolving any stranded sugar crystals there.

• Leave the pan alone. Do not stir or swirl the syrup around. These motions can introduce foreign particles or air into the boiling syrup, and can agitate the sugar solution, causing seeds to develop in the syrup itself.

• Cook the syrup over high heat. The longer it takes for the caramel to get to 325°F, the more likely it is that the syrup will crystallize.

Burnt Caramel

Sometimes sugar caramelizes so quickly that it burns or becomes too dark and bitter.

• Remove your caramel from the heat when it is a light golden brown (approximately 325°F on a candy thermometer). Let it sit for 30 seconds; the caramel will be so hot that it will continue to cook even off the heat. Then check for color; if the caramel is not dark enough, return the pan to medium heat for a few more seconds. Repeat until you have achieved a nice rich, brown caramel. (Note that in order to assess the color visually you need to use a white enamel, stainless-steel, or aluminum-coated pan. Dark enamels, Calphalon, Teflon coating, and copper disguise the color brown.)

• When the syrup starts to boil, place a bowl of ice water big enough to hold your pan next to the stove. If the caramel is coloring too rapidly, dip the bottom of the pan in the ice water to quickly stop the cooking process.

Bittersweet Chocolate Mousse

5 ounces bittersweet chocolate (66 to 85 percent cocoa solids)

1 ounce unsweetened chocolate

1 cup heavy cream

4 eggs

¼ teaspoon salt

½ cup plus 2 tablespoons sugar

¼ teaspoon cream of tartar

2 tablespoons brewed espresso, at room temperature

2 tablespoons Kahlúa

SPECIAL TOOLS AND PANS

Bain-marie (see page 10)

Stand mixer

YIELD

2 quarts, serves 8 to 10

Like many of my chocolate desserts, this one uses caramel as an underlying sweetener, giving the dessert a dark, rich flavor and a creamy texture. Versatile and delicious, this mousse can be eaten plain or combined with other elements in a larger dessert.

Melt the chocolate and separate the eggs.
In a bain-marie, melt the chocolate, stirring occasionally with a rubber spatula (this will take about 5 minutes). In another bowl, whip the cream and set it aside in the refrigerator.

Make the caramel syrup.
See BEYOND THE BASICS: *Cooking caramel successfully, page 107.*

Separate the eggs, and put the yolks in the bowl of a stand mixer and the whites in a separate bowl. Add the salt to the egg yolks and beat on medium-high speed until combined.

Combine ½ cup of the sugar, ⅛ teaspoon cream of tartar, and 3 tablespoons water in a heavy-bottomed saucepan. Cover and bring to a rapid boil over medium-high heat. Once boiling, uncover the pan and cook the sugar until deep golden brown. Turn off the heat and very carefully pour 2 tablespoons water into the hot caramel. Stand back—the caramel will hiss and bubble and spurt.

Add the caramel to the yolks.
Once you have added the water, the caramel syrup will come back to a rolling boil from the residual heat. When the caramel syrup stops boiling, slowly pour it into the egg yolks with the mixer running on medium-high speed. Whisk the mixture for 5 minutes and then add the coffee and Kahlúa. Continue to whisk on medium-high speed until the egg yolks triple in volume and cools to room temperature. Set the bowl aside.

Beat the egg whites.
See BEYOND THE BASICS: *Acid in egg white foams, page 123.*

In another bowl on the stand mixer, whisk the egg whites on medium-high speed. Once the egg whites begin to foam up, add the remaining ⅛ teaspoon cream of tartar. When the egg whites are completely foamy and begin to hold the lines of a whisk, begin adding the remaining 2 tablespoons of sugar, 1 teaspoon at a time, whisking for 1 minute after each addition. The meringue is done when it has gained 8 to 10 times its original volume.

Finish the mousse.
Whisk together the caramel–egg yolks mixture and melted chocolate. Once this mixture is shiny and smooth, scrape the lightly whipped cream over the chocolate-mousse base. Fold the cream into the chocolate-mousse base using a spatula or bowl scraper: place the spatula in the center of the bowl, scrape the bottom, and bring the bottom over the top. Rotate the bowl 45 degrees and continue folding until all the cream is incorporated. Repeat this process to incorporate the meringue.

If you want to serve the mousse in a casual manner, let the mousse chill and gel in a large bowl in the refrigerator for at least 2 hours before dolloping it out onto individual plates. Alternatively, for a more finished look, pour the mousse into 6 to 8 small serving dishes and let it set in the refrigerator for at least 2 hours before serving.

Serving Suggestions
This mousse can be served with a dollop of whipped cream and a few chopped nuts for crunch. With a little added gelatin, this mousse can also be used as a filling between cake layers or frozen in parfait glasses.

Storage
This mousse keeps, refrigerated, for 3 days, and frozen for 1 week.

Sesame Milk Chocolate Mousse

Halvah, a traditional Middle Eastern candy made with sesame seeds, is one of my favorite over-the-counter treats. I use it in both chocolate and coffee desserts at Chanterelle. Sometimes I just place shavings of halvah on a plate to finish a dessert. In this recipe, I take a simple milk chocolate mousse and add halvah, giving it another dimension of flavor and sophistication.

Melt the chocolate and dissolve the gelatin.
In a bain-marie, melt the chocolate, stirring occasionally with a rubber spatula (this will take about 10 minutes). In a small bowl, sprinkle the gelatin over 3 teaspoons of water and set it aside. In another bowl, whip the cream and set it aside in the refrigerator.

Make the sabayon.
See BEYOND THE BASICS: *Egg yolk foams and sabayons, page 216.)*

While the chocolate is melting, vigorously whisk the egg yolks and egg in a stainless-steel bowl until they lighten in color a bit, 2 minutes. Crumble the halvah with your hands or chop it with a knife. Add the sugar, white wine, salt, and halvah to the eggs.

Once the chocolate has melted, remove from the bain-marie and replace it with the bowl containing the egg mixture. Whisk briskly until the mixture has thickened, doubled in volume, and holds the lines of a whisk, 5 to 8 minutes. (As you whisk your sabayon you will smell the alcohol in the wine evaporating.) Remove the bowl from the heat and add the softened gelatin. Continue to whisk until the gelatin is dissolved. Scrape the sabayon into the bowl of melted milk chocolate and whisk until the mixture is thoroughly combined and becomes shiny and smooth, and holds the lines of a whisk.

Incorporate the cream.
Scrape the lightly whipped cream over the chocolate sabayon. Fold the two together with a spatula or bowl scraper: place the spatula in the center of the bowl, scrape the bottom, and bring the bottom over the top. Rotate the bowl 45 degrees and continue folding until all the whipped cream is incorporated.

If you want to serve the mousse in a casual manner, let the mousse chill and gel in a large bowl or plastic container in the refrigerator for at least 2 hours before dolloping it out onto individual plates. Alternatively, for a more finished look, pour the mousse into 10 small serving dishes and let it set in the refrigerator for at least 2 hours before serving.

Serving Suggestions
Serve this mousse with some toasted pignoli nuts or some crushed toffee (page 194) sprinkled over the top.

7 ounces milk chocolate (36 percent or higher cocoa solids)

1 teaspoon unflavored gelatin

2 cups heavy cream

3 egg yolks

1 egg

2 ounces sesame halvah

2 tablespoons sugar

¼ cup white wine

¼ teaspoon of salt

SPECIAL TOOLS AND PANS
Bain-marie (see page 10)

YIELD
6 cups, serves 6 to 8

SOUFFLÉS

CHAPTER FIVE

Soufflé Guidelines

There is something magical about a soufflé—the dramatic rise and fall, the seductively warm, light, yet richly flavored interior—that makes it the perfect ending to a romantic evening. Many home cooks hear scary tales about the difficulty of making soufflés, so they give up attempting one in their own kitchens, believing soufflés are something to be savored only when dining out.

Yet it is possible to make soufflés that are just as delicious, sensuous, and showstopping as the ones found at the best restaurants. Like most things, making a soufflé is a matter of technique and of understanding the reasons behind the technique.

"Soufflé" generally refers to a light, airy, creamy baked mousse that rises significantly in the oven and then deflates a few minutes after it has been removed. It is rushed to the table so diners can enjoy the soufflé's hot, inflated, dramatic state before it collapses.

To produce a soufflé you need to combine a thick flavor base with an egg white foam (some form of whipped egg whites). Sometimes the thick flavor base is simply jam or chocolate ganache, but more often it is a pastry cream. All of our soufflés at Chanterelle are a combination of an Italian meringue, instead of plain beaten egg whites, and a flavored pastry cream.

An Italian meringue holds air for a much longer period of time than does a French meringue or plain beaten egg whites, so I am able to prepare the soufflés in the morning and bake them in the evening. Even though making the meringue seems like a complicated process, it similarly allows you to prepare these wonderful, light, seemingly *à la minute* desserts ahead of time. When you are ready for dessert, you simply place the prepared individual soufflé molds in the oven, bake, and then serve.

"Meringue" is a generic term for an egg white foam whipped with sugar. (*See* BEYOND THE BASICS: *A French meringue and egg white foams, page 75, to understand how egg white proteins form foams through agitation and the effect of added sugar.*)

There are three common types of meringues: a French meringue is an egg white foam with granulated or powdered sugar; a Swiss meringue is an egg white foam that is first heated with sugar until all the sugar dissolves (at around 110°F to 120°F) and then whipped; an Italian meringue is an egg white foam with a sugar syrup cooked to 248°F. A crunchy meringue cookie or the topping of a lemon meringue pie is simply the baked version of any one of these whipped egg white foams.

The finished characteristics of a whipped Italian meringue differ from those of the French and Swiss meringues. If you leave an Italian meringue and a French meringue in separate bowls on the counter for 6 hours at room temperature, you will notice a complete difference between the two bowls at the end of this time. One will contain the same whipped egg whites you made 6 hours ago (Italian), and the other will look slightly foamy but mostly like unbeaten egg whites (French).

There are numerous proteins in egg whites that form liquid and air-holding scaffolding structures (gelled foams) under different conditions (some respond to heat, some to agitation). The combined process of beating and cooking that takes place while making an Italian meringue produces a very stable whipped meringue in which almost all the proteins have gelled, leaving you with a voluminous and stable meringue.

A properly whipped egg white foam (in our case an Italian meringue) gently incorporated into a thick flavor base (in our case a pastry cream sometimes containing added raw egg yolks) is a soufflé waiting to be baked. Once the soufflé goes into the oven, air trapped in the egg white foam structure expands, making the soufflé rise above the rim of the dish. Depending on the ingredients in the thick flavor base, the soufflé may also attain height through other protein reactions in the flavor base.

Meyer Lemon Soufflé

5 tablespoons (2 ½ ounces) butter, at room temperature

1 cup plus 2 tablespoons sugar

½ cup heavy cream

½ cup Meyer lemon juice (from approximately 3 to 4 lemons)

2 teaspoon Meyer lemon zest

8 eggs

¼ teaspoon salt

2 tablespoons plus 1 teaspoon flour

Pinch of cream of tartar

SPECIAL TOOLS AND PANS

Stand mixer

Eight to twelve 4-ounce or eight 5-ounce ramekins

Candy thermometer

See Soufflé Guidelines (page 112).

YIELD

Twelve 4- to 5-ounce soufflés

Meyer lemon soufflé—hot, creamy, light, bursting with the tartness and flavor of Meyer lemon zest—is simply a marvelous lemon dessert. The juice and the precious zest of the Meyer lemon make a lemon pastry cream flavor base. This base is folded into an Italian meringue (egg white foam stabilized with hot sugar syrup) and spooned into ramekins, which are then tucked away until you are ready to bake them. (*See* INGREDIENT: *Meyer lemons, page 18*)

This soufflé is delicious on its own. At Chanterelle, one way I dress it up is to bake the soufflés free-form, without any dish, to order on top of individual-sized lemon curd tarts with fresh raspberries; the contrast of the hot, airy, light lemon soufflé on top of the creamy, richer lemon curd sets off the delicately warmed raspberries and flaky crust. When it comes out of the oven, I serve the soufflé with a scoop of Pineapple-Rosemary Sorbet (page 146), adding another temperature, texture, and flavor.

Prepare the soufflé molds.

Melt 3 tablespoons of the butter and generously grease your soufflé ramekins. Refrigerate the buttered ramekins and then butter them again. Dust the insides of the ramekins with 3 tablespoons of the sugar and return them to the refrigerator. Keep the remaining butter at room temperature.

Make the lemon pastry cream base.

In a heavy-bottomed saucepan over medium heat, combine the cream, lemon juice, lemon zest, and 1 tablespoon of the sugar and heat through.

Meanwhile, separate 8 eggs, reserving the whites; place 5 yolks in a medium-sized bowl, 2 yolks in a small glass to hold for later, and discard the remaining yolk or use it for something else. Whisk the 5 egg yolks with 2 tablespoons of the sugar and the salt. Briskly whisk in the flour, making sure that the mixture is smooth with no lumps or streaks of white. While continually whisking, add about half of the lemon cream to the egg yolk mixture to warm it, then whisk the egg yolk mixture into the remaining lemon cream in the pan.

Bring the custard to a boil over medium-high heat, whisking continuously and making sure to scrape the bottom of the entire pan. Once the mixture boils for 20 seconds and thickens, remove it from the heat and stir in 2 tablespoons butter. Transfer the custard to a clean stainless-steel bowl and allow the mixture to cool.

Make the meringue.

See BEYOND THE BASICS: *Acid in egg white foams, page 123.*

Combine ½ cup plus 2 tablespoons of sugar and 3 tablespoons water in a small saucepan over medium heat and attach a candy thermometer to the side of the pan. Simultaneously place the 8 egg whites in the bowl of a stand mixer and whisk on medium-high speed. Once the egg whites begin to foam up, add the cream of tartar.

When the egg whites are completely foamy and begin to hold the lines of a whisk, turn the heat under the pan of sugar syrup to high. Once the sugar syrup has come to a rolling boil and reaches 225°F to 230°F, gradually add the remaining 2 tablespoons of sugar, 1 teaspoon at a time, to the egg whites. As you add the sugar, the whites should become shiny and gain volume. If you see the whites beading (small lumps of egg whites forming on the side of the bowl), you have whipped them too dry; slow the machine down and add the remaining sugar.

Once the sugar syrup on the stove reaches 248°F quickly, in a slow continuous stream, pour the hot syrup into the egg whites with the mixer set on a medium-high speed. The whites should still gain more volume and take on a satiny white color. Continue to whip the meringue on medium-high speed until it stiffens and cools, 3 to 5 minutes.

Fold the meringue into the lemon pastry cream base.

See BEYOND THE BASICS: *Raw egg yolks in pastry cream for soufflé, page 127.*

Once the meringue is done, whisk the remaining 2 raw egg yolks into the lemon pastry cream. Add about a quarter of the meringue to the lemon custard to lighten it and then add the remaining meringue. Place a spatula in the center of the bowl, scrape the bottom, and bring the bottom over the top. Rotate the bowl 45 degrees and continue folding until all the egg whites are incorporated.

Fill the prepared ramekins.

Using a rubber or plastic spatula, fill the prepared ramekins with the mousse, avoiding leaving any air pockets under the mousse in the ramekins. Flatten the tops of the ramekins with a metal spatula, scraping any excess mousse back into the bowl. Clean off any bits of mousse that might have dripped onto the sides of the ramekins.

Bake the soufflé.

You can now either bake your soufflés or place them in the refrigerator, covered, for up to 4 hours or in the freezer for up to 24 hours. Before baking frozen soufflés, allow them to sit out at room temperature for 1 hour. When you are ready to bake the soufflés, preheat the oven to 375°F. Bake the soufflés until they rise over the rims by about ½ their original volume, 9 to 12 minutes in a convection oven or 15 to 20 minutes in a regular oven without a fan.

Serving Suggestions

Serve the soufflés as soon as they come out of the oven. Often in fancy restaurants a waiter arrives at your table with not only the soufflé but also a scoop of ice cream or a tureen of sauce and a spoon. The waiter sticks the spoon right in the middle of your soufflé and creates a pocket in which he inserts the ice cream or sauce. We never do this at Chanterelle. I always serve the ice cream, sauce, or whipped cream or crème fraîche on the side. I think it is more exciting to let Chanterelle's clients do the garnishing of their own soufflés.

Serve this soufflé with Spiced Mandarin Ice Cream (page 136), Mandarin Orange Sorbet (page 144), Strawberry and Tarragon Sorbet (page 148), or Guava Sorbet (page 152). Or pass around a small bowl of whipped crème fraîche or whipped cream for guests to dollop on top of their soufflés after they have taken that first aerated spoonful.

Goat Cheese and Purple Basil Soufflé

6 tablespoons (3 ounces) butter

⅓ cup plus 7 tablespoons sugar

¾ cup whole milk

7 eggs

¼ teaspoon salt

1 tablespoon plus 2 teaspoons flour

8 ounces fresh goat cheese, at room temperature

2 tablespoons finely chopped purple basil

Pinch of cream of tartar

SPECIAL TOOLS AND PANS

Twelve 4-ounce or seven 5-ounce ramekins

Stand mixer

Candy thermometer

See Soufflé Guidelines (page 112).

YIELD

Twelve 4-ounce soufflés or seven 5-ounce soufflés

This is a grown-up dessert: barely sweet, herbaceous, and complex. The tanginess of the goat cheese complements the refreshing clarity of the basil, making this a truly sophisticated ending for a summer dinner party.

Purple basil is a strain of the species that features the spicy flavor and aroma we expect from ordinary basil, but its stunningly colored purple leaves make for an exciting and exotic presentation. That said, if your local market doesn't stock purple basil, the green variety will produce the same flavors in this soufflé.

Prepare the soufflé molds.

Melt 3 tablespoons of the butter and generously grease your soufflé ramekins. Refrigerate the buttered ramekins and then butter them again. Dust the insides of the ramekins with 3 tablespoons of the sugar and return them to the refrigerator. Keep the remaining butter at room temperature.

Make the pastry cream.

Heat the milk in a heavy-bottomed saucepan.

Meanwhile, separate the eggs, reserving the whites in the bowl of your stand mixer. Place 4 of the yolks in a medium bowl, 2 in a small bowl to be used later, and either discard the remaining yolk or use it for something else. Whisk the 4 yolks with 1 tablespoon of the sugar and the salt. Briskly whisk in the flour, making sure that the mixture is smooth with no lumps or streaks of white. While continually whisking, add about half the hot milk to the egg yolk mixture to warm it, then whisk the yolk mixture back into the remaining milk in the pan.

Bring the custard to a boil over medium-high heat, whisking continuously and making sure to scrape the bottom of the entire pan. Once the mixture boils (20 seconds) and thickens, remove it from the heat and stir in 2 tablespoons butter. Transfer the custard to a clean stainless-steel bowl and allow the mixture to cool for 5 minutes. Whisk in the goat cheese, basil, and remaining 2 egg yolks. Cover the goat cheese cream with plastic wrap while you make the meringue.

Make the meringue.

See BEYOND THE BASICS: *Acid in egg white foams, page 123.*

Combine ⅓ cup plus 3 tablespoons of sugar and 3 tablespoons water in a small saucepan over medium heat and attach a candy thermometer to the side of the pan. Simultaneously place the 7 egg whites in the bowl of a stand mixer and whisk on medium-high speed. Once the egg whites begin to foam up, add the cream of tartar.

When the egg whites are completely foamy and begin to hold the lines of a whisk, turn the heat under the pan of sugar syrup to high. Once the sugar syrup has come to a rolling boil and reaches 225°F to 230°F, gradually add the remaining 2 tablespoons of sugar, 1 teaspoon at a time, to the egg whites. As you add the sugar, the whites should become shiny and gain volume. If you see the whites beading (small lumps of egg whites forming on the side of the bowl), you have whipped them too dry; slow the machine down and add the remaining sugar.

Once the sugar syrup on the stove reaches 248°F quickly, in a slow continuous stream, pour the hot syrup into the egg whites with the mixer set on a medium-high speed. The whites should still gain more volume and take on a satiny white color. Continue to whip the meringue on medium-high speed until it stiffens and cools, 3 to 5 minutes.

Goat Cheese and Purple Basil Soufflé

Fold the meringue into the pastry cream.

Give the goat cheese cream a few hard and fast strokes with the whisk to smooth out the mixture. Add about a quarter of the meringue to the goat cheese custard to lighten it and then add the remaining meringue. Place a spatula in the center of the bowl, scrape the bottom, and bring the bottom over the top. Rotate the bowl 45 degrees and continue folding until all the egg whites are incorporated.

Fill the prepared ramekins.

Using a rubber or plastic spatula, fill the prepared ramekins with the mousse, avoiding leaving any air pockets under the mousse in the ramekins. Flatten the tops of the ramekins with a metal spatula, scraping any excess mousse back into the bowl. Clean off any bits of mousse that might have dripped onto the sides of the ramekins.

Bake the soufflé.

You can now either bake your soufflés or place them in the refrigerator, covered, for up to 4 hours or in the freezer for up to 24 hours. Before baking frozen soufflés, allow them to sit out at room temperature for 1 hour. When you are ready to bake the soufflés, preheat the oven to 375°F. Bake the soufflés until they rise over the rims by about ½ their original volume, 9 to 12 minutes in a convection oven or 15 to 20 minutes in a regular oven without a fan.

Serving Suggestions

Serve these soufflés as soon as they come out of the oven. Place some dried fruits or fresh grapes on a side dish. Or pass around a small bowl of whipped crème fraîche for guests to dollop on top of their soufflés after they have taken that first aerated spoonful.

Chocolate Soufflé

Like many of the chocolate recipes in this book, this soufflé features a dark caramel flavor in the background, which helps to intensify the richness of the chocolate. As always, great chocolate makes for a great result, so use the good stuff.

Prepare the soufflé molds.
Melt 3 tablespoons of the butter and generously grease your soufflé ramekins. Refrigerate the buttered ramekins and then butter them again. Dust the insides of the ramekins with 3 tablespoons of the sugar and return them to the refrigerator.

Melt the chocolate and the butter.
In a bain-marie, melt the dark and unsweetened chocolate and the remaining 4 tablespoons of butter, stirring occasionally with a rubber spatula (this will take about 10 minutes). Set the melted chocolate aside.

Whip the yolks with the hot caramel syrup.
See BEYOND THE BASICS: *Cooking caramel successfully, page 107.*

Separate the eggs, putting the whites in the bowl of a stand mixer. Place 5 yolks in a medium-sized stainless-steel bowl and discard the remaining 3 yolks or use them for something else. Place a damp towel under the bowl of egg yolks to hold it in place while you whisk.

Combine ½ cup of the sugar, 1 pinch of cream of tartar, and 3 tablespoons water in a heavy-bottomed saucepan. Cover and bring to a rapid boil over medium-high heat. Once boiling, uncover the pan and cook the sugar until deep golden brown. Turn off the heat and very carefully pour 2 tablespoons water into the hot caramel. Stand back—the caramel will hiss and bubble and spurt.

Once you have added the water, the caramel syrup will come back to a rolling boil from the residual heat. When the caramel syrup stops boiling, slowly pour it into the egg yolks while simultaneously whisking them by hand (you can also use a hand mixer). Beat for 2 minutes, until the egg yolks thicken and double in volume.

Add the coffee, rum, and salt and continue to whisk until the yolk mixture is lukewarm. Set aside.

Make the meringue.
See BEYOND THE BASICS: *Acid in egg white foams, page 123.*

Combine ½ cup plus 2 tablespoons of sugar and 3 tablespoons water in a small saucepan over medium heat and attach a candy thermometer to the side of the pan. Simultaneously place the 8 egg whites in the bowl of a stand mixer and whisk on medium-high speed. Once the egg whites begin to foam up, add the cream of tartar.

When the egg whites are completely foamy and begin to hold the lines of a whisk, turn the heat under the pan of sugar syrup to high. Once the sugar syrup has come to a rolling boil and reaches 225°F to 230°F, gradually add the remaining 2 tablespoons of sugar, 1 teaspoon at a time, to the egg whites. As you add the sugar, the whites should become shiny and gain volume. If you see the whites beading (small lumps of egg whites forming on the side of the bowl), you have whipped them too dry; slow the machine down and add the remaining sugar.

Once the sugar syrup on the stove reaches 248°F quickly, in a slow continuous stream, pour the hot syrup into the egg whites with the mixer set on a medium-high speed. The whites should still gain more volume and take on a satiny white color. Continue to whip the meringue on medium-high speed until it stiffens and cools, 3 to 5 minutes.

Add the chocolate to the whipped egg yolk base.
Add the whipped egg yolk mixture to the bowl with the melted chocolate. Whisk the chocolate and the yolks until the mixture is smooth, shiny, and thoroughly combined.

---

7 tablespoons (3½ ounces) butter

1 cup plus 5 tablespoons sugar

6½ ounces dark chocolate (66 to 85 percent cocoa solids)

1 ounce unsweetened chocolate (99 to 100 percent cocoa solids)

8 eggs

2 pinches (½ teaspoon) cream of tartar

2 tablespoons brewed espresso

1 tablespoon dark rum

¼ teaspoon salt

SPECIAL TOOLS AND PANS

Twelve 4-ounce or eight 5-ounce ramekins

Bain-marie (see page 10)

Candy thermometer

Stand mixer

See Soufflé Guidelines (page 112).

YIELD

Twelve 4-ounce soufflés

Fold the meringue into the chocolate-yolk base.

Add about a quarter of the meringue to the chocolate mixture to lighten it and then add the remaining meringue. Place a spatula in the center of the bowl, scrape the bottom, and bring the bottom over the top. Rotate the bowl 45 degrees and continue folding until all the egg whites are incorporated.

Fill the prepared ramekins.

Using a rubber or plastic spatula, fill the prepared ramekins with the mousse, avoiding leaving any air pockets under the mousse in the ramekins. Flatten the tops of the ramekins with a metal spatula, scraping any excess mousse back into the bowl. Clean off any bits of mousse that might have dripped onto the sides of the ramekins.

Bake the soufflé.

You can now either bake your soufflés or place them in the refrigerator, covered, for up to 4 hours or in the freezer for up to 24 hours. Before baking frozen soufflés, allow them to sit out at room temperature for 1 hour. When you are ready to bake the soufflés, preheat the oven to 375°F. Bake the soufflés until they rise over the rims by about ½ their original volume, 9 to 12 minutes in a convection oven or 15 to 20 minutes in a regular oven without a fan.

Serving Suggestions

Serve these soufflés as soon as they come out of the oven. If you have extra time, a small dish of Fresh Cherry Vanilla Compote (page 170) is a wonderful accompaniment. The Rum Caramel Sauce (page 213), the Cinnamon Caramel Mousse (page 106), and the Toffee Sauce (page 214) are excellent with it as well.

Freestanding Chocolate Soufflé with Fresh Cherry Vanilla Compote

Maple Walnut Soufflé

5 tablespoons (2 ½ ounces) butter

²⁄₃ cup plus 4 tablespoons sugar

1¼ cups maple syrup

1 cup (4 ounces) finely chopped walnuts

1 cup whole milk

9 eggs

3 tablespoons plus 1 teaspoon flour

¼ teaspoon salt

1 tablespoon cornstarch

1 tablespoon brandy

Pinch of cream of tartar

SPECIAL TOOLS AND PANS

Twelve 4-ounce or eight 5-ounce ramekins

Candy thermometer

Stand mixer

See Soufflé Guidelines (page 112).

YIELD

Eight to twelve 4- to 5-ounce individual soufflés

One of the first soufflés I learned to make during an apprenticeship in France was a classic French walnut soufflé. When I returned home, I longed to add another layer of flavor to the original. Maple walnut ice cream is a classic American treat, so I turned to this traditional combination for inspiration. In a soufflé, the buttery luxuriousness of maple syrup turns into a light, airy confection that perfectly marries with the earthy richness of walnuts.

Prepare the soufflé molds.
Melt 3 tablespoons of the butter and generously grease your soufflé ramekins. Refrigerate the buttered ramekins and then butter them again. Dust the insides of the ramekins with 3 tablespoons of the sugar and return them to the refrigerator. Keep the remaining butter at room temperature.

Make the pastry cream.
Boil the maple syrup in a heavy-bottomed saucepan over medium-high heat until the syrup reduces by half and registers 240°F on a candy thermometer. If you do not have a thermometer, test the syrup after it has boiled, foamed, and reduced somewhat. Drop a fork tong of syrup on the counter—if it dries in a mound, scrapes off the counter cleanly with your fingernail, and is somewhat pliable and gummy between two fingers, it is ready. Remove from the heat and let cool for 5 minutes. Add the walnuts and milk and reheat until the syrup dissolves in the milk.

Meanwhile, separate the 9 eggs, placing the whites in the bowl of a stand mixer; place 7 of the yolks in a medium bowl, and reserve 2 yolks in a small bowl to use later in the recipe. Briskly whisk the 7 yolks with the flour, salt, and cornstarch, making sure that the mixture is smooth with no lumps or streaks of white remaining. While continually whisking, add about half the hot milk mixture to the egg yolk mixture to warm it, then whisk the yolk mixture into the remaining hot milk in the pan.

Bring the custard to a boil over medium-high heat, whisking continuously and making sure to scrape the bottom of the entire pan. Once the mixture boils for 20 seconds and thickens, remove it from the heat and stir in the remaining butter and the alcohol. Transfer the custard to a clean stainless-steel bowl and allow the mixture to cool, stirring every 2 to 3 minutes.

Make the meringue.
See BEYOND THE BASICS: *Acid in egg white foams, page 123.*

Combine ²⁄₃ cup plus 1 tablespoon of sugar and 3 tablespoons water in a small saucepan over medium heat and attach a candy thermometer to the side of the pan. Simultaneously place the 9 egg whites in the bowl of a stand mixer and whisk on medium-high speed. Once the egg whites begin to foam up, add the cream of tartar.

When the egg whites are completely foamy and begin to hold the lines of a whisk, turn the heat under the pan of sugar syrup to high. Once the sugar syrup has come to a rolling boil and reaches 225°F to 230°F, gradually add the remaining 2 tablespoons of sugar, 1 teaspoon at a time, to the egg whites. As you add the sugar, the whites should become shiny and gain volume. If you see the whites beading (small lumps of egg whites forming on the side of the bowl), you have whipped them too dry; slow the machine down and add the remaining sugar.

Once the sugar syrup on the stove reaches 248°F quickly, in a slow continuous stream, pour the hot syrup into the egg whites with the mixer set on a medium-high speed. The whites should still gain more volume and take on a satiny white color. Continue to whip the meringue on medium-high speed until it stiffens and cools, 3 to 5 minutes.

Fold the meringue into the pastry cream.

See BEYOND THE BASICS: *Raw egg yolks in pastry cream for soufflé, page 127.*

Whisk the remaining 2 egg yolks into the maple walnut pastry cream. Add about a quarter of the meringue to the maple walnut pastry cream to lighten it and then add the remaining meringue. Place a spatula in the center of the bowl, scrape the bottom, and bring the bottom over the top. Rotate the bowl 45 degrees and continue folding until all the egg whites are incorporated.

Fill the prepared ramekins.

Using a rubber or plastic spatula, fill the prepared ramekins with the mousse, avoiding leaving any air pockets under the mousse in the ramekins. Flatten the tops of the ramekins with a metal spatula, scraping any excess mousse back into the bowl. Clean off any bits of mousse that might have dripped onto the sides of the ramekins.

Bake the soufflé.

You can now either bake your soufflés or place them in the refrigerator, covered, for up to 4 hours or in the freezer for up to 24 hours. Before baking frozen soufflés, allow them to sit out at room temperature for 1 hour. When you are ready to bake the soufflés, preheat the oven to 375°F. Bake the soufflés until they rise over the rims by about ½ their original volume, 9 to 12 minutes in a convection oven or 15 to 20 minutes in a regular oven without a fan.

Serving Suggestions

Serve these soufflés as soon as they come out of the oven with a dollop of vanilla ice cream or crème fraîche.

BEYOND THE BASICS
Acid in egg white foams

Whenever you are instructed to beat egg whites into a foam (for a meringue, a mousse, or a soufflé), the recipe usually calls for a pinch of vinegar, lemon juice, or cream of tartar. In BEYOND THE BASICS: *The unique consistency of citrus curds (page 20)*, I point out that acid has three major effects on egg proteins: it causes proteins to denature, enables them to make early bonds (aggregations), and reduces the likelihood of sulfur bonding, a strong protein bond. Adding a small amount of acid to whipping egg whites has the same effect: it helps to denature the egg whites during the early stages of agitation, making them easier to whip up; it greatly reduces the likelihood of complete coagulation of egg white proteins—which produces a grainy, lumpy, watery, weak egg white foam. Added acid makes it possible to whisk the egg whites vigorously for a set time period without any signs of dryness or beading (little clumps of coagulated proteins) forming on the sides of the bowl.

Similarly, the secret behind the use of copper bowls for whipping egg whites is that copper reduces the likelihood of sulfur bonding, enabling you to beat your egg whites with a reduced risk of over-coagulation. But a touch of acid has the same effect.

Brandied Dried Fig and Vanilla Soufflé

MACERATED FIGS

6 (5 ounces) dried figs

¼ cup brandy

SOUFFLÉ

7 tablespoons (3 ½ ounces) butter

1 cup plus 5 tablespoons sugar

1 vanilla bean or 1 teaspoon vanilla extract

1 cup whole milk

9 eggs

Pinch of salt

3 tablespoons flour

Pinch of cream of tartar

SPECIAL TOOLS AND PANS

Twelve 4-ounce or nine 5-ounce ramekins for baking

Candy thermometer

Stand mixer

See Soufflé Guidelines (page 112).

YIELD

Twelve 4-ounce soufflés

The combination of fig and vanilla is one of my absolute favorite flavors. I use it in my Stuffed Roasted Fall Apples (page 182) and Fresh Fig and Madeira Compote (page 170), and I often include figs and vanilla along with the apples in the Thanksgiving apple pie I make for my family.

I came up with this dessert when I received a particularly extraordinary shipment of Bourbon vanilla beans from Madagascar, and I was determined to make a vanilla soufflé, but it just didn't work on its own. I added some chopped figs marinated in brandy, and suddenly the flavors came into focus.

24 hours ahead of time: Macerate the figs.
Chop the hard stem off the end of each fig and dice the figs. Place the chopped figs and brandy in a sealed container and marinate overnight.

Prepare the soufflé molds.
Melt 3 tablespoons of the butter and generously grease your soufflé ramekins. Refrigerate the buttered ramekins and then butter them again. Dust the insides of the ramekins with 3 tablespoons of the sugar and return them to the refrigerator. Keep the remaining butter at room temperature.

Make the pastry cream.
Run a paring knife down the center of the vanilla bean. Split it open with your fingers and use the knife to scrape out the tiny black seeds into a heavy-bottomed saucepan. (If you are using vanilla extract, add it later, as directed below.) Add the milk and 1 tablespoon of the sugar to the saucepan and heat to just below a simmer.

Meanwhile, separate the 9 eggs, reserving the whites in the bowl of a stand mixer. Place 7 yolks in a medium bowl, reserving the remaining 2 yolks to use later in the recipe. Whisk the 7 yolks with 1 tablespoon of the sugar and the salt. Briskly whisk in the flour, making sure that the mixture is smooth with no lumps or streaks of white. While continually whisking, add about half of the hot milk to the egg yolk mixture to warm it, then whisk the egg yolk

mixture into the remaining hot milk in the pan.

Bring the custard to a boil over medium-high heat, whisking continuously and making sure to scrape the bottom of the entire pan. Once the mixture boils (20 seconds) and thickens, remove it from the heat and stir in 4 tablespoons butter. Transfer the custard to a clean stainless-steel bowl and remove the vanilla bean with a fork; rinse it and save it for another use. (If using vanilla extract, add it at this point.) Whisk in the macerated figs and brandy. Set the pastry cream aside to cool.

Make the meringue.
See BEYOND THE BASICS: *Acid in egg white foams, page 123.*

Combine all but 2 tablespoons of the remaining sugar and 3 tablespoons water in a small saucepan over medium heat and attach a candy thermometer to the side of the pan. Simultaneously place the 9 egg whites in the bowl of a stand mixer and whisk on medium-high speed. Once the egg whites begin to foam up, add the cream of tartar.

When the egg whites are completely foamy and begin to hold the lines of a whisk, turn the heat under the pan of sugar syrup to high. Once the sugar syrup has come to a rolling boil and reaches 225°F to 230°F, gradually add the remaining 2 tablespoons of sugar, 1 teaspoon at a time, to the egg whites. As you add the sugar, the whites should become shiny and gain volume. If you see the whites beading (small lumps of egg whites forming on the side of the bowl), you have whipped them too dry; slow the machine down and add the remaining sugar.

Once the sugar syrup on the stove reaches 248°F quickly, in a slow continuous stream, pour the hot syrup into the egg whites with the mixer set on a medium-high speed. The whites should still gain more volume and take on a satiny white color. Continue to whip the meringue on medium-high speed until it stiffens and cools, 3 to 5 minutes.

Fold the meringue into the pastry cream.

See BEYOND THE BASICS: *Raw egg yolks in pastry cream for soufflé, page 127.*

Whisk the remaining 2 egg yolks into the brandied fig pastry cream. Add about a quarter of the meringue to the pastry cream to lighten it and then add the remaining meringue. Place a spatula in the center of the bowl, scrape the bottom, and bring the bottom over the top. Rotate the bowl 45 degrees and continue folding until all the egg whites are incorporated.

Fill the prepared ramekins.

Using a rubber or plastic spatula, fill the prepared ramekins with the mousse, avoiding leaving any air pockets under the mousse in the ramekins. Flatten the tops of the ramekins with a metal spatula, scraping any excess mousse back into the bowl. Clean off any bits of mousse that might have dripped onto the sides of the ramekins.

Bake the soufflé.

You can now either bake your soufflés or place them in the refrigerator, covered, for up to 4 hours or in the freezer for up to 24 hours. Before baking frozen soufflés, allow them to sit out at room temperature for 1 hour. When you are ready to bake the soufflés, preheat the oven to 375°F. Bake the soufflés until they rise over the rims by about ½ their original volume, 9 to 12 minutes in a convection oven or 15 to 20 minutes in a regular oven without a fan.

Serving Suggestions

Serve these soufflés as soon as they come out of the oven. Good accompaniments are some dried fruits or fresh grapes on the side. Or pass around a small bowl of whipped crème fraîche for guests to dollop on top of their soufflés after they have taken that first aerated spoonful.

Pumpkin Soufflé

4 tablespoons (2 ounces) butter

¾ cup plus 3 tablespoons sugar

½ cup maple syrup

½ cup plus 2 tablespoons canned, unsweetened pumpkin puree

¼ cup plus 2 tablespoons half-and-half

½ teaspoon cinnamon

1 teaspoon powdered ginger

¼ teaspoon clove

¼ teaspoon allspice

Pinch of nutmeg

Pinch of white pepper

½ teaspoon salt

7 eggs

3 tablespoons flour

Pinch of cream of tartar

SPECIAL TOOLS AND PANS

Twelve 4- to 5-ounce or ten 5-ounce ramekins for baking

Candy thermometer

Stand mixer

See Soufflé Guidelines (page 112).

YIELD

Twelve 4-ounce soufflés

I make this soufflé every fall at Chanterelle. It is the perfect pumpkin dessert, marrying the traditional flavors of American pumpkin pie with the classic elegance of the French soufflé. Warm, light, and creamy, it's a wonderful dessert for the early cold weather months.

Prepare the soufflé molds.

Melt 3 tablespoons of the butter and generously grease your soufflé ramekins. Refrigerate the buttered ramekins and then butter them again. Dust the insides of the ramekins with 3 tablespoons of the sugar and return them to the refrigerator. Keep the remaining butter at room temperature.

Make the pumpkin pastry cream.

In a heavy-bottomed saucepan, bring the maple syrup to a boil and reduce it by almost half. A thermometer inserted in the maple syrup should read 140°F when the syrup is fully reduced. Remove the syrup from the heat and allow it to cool in the pan for 10 minutes.

Add the pumpkin puree, half-and-half, and all the spices including the salt to the pan with the maple syrup. Heat the mixture on low, stirring with a whisk, until the maple syrup softens and incorporates into the pumpkin mixture.

Meanwhile, separate the 7 eggs, reserving the whites in the bowl of a stand mixer. Place 4 egg yolks in a medium bowl, reserve 2 egg yolks in a small glass to hold for later, and either discard the remaining yolk or use it for something else. Whisk 2 tablespoons of the warm pumpkin mixture into the egg yolks, and then briskly whisk in the flour, making sure that the mixture is smooth with no lumps or streaks of white, 2 to 3 minutes. While continually whisking, add about half of the remaining hot pumpkin mixture to the egg yolk mixture to warm it, then whisk the egg yolk mixture into the remaining pumpkin mixture in the pan.

Bring the custard to a boil over medium-high heat, whisking continuously and making sure to scrape the bottom of the entire pan.

Once the mixture boils for 20 seconds and thickens, remove it from the heat and stir in the remaining 1 tablespoon of butter. Transfer the custard to a clean stainless-steel bowl and allow the mixture to cool.

Make the meringue.

See BEYOND THE BASICS: *Acid in egg white foams, page 123.*

Combine all but 2 tablespoons of the remaining sugar and 4 tablespoons water in a small saucepan over medium heat and attach a candy thermometer to the side of the pan. Simultaneously place the 7 egg whites in the bowl of a stand mixer and whisk on medium-high speed. Once the egg whites begin to foam up, add the cream of tartar.

When the egg whites are completely foamy and begin to hold the lines of a whisk, turn the heat under the pan of sugar syrup to high. Once the sugar syrup has come to a rolling boil and reaches 225°F to 230°F, gradually add the remaining 2 tablespoons of sugar, 1 teaspoon at a time, to the egg whites. As you add the sugar, the whites should become shiny and gain volume. If you see the whites beading (small lumps of egg whites forming on the side of the bowl), you have whipped them too dry; slow the machine down and add the remaining sugar.

Once the sugar syrup on the stove reaches 248°F quickly, in a slow continuous stream, pour the hot syrup into the egg whites with the mixer set on a medium-high speed. The whites should still gain more volume and take on a satiny white color. Continue to whip the meringue on medium-high speed until it stiffens and cools, 3 to 5 minutes.

Fold the meringue into the pastry cream.

See BEYOND THE BASICS: *Raw egg yolks in pastry cream for soufflé, page 127.*

Once the meringue is done, whisk the remaining 2 egg yolks into the pumpkin pastry cream. Add about a quarter of the meringue to the pumpkin custard to lighten it and then add the remaining meringue. Place a spatula in the center of the bowl, scrape the bottom, and bring the bottom over the top. Rotate the bowl 45 degrees and continue folding until all the egg whites are incorporated.

Fill the prepared ramekins.

Using a rubber or plastic spatula, fill the prepared ramekins with the mousse, avoiding leaving any air pockets under the mousse in the ramekins. Flatten the tops of the ramekins with a metal spatula, scraping any excess mousse back into the bowl. Clean off any bits of mousse that might have dripped onto the sides of the ramekins.

Bake the soufflé.

You can now either bake your soufflés or place them in the refrigerator, covered, for up to 4 hours or in the freezer for up to 24 hours. Before baking frozen soufflés, allow them to sit out at room temperature for 1 hour. When you are ready to bake the soufflés, preheat the oven to 375°F. Bake the soufflés until they rise over the rims by about ½ their original volume, 9 to 12 minutes in a convection oven or 15 to 20 minutes in a regular oven without a fan.

Serving Suggestions

Serve these soufflés as soon as they come out of the oven. I recommend serving this soufflé with Maple-Ginger Ice Cream (page 139) and crispy Gingersnaps (page 59). You can also serve it with vanilla ice cream and a plain wafer. Caramel or cinnamon ice cream makes a nice accompaniment. Or pass around a small bowl of whipped crème fraîche or cream for guests to dollop on top of their soufflés after they have taken that first aerated spoonful.

BEYOND THE BASICS
Raw egg yolks in pastry cream for soufflé

In most of my soufflé recipes I add raw egg yolks to my pastry cream or soufflé base. These raw egg yolks introduce uncooked proteins into the prepared soufflé about to enter the oven. Your soufflé already contains an elastic egg white foam that, through exposure to intense heat, will rise and stretch as the air trapped in the egg white protein network expands. The raw egg yolk proteins will, through exposure to heat, create their own, new, strong network of scaffolding-like structures that will push out against the stable, elastic, expanding egg white foam, giving the soufflé an intense push up as well as some stability when it is removed from the oven.

ICE CREAMS, SORBETS, AND FROZEN DESSERTS

CHAPTER SIX

Ice Cream and Sorbet Guidelines

Ice cream is one of the most versatile desserts. Laden with milk and cream, an ice cream base (a lightly thickened custard) can be infused with almost any flavor—from fresh herbs, dried spices, fragrant fruits, and chocolates of all types to numerous alcohols. Ice cream is usually frozen at temperatures well below freezing (32°F), and, yet, at these freezing temperatures, it is soft and scoopable, and its seemingly creamy and cool impression is magically pleasurable to our tongue. It can easily be combined with a crunchy candy or nuts or it can be served with a delightful crisp cookie or wafer. Ice cream satisfies the palate by appealing to our senses of temperature and texture and taste simultaneously. It is truly one of the world's favorite desserts. And mine as well.

Some Science Involved in Ice Cream Making

That said, producing smooth and creamy ice cream at home is a challenge. Every dessert cookbook provides recipes for this or that flavor, but what's important about ice cream is understanding how the machinery and the ingredients interact to make ice cream.

Commercial ice cream makers produce their uniformly smooth and creamy ice cream by taking advantage of a number of factors that are, for the most part, inaccessible to the home cook. Machinery is the first of them, and, for reasons I'll explore below, expensive industrial-strength ice cream machines simply do the job better than smaller units designed for home use. Commercial ice cream makers also use a wide range of thickening, gelling, and stabilizing agents that are essentially outside the purview of the home cook.

In order to extract the most decadent and delicious ice creams from our home machines we must consider the role played by the ingredients we do use. Ice cream is a complicated emulsion of water, sugar, protein, fat, and flavoring, with the special and unique properties of water acting as the principal player in the transmutation of custard into a frozen confection.

Controlling ice crystal formation, in terms of both their size and their number, is the essential secret to making good ice cream and sorbet as well. When pure water freezes, at 0°C (32°F), it forms hexagonal-shaped crystals with sharp edges that, if left alone, can grow quite large, becoming visible to the eye and clearly discernible on the tongue. In ice cream, neither large crystals nor sharp edges are desirable, so finding ways to make the crystals small enough so that we don't taste or identify the individual crystals is the name of the game.

Before considering how the ingredients affect ice crystal formation, let's look briefly at how ice cream machines function and their effect on ice crystal formation. These machines simultaneously chill and whip custards by rapid spinning with a sharp blade. In general, it's the combination of a strong cooling mechanism, the speed and sharpness of the whipping blade (called a dasher), and the amount of air pumped into the mixture that produces the smaller ice crystals that give the final product a smoother texture. Commercial ice cream machines have these key features, while even the best home machines, for the most part, have weak cooling mechanisms, blunt plastic dashers, and minimal air circulation—never mind active air pumping.

What role do the ingredients play, then, in home ice cream making? Adding soluble ingredients—such as sugar or salt—lowers the freezing point of water. That's why we put salt on ice in the winter: the salt lowers the freezing point of water, so that the ice melts because its freezing point has dropped below the air temperature. The same is true of sugar, the ingredient in ice cream base that actively lowers its freezing point. The lower the freezing point of a fluid, the more ice crystals will form (in a given volume) during freezing, and the smaller each individual crystal will become. That is, sugar directly results in smaller ice crystals and improved texture. Liquid sugars (or inverted sugars)—honey, corn syrup and its derivatives, caramel, maple syrup, malt syrup, and molasses, for example— lower the freezing point of a fluid even more powerfully. The addition of liquid sugars helps ice cream bases and sorbet bases obtain a potentially smoother texture than they would otherwise with the addition of just ordinary table sugar (sucrose).

Another ingredient that affects the freezing process is protein, which is present in ice cream base from dairy and eggs. Proteins are large molecules that literally get in the way of ice crystal formations; under certain conditions, proteins absorb water, forming a gel, thereby preventing existing ice crystals from growing larger. Every ice cream recipe in this chapter begins with a crème anglaise—a custard made of eggs, milk, cream, and sugar. The proteins in the mixture are heated and agitated (denatured), which allows them to form a gel. Water locked into a gel cannot migrate over to existing ice crystals—thereby increasing their size—or form its own ice crystals at normal freezer temperatures. Interestingly, most ice cream is hard enough to scoop at –15°F, and at that temperature only 70 percent of the water in the ice cream is present in the form of ice crystals.

Skim milk powder, a primary ingredient in good quality commercial ice cream and one that I also recommend depending on the recipe, is a convenient means of adding protein as well as sugar and other molecules to the ice cream base; these molecules get in the way of ice crystal formation, controlling crystal size and improving the final texture of the frozen dessert. Egg whites are often added to sorbet mixtures. Proteins in egg whites function similarly to proteins in skim milk powder, improving the texture of sorbet.

Some commercial ice creams and sorbets utilize stabilizers, both natural and otherwise, to improve texture. An important class of stabilizers is the polysaccharides (including pectin, carrageenan, guar gum, locust bean gum, and cellulose gum). These molecules function similarly to proteins in one respect: they absorb water when gelled, thereby preventing water from migrating through the mixture to freeze onto existing ice crystals. Different stabilizers absorb more or less water, but almost all are effective in very small amounts.

The last ingredient that affects ice crystal formation is fat. Fat in ice cream comes from dairy and eggs. Just like proteins, fats are large molecules that physically block ice crystals from growing in size. In addition, whipped fat is an excellent vehicle for holding air pockets, and air lightens texture by increasing volume. Too much cream, however, can produce a grainy ice cream—the dasher (whipping blade) causes the high concentration of fat molecules to coalesce (as tiny flecks of hard butterfat), abandoning the air pockets they surround and breaking the creamy emulsion usually created in ice cream.

Dairy fat also contains natural emulsifiers, which are molecules that bind to both fat and water, improving texture and stability in ice cream base. In the ice cream recipes that follow, the principal emulsifier is lecithin, which is naturally found in egg yolks. In commercial ice creams, artificial emulsifiers such as those mysterious mono- and diglycerides one always sees in ingredient lists are added to increase the number of water molecules that are bound to fat rather than remaining on their own.

The Ins and Outs of Ice Cream Machines

I've had less than wonderful experiences with expensive "gourmet" home ice cream machines that have their own cooling mechanisms. They're heavy, they take up an enormous amount of cabinet and counter space, and, frankly, they're just not powerful enough to freeze ice cream. Some of these machines take 30 minutes to churn the ice cream, and that's just too long; ideally, your ice cream should churn and set, at home, in 10 to 15 minutes at most.

I used one of these fancy machines at my first job as a pastry chef at the much-beloved Firefly in San Francisco, a small restaurant with a tiny, hot kitchen. For months, my ice cream was grainy, and I was convinced that I did not know how to make crème anglaise properly. I read every book available, trying to perfect my ice cream base. But no matter what I tried, the ice cream never came out smooth and creamy. Looking back, I realize that the problem wasn't my crème anglaise, it was the ice cream maker, which, in the hot environment of Firefly's kitchen, took about 40 minutes to churn each batch of ice cream. There's just no hope that ice cream will come out well under such circumstances. But at the time, it drove me nuts.

There is a machine that I think works remarkably well, and, ironically enough, it's one of the cheapest machines on the market, and it also takes the least amount of space in your kitchen. A number of manufacturers, including Cuisinart and Krups, make this unit, which consists of a canister, which is filled with a refrigerant (like Freon) that is prechilled for 24 hours in your freezer, and a small motor and blade upon which the canister sits. The blade is nothing special, and the speed of the motor is not terrific either (though that's not surprising given the cost of the machine), but the canister, if chilled for a full day before use, is far more powerful than any self-contained chilling mechanism and will churn ice cream in no more than 15 minutes. It's one of my favorite home tools, and I highly recommend that if you're going to make ice cream, you acquire one. It will set you back less than eighty dollars, and it's worth every penny.

Always remember that the time a machine takes to churn ice cream is a critical factor in the final consistency and texture of the ice cream. Make sure the ice cream base is first chilled on ice and then refrigerated for at least 2 hours and ideally 12 hours or overnight. Room-temperature or warm ice cream base increases freezing time. Also, ice cream base, as it sits in the refrigerator, increases in viscosity and this slightly thickened base has more body, yielding a creamier ice cream. A second recommendation for adhering to shorter freezing times is to make sure you are using the correct amount of base called for in your particular machine's instructions. If you can, churn a little less ice cream base than the machine recommends and the ice cream will freeze faster, resulting in creamier ice cream.

All of the ice cream recipes in this book can be prepared ahead of time and chilled for a maximum of 2 days before churning. Churn the ice cream the day you plan to serve it. The natural emulsifiers present in these ice cream recipes are most effective in the first 24 hours after the ice cream is churned, lending the ice cream a luscious creamy texture. As churned ice cream sits in the freezer, ice crystals begin to grow and increase in size, attracting water molecules and pulling the ice cream out of emulsion. Unlike commercial ice creams, those made at home are not meant to sit in the freezer for long periods of time. At Chanterelle, even with my industrial-strength machine, I churn my ice cream every day. While the ice creams you make following my recipes can be stored for several days, they are best eaten within the first 24 hours.

Coconut Cream Cheese Ice Cream

Coconut, with its round, mellow flavor and low acidity, blends beautifully with cultured dairy products such as sour cream, cream cheese, and buttermilk, all of which have a wonderful sour/acidic note.

This ice cream has a creamy, full-bodied consistency. Cultured dairy products add viscosity to ice cream base, not only because of their natural thickness and innate characteristics, but also because commercially available cultured dairy products almost invariably are stabilized with emulsifiers and gums which make for a creamier ice cream.

Make the crème anglaise.

Follow the TECHNIQUE TIP: *Cooking a stirred custard and testing for doneness, page 96.*

In a heavy-bottomed medium saucepan, heat the milk, coconut milk, shredded coconut, and ½ cup of the sugar. Once the coconut cream begins to steam, take the pan off the heat. In a mixing bowl, combine the egg yolks and remaining sugar and briskly whisk for 1 minute. Using a ladle, slowly whisk some of the hot coconut cream into the egg yolk mixture to warm it. Gradually pour the warmed egg mixture into the hot coconut cream mixture, whisking constantly as you pour. Cook the custard over medium heat, stirring continuously and scraping the bottom with a rubber spatula or wooden spoon until the custard thickens enough to coat the back of the spoon. Remove from the heat and place in the ice bath to cool until it is warm to the touch. Whisk in the sour cream and the cream cheese.

Chill the crème anglaise and churn it.

Return the crème anglaise (ice cream base) to the ice bath to cool completely. Transfer to the refrigerator and chill a minimum of 2 hours and up to 2 days before churning it in an ice cream machine. Churn the crème anglaise in an ice cream maker according to the machine manufacturer's instructions. The ice cream is finished once it has increased in volume and it holds the lines from the stirring mechanism and mounds like softly whipped cream. Transfer to the freezer for 4 hours to attain a scoopable consistency.

Serving Suggestions

Coconut Cream Cheese Ice Cream is a great accompaniment to carrot cake. I also love to serve it with the Date Cake (page 45) or the Chocolate Layer Cake (page 52).

Storage

This ice cream is best if you serve it 4 to 6 hours after churning, but will keep in the freezer for up to 1 week.

½ cup whole milk

1 (13.5-ounce) can coconut milk

1 cup shredded unsweetened coconut

1 cup plus 1 tablespoon sugar

8 egg yolks

10 ounces (1 ¼ cups) cream cheese, at room temperature

10 ounces (1 ¼ cups) sour cream, at room temperature

SPECIAL TOOLS AND PANS

Ice bath

Ice cream machine

See Ice Cream and Sorbet Guidelines (page 130).

YIELD

1½ quarts churned ice cream

Mandarin Ice Cream

2 cups heavy cream

1 cup half-and-half

¾ cup sugar

Zest of 1 mandarin

7 egg yolks

2 eggs

¼ teaspoon salt

¼ cup skim milk powder

1 cup strained mandarin
juice (from approximately
3 mandarins)

SPECIAL TOOLS AND PANS

Ice bath

Fine-mesh strainer

Ice cream maker

See Ice Cream and Sorbet
Guidelines (page 130).

YIELD

1 ½ quarts churned ice cream

VARIATION

Spiced Mandarin Ice Cream:
Add 1 cinnamon stick and
3 star anise to infuse the
cream. Allow the cream to
steep for 15 minutes with the
spices and the zest.

Satsuma and honey mandarins are my favorite types of citrus for this recipe. You can, however, use any type of tangerine. The zest is used to infuse the cream, producing a mellow, round mandarin flavor. If you like Creamsicles, you will love this ice cream. It goes wonderfully with any citrus or chocolate dessert or stands alone on a hot summer day.

I have added some dry skim milk powder to this recipe. It helps to absorb some of the extra water from the fresh tangerine juice, lending the ice cream a creamier texture.

Infuse the cream and make a créme anglaise.
Follow the TECHNIQUE TIP: *Cooking a stirred custard and testing for doneness, page 96.*

In a heavy-bottomed saucepan, heat the cream, half-and-half, ¼ cup of the sugar, and the mandarin zest. Once the cream begins to steam, remove the pot from the heat and set it aside for 5 minutes. In a mixing bowl, combine the egg yolks, eggs, salt, skim milk powder, and the remaining sugar and briskly whisk for 1 minute. Using a ladle, slowly whisk some of the hot cream mixture into the egg yolk mixture to warm it. Gradually pour the warmed egg mixture into the hot cream mixture, whisking constantly as you pour. Whisk in the mandarin juice. Cook the custard over medium heat, stirring continuously and scraping the bottom with a rubber spatula or wooden spoon until the custard thickens enough to coat the back of the spoon. Remove from the heat and strain the custard through a mesh strainer to remove the tangerine zest.

Chill the créme anglaise and churn it.
Place the créme anglaise (ice cream base) in an ice bath to cool. Transfer to the refrigerator and chill a minimum of 2 hours and up to 2 days before churning it in an ice cream machine. Churn the crème anglaise in an ice cream maker

according to the machine manufacturer's instructions. The ice cream is finished once it has increased in volume and it holds the lines from the stirring mechanism and mounds like softly whipped cream. Transfer to the freezer for 4 hours to attain a scoopable consistency.

Serving Suggestions
Serve this ice cream by itself or with a crisp cookie; the Crispy Bittersweet Chocolate Wafer (page 65) and the Hazelnut Shortbread (page 66) are both great accompaniments. The Meyer Lemon Curd Tart (page 18) and the Roasted Medjool Dates Stuffed with Cashews, Currants, and Candied Citrus (page 165) go well with this ice cream too.

Storage
This ice cream is best if you serve it 4 to 6 hours after churning, but will keep in the freezer for up to 1 week.

Banana Malt Ice Cream

I discovered Fox Brand malt syrup (half malt syrup and half corn syrup) at one of my first restaurant jobs where we made malted meringues. Later, at another job, I began to make a walnut-rye levain bread that called for organic barley malt syrup. After tasting this syrup, I never looked back, and I now use pure malt syrup in numerous desserts.

In a sense, my discovery of malt was really a rediscovery. Many of the treasured flavors of my childhood featured malt, either as a main flavor or as the foundation for another, like chocolate malted milk balls, Ovaltine, ice cream parlor milk shakes, and Grapenuts. I had just forgotten, during my early adulthood, how much I loved the flavor.

Malt is the perfect sweetener for banana. It adds a slight note of acidity with a warm, round flavor that makes the banana shine. Aside from flavor, the malt syrup adds a creamy dimension to this ice cream.

5 small ripe bananas or 2 to 3 large bananas (10 to 12 ounces)

2 cups heavy cream

1 cup whole milk

¾ cup sugar

8 egg yolks

2 eggs

¼ teaspoon salt

2 tablespoons malt syrup (barley malt)

SPECIAL TOOLS AND PANS

Fine-mesh strainer

Ice bath

Ice cream machine

See Ice Cream and Sorbet Guidelines (page 130).

YIELD

1½ quarts churned ice cream

Infuse the cream and make a crème anglaise.

Follow the TECHNIQUE TIP: *Cooking a stirred custard and testing for doneness, page 96.*

Chop the bananas into ½-inch pieces. In a heavy-bottomed saucepan, heat the cream, milk, ½ cup of the sugar, and the bananas. Once the cream begins to boil remove the pot from the heat and set it aside for 10 minutes. In a mixing bowl, combine the egg yolks, eggs, salt, and remaining sugar and briskly whisk for 1 minute. Whisk in the malt syrup. Using a ladle, slowly whisk some of the hot cream mixture into the egg mixture to warm it. Gradually pour the warmed egg mixture into the hot cream mixture, whisking constantly as you pour.

Cook the custard over medium heat, stirring continuously and scraping the bottom with a rubber spatula or wooden spoon until the custard thickens enough to coat the back of the spoon. Remove from the heat and strain the custard through a fine-mesh strainer to remove the banana pieces. Using the back of a ladle, squeeze through as much of the cooked banana as possible. Discard any pieces of banana left in the strainer.

Chill the crème anglaise and churn it.

Place the crème anglaise (ice cream base) in an ice bath to cool completely. Transfer to the refrigerator and chill a minimum of 2 hours and up to 2 days before churning it in an ice cream machine. Churn the crème anglaise in an ice cream maker according to the machine manufacturer's instructions. The ice cream is finished once it has increased in volume and it holds the lines from the stirring mechanism and mounds like softly whipped cream. Transfer to the freezer for 4 hours to attain a scoopable consistency.

Serving Suggestions

Serve this ice cream by itself with a crispy cookie; the Crispy Bittersweet Chocolate Wafer (page 65) and the Hazelnut Shortbread (page 66) are both great accompaniments. Or sprinkle some crushed toffee over each serving. The Chocolate Caramel Tart (page 29), the Passion-Fruit Curd Tart (page 21), and the Chocolate Bête Noire (page 47) are also all delicious with this ice cream.

Storage

This ice cream is best if you serve it 4 to 6 hours after churning, but will keep in the freezer for up to 1 week.

Espresso Ice Cream

1 cup minus 1 tablespoon sugar

Pinch of cream of tartar

2 cups heavy cream

½ cup whole milk

½ cup freshly brewed, strong espresso

1 egg

6 egg yolks

Pinch of salt

1 tablespoon instant espresso powder (I use Medaglia D'Oro)

SPECIAL TOOLS AND PANS

Fine-mesh strainer

Ice bath

Ice cream machine

See Ice Cream and Sorbet Guidelines (page 130).

YIELD

1 quart churned ice cream

During my travels in Italy I tasted the most wonderful espresso gelato. Ever since that day I have strived to make an espresso ice cream with the robustness of flavor that I associated with that gelato. One day I was reading one of Lidia Bastianich's cookbooks and I found a recipe for espresso mousse that involved first making a dark caramel to be incorporated into an espresso anglaise, the flavor base for this mousse. After reading this recipe I realized what flavor was missing from my espresso ice cream—dark caramel. This deep, dark, rich, round, creamy espresso ice cream depends on dark caramel not only as an underlying flavor but also as a high concentration of an inverted sugar, significantly lowering the freezing temperature and improving texture dramatically.

Make the caramel.
See BEYOND THE BASICS: *Cooking caramel successfully, page 107.*

Combine the sugar, cream of tartar, and ⅓ cup water in a heavy-bottomed saucepan. Cover and bring to a rapid boil over medium-high heat. Once boiling, uncover the pan and cook the sugar until light golden brown, about 5 minutes. Remove from the heat; the sugar will continue to cook. When the caramel is a deep amber brown, stand back and carefully add the cream. The caramel will erupt with bubbles and steam. Return the pan to medium-high heat and whisk the cream until dissolved and the caramel is completely smooth. Whisk in the milk and espresso, remove from the heat, and set aside.

Make the crème anglaise.
In a bowl, combine the egg, egg yolks, and salt and whisk for 1 minute. Using a ladle, slowly whisk ⅓ of the hot espresso cream into the egg mixture to warm it. Gradually, pour the warmed egg mixture into hot espresso cream, whisking constantly as you pour. Cook the custard over medium heat, stirring continuously and scraping the bottom with a rubber spatula or wooden spoon until the custard thickens enough to coat the back of a spoon. (This ice cream base has a high concentration of sugar, which raises the temperature at which the eggs coagulate, increasing the time it takes to cook and thicken the custard.) Remove from the heat and stir in the instant espresso powder. Strain the crème anglaise through a fine-mesh strainer into a bowl.

Chill the crème anglaise and churn it.
Place the crème anglaise (ice cream base) in an ice bath to cool completely. Transfer to the refrigerator and chill a minimum of 2 hours and up to 2 days before churning it in an ice cream machine. Churn the crème anglaise in an ice cream maker according to the machine manufacturer's instructions. The ice cream is finished once it has increased in volume and it holds the lines from the stirring mechanism and mounds like softly whipped cream. Transfer to the freezer for 4 hours to attain a scoopable consistency.

Serving Suggestions
Serve this ice cream with a crunchy light cookie such as the Crispy Bittersweet Chocolate Wafer (page 65). The Chocolate Caramel Tart (page 29) and the Hazelnut Cake (page 39) are also delicious with this ice cream.

Storage
This ice cream will keep in the freezer for 1 week.

Maple-Ginger Ice Cream

To use maple syrup in desserts, it must be boiled down in order to intensify the maple flavor but not increase the liquid content in whatever you are making. The reducing process is a great opportunity to infuse another flavor into the syrup, as in the Maple–Star Anise Mousse on page 104. There is really no limitation on the spices or flavor you can infuse into the maple syrup.

  This ice cream is only slightly gingery, with the hint of flavor somehow heightening the exoticism of the maple flavor and giving it crispness, clarity, and depth. The reduced maple syrup not only delivers an intense, concentrated maple flavor, but also, since it is an inverted sugar, helps to produce a singularly smooth texture in the finished ice cream.

Infuse and reduce the maple syrup.
If you are using regular ginger with a thin woody brown skin, peel it. Slice the ginger into nickel-size coins. In a heavy-bottomed saucepan over medium-high heat, combine the maple syrup and ginger and attach a candy thermometer to the side of the pan. Cook until the syrup reduces by half and registers 240°F on a candy thermometer. Gradually whisk in the cream until completely incorporated. Add the milk and bring the mixture to a simmer.

Make the maple-ginger crème anglaise.
Follow the TECHNIQUE TIP: *Cooking a stirred custard and testing for doneness, page 96.*

In a mixing bowl, combine the egg yolks, eggs, and salt and briskly whisk for 1 minute. Using a ladle, slowly whisk some of the hot maple-ginger cream into the egg yolk mixture to warm it. Gradually pour the warmed egg mixture into the hot maple-ginger cream, whisking constantly as you pour. Cook the custard over medium heat, stirring continuously and scraping the bottom with a rubber spatula or wooden spoon until the custard thickens enough to coat the back of the spoon. Strain the custard through a fine-mesh strainer to remove the ginger.

Chill the crème anglaise and churn it.
Place the maple-ginger crème anglaise (ice cream base) in an ice bath to cool completely. Transfer to the refrigerator and chill a minimum of 2 hours and up to 2 days before churning it in an ice cream machine. Churn the crème anglaise in an ice cream maker according to the machine manufacturer's instructions. The ice cream is finished once it has increased in volume and it holds the lines from the stirring mechanism and mounds like softly whipped cream. Transfer to the freezer for 4 hours to attain a scoopable consistency.

Serving Suggestions
This ice cream flavor speaks for itself. A crunchy cookie is always a nice accompaniment. I recommend the Hazelnut Shortbread (page 66) and the Gingersnaps (page 59).

Storage
This ice cream is best if you serve it 4 to 6 hours after churning, but will keep in the freezer for up to 1 week.

---

4 ounces fresh ginger (preferably young)

2 cups maple syrup

3 cups heavy cream

1½ cups whole milk

8 egg yolks

2 eggs

¼ teaspoon salt

SPECIAL TOOLS AND PANS

Candy thermometer

Fine-mesh strainer

Ice bath

Ice cream maker

See Ice Cream and Sorbet Guidelines (page 130).

YIELD

1½ quarts churned ice cream

VARIATION

Maple–Star Anise, Maple Cinnamon, Maple Vanilla Ice Cream: Substitute 8 star anise, or 5 cinnamon sticks, or 1 good vanilla bean for the ginger.

Port Plum Ice Cream

PLUM PUREE

6 medium (1¼ pounds) red,
purple, or black plums

¾ cup sugar

ICE CREAM

⅓ cup whole milk

2 cups heavy cream

¾ cup sugar

8 egg yolks

1 egg

¼ cup port

SPECIAL TOOLS AND PANS

Fine-mesh strainer

Ice bath

Ice cream machine

See Ice Cream and Sorbet
Guidelines (page 130).

YIELD

1¼ quarts churned ice cream

This is my daughter's favorite dessert, in no small part because of the striking color: she calls it "pink ice cream" and will happily devour it whenever it is sitting in the freezer.

The color derives from the plum skins. As many types of plums ripen, the intense color of the skin leaches into the flesh, which is initially yellow or white but becomes increasingly and beautifully colored by the skin with a lovely range of purple, red, and pink tones. This same process, the color leaching out of the skin, occurs further along during the cooking process, producing a rich and dark purple plum puree.

The port mellows the tart, assertive plum flavor, yielding a unique and complex fruit-flavored ice cream. The added alcohol also lowers the freezing temperature of the ice cream base. The overall effect is a creamier, softer ice cream.

Make the plum puree.
Quarter the plums, discarding the pits. Combine the sugar and plums in a stainless-steel-lined pan over medium heat. Bring the fruit to a boil, turn the heat down to low and simmer for 10 to 15 minutes. Pass the cooked plums and their cooking liquid through a fine-mesh strainer into a bowl and discard the skins. Use the back of a ladle or rubber spatula to push as much of the fruit through as possible. Place the puree in an ice bath to cool.

Make the crème anglaise.
Follow the TECHNIQUE TIP: *Cooking a stirred custard and testing for doneness, page 96.*

In a heavy-bottomed medium saucepan, heat the milk, cream, and ½ cup of the sugar. Once the cream begins to steam, take the pan off the heat. In a mixing bowl, combine the egg yolks, egg, and remaining sugar and briskly whisk for 30 seconds. Using a ladle, slowly whisk some of the hot cream into the egg yolk mixture to warm it. Gradually pour the warmed egg mixture into the hot cream, whisking constantly as you pour. Cook the custard over medium heat, stirring continuously and scraping the bottom with a rubber spatula or wooden spoon until the custard thickens enough to coat the back of the spoon. Remove from the heat and place in the ice bath to cool until it is warm to the touch. Stir in the plum puree and port.

Chill the crème anglaise and churn it.
Transfer the plum-port crème anglaise to the refrigerator and chill a minimum of 2 hours and up to 2 days before churning it in an ice cream machine. Churn the crème anglaise in an ice cream maker according to the machine manufacturer's instructions. The ice cream is finished once it has increased in volume and it holds the lines from the stirring mechanism and mounds like softly whipped cream. Transfer to the freezer for 4 hours to attain a scoopable consistency.

Serving Suggestions
Serve this ice cream by itself as a refreshing treat. It also goes beautifully with the Plum and Almond Tart (page 26) and the Fresh Huckleberry and Fig Tart (page 24).

Storage
This ice cream is best if you serve it 4 to 6 hours after churning, but will keep in the freezer for up to 1 week.

Apple Cider and Caramel Ice Cream

A French friend of mine tasted this ice cream and said, delightedly, "It tastes like Tarte Tatin!" Not a surprising reaction, given that caramel and caramelized apples are the primary flavors of the classic French pastry.

I've long made a cider caramel sauce finished with butter that I serve alongside my apple desserts. These flavors translate into a unique and enticing ice cream, and I've been making this ever since I first tried it.

5 cups fresh apple cider

¾ cup sugar

Pinch of cream of tartar

1½ cups heavy cream

1 cup whole milk

8 egg yolks

1 egg

Pinch of salt

SPECIAL TOOLS AND PANS

Fine-mesh strainer

Ice bath

Ice cream maker

See Ice Cream and Sorbet Guidelines (page 130).

YIELD

1½ quarts churned ice cream

Reduce the apple cider.

Place the apple cider in a saucepan over medium heat. Bring to a boil and cook until it reduces to 1½ cups. Remove from the heat and set aside.

Make the caramel.

See BEYOND THE BASICS: *Cooking caramel successfully, page 107.*

Combine the sugar, cream of tartar, and ⅓ cup water in a heavy-bottomed saucepan. Cover and bring to a rapid boil over medium-high heat. Once boiling, uncover the pan and cook the sugar until light golden brown, about 5 minutes. Remove from the heat; the sugar will continue to cook. When the caramel is a deep amber brown, stand back and carefully add the reduced cider. The caramel will erupt with bubbles and steam. Return the pan to medium-high heat and whisk the cider until dissolved and the caramel is completely smooth. Whisk in the cream and milk, and continue cooking until the mixture comes to just under a boil.

Make the crème anglaise.

Follow the TECHNIQUE TIP: *Cooking a stirred custard and testing for doneness, page 96.*

In a mixing bowl, combine the egg yolks, egg, and salt and briskly whisk for 1 minute. Using a ladle, slowly whisk some of the hot cider cream into the egg yolk mixture to warm it. Gradually pour the warmed egg mixture into the hot cider cream, whisking constantly as you pour. Cook the custard over medium heat, stirring continuously and scraping the bottom with a rubber spatula or wooden spoon until the custard thickens enough to coat the back of the spoon. Strain the crème anglaise through a fine-mesh strainer.

Chill the crème anglaise and churn it.

Place the créme anglaise (ice cream base) in an ice bath to cool completely. Transfer to the refrigerator and chill a minimum of 2 hours and up to 2 days before churning it in an ice cream machine. Churn the crème anglaise in an ice cream maker according to the machine manufacturer's instructions. The ice cream is finished once it has increased in volume and it holds the lines from the stirring mechanism and mounds like softly whipped cream. Transfer to the freezer for 4 hours to attain a scoopable consistency.

Serving Suggestions

This ice cream is delicious on its own or serve it with the Walnut, Currant, and Cinnamon Rugelach (page 73).

Storage

Because of the caramel, this ice cream keeps better than others. It will keep in the freezer for 1 week.

Basil Ice Cream

1 ½ ounces basil leaves
or 30 leaves

2 cups heavy cream

2 cups whole milk

1 cup sugar

8 egg yolks

1 whole egg

Pinch of salt

¼ cup skim milk powder

SPECIAL TOOLS AND PANS

Fine-mesh strainer

Ice bath

Ice cream machine

See Ice Cream and Sorbet
Guidelines (page 130).

YIELD

1 ½ quarts churned ice cream

VARIATIONS

Fig Leaf Ice Cream: Use 3 fig tree leaves, cut into small pieces, instead of the basil.

Black Mint Ice Cream: Use 1 ounce of black mint leaves instead of the basil.

Lemon Verbena Ice Cream: Use 1 ounce of fresh lemon verbena leaves or 3 lemon verbena tea bags instead of the basil.

(Continued on next page.)

In late summer, when basil is abundant at the market, try making this ice cream. Basil is refreshing and soothing like mint, but it has a sweeter, rounder flavor that mellows in your mouth as you savor it.

For scientific reasons that I mentioned in the ice cream guidelines section, ice cream has the interesting quality of disguising its temperature on the tongue. If we place an ice cube in our mouths, it feels unpalatably cold; ice cream, out of the same freezer, is a pure pleasure for our senses. One of the holy grails of an ice cream flavor, to my mind, is finding those tastes that subtly enhance this characteristic. Basil may be the perfect match, lending its combination of invigorating mint-like qualities and full-bodied warmth of flavor.

Infuse the cream.
Wash and dry the basil leaves. In a heavy-bottomed saucepan, heat the cream, milk, and ½ cup of the sugar. Once the cream begins to boil, add the basil leaves, remove the pot from the heat, and set it aside for 10 minutes.

Make the crème anglaise.
Follow the TECHNIQUE TIP: *Cooking a stirred custard and testing for doneness, page 96.*

In a mixing bowl, combine the egg yolks, egg, salt, skim milk powder, and remaining sugar and briskly whisk for 1 minute. Using a ladle, slowly whisk some of the hot cream into the egg yolk mixture to warm it. Gradually pour the warmed egg mixture into the hot cream, whisking constantly as you pour. Cook the custard over medium heat, stirring continuously and scraping the bottom with a rubber spatula or wooden spoon until the custard thickens enough to coat the back of the spoon. Strain the custard through a fine-mesh strainer and remove the basil leaves.

Chill the crème anglaise and churn it.
Place the basil crème anglaise (ice cream base) in the ice bath to cool completely. Transfer to the refrigerator and chill a minimum of 2 hours and up to 2 days before churning it in an ice cream machine. Churn the crème anglaise in an ice cream maker according to the machine manufacturer's instructions. The ice cream is finished once it has increased in volume and it holds the lines from the stirring mechanism and mounds like softly whipped cream. Transfer to the freezer for 4 hours to attain a scoopable consistency.

Serving Suggestions
This ice cream is delicious all by itself. It also goes beautifully with the Meyer Lemon Curd Tart (page 18) or the Fresh Apricot and Almond Tart (page 26).

Storage
This ice cream is best if you serve it 4 to 6 hours after churning, but will keep in the freezer for up to 1 week.

THE SWEET LIFE

VARIATIONS (CONT.)

Cardamom, Cinnamon, Star Anise, Black Pepper Ice Creams: Infuse the cream with any of these spices instead of the basil: 15 crushed cardamom pods; 2 cinnamon sticks and 1 teaspoon ground cinnamon; 8 large star anise; 2 tablespoons crushed peppercorns and 1 teaspoon finely ground black pepper.

Plum or Apricot Pit (Bitter Almond) Ice Cream: Smash 15 apricot or plum pits with a mallet and remove the almond-like nut from inside. Chop up the almond-like nuts and steep them in the hot milk as you would the basil. (*See* INGREDIENT: *Plum pits and other stone fruit pits, page 175.*)

BEYOND THE BASICS
Enzymatic browning in fruit

An important enzyme in fruits such as bananas, apples, pears, and white grapes is polyphenol oxidase (PPO). When this enzyme is exposed to air it causes an unappealing browning through the production of melanins, which are dark pigments. Melanins are responsible for the deep colors of cocoa, tea, coffee, prunes, and raisins, to name a few.

To prevent enzymatic browning in pear, apple, and grape sorbet or in apple or pear chips, you must deactivate polyphenol oxidase. Enzymes are proteins and anything that denatures proteins will also inactivate enzymes. Acid, salt, extreme cold, and heat are all agents in the denaturing process. Whenever you are slicing apples for a pie, you are invariably encouraged to squeeze lemon juice over the apples, but I prefer not to do so as this changes the flavor of the fruit and ultimately, fruit tossed with lemon juice, especially in sorbet, will still turn brown. The best way to denature the PPO enzymes without significantly altering a fruit's flavor, is a combination of fast heating and rapid chilling. I use this technique in the apple, pear, and grape sorbets and in the apple and pear chips.

Mandarin Orange Sorbet

Zest of 3 tangerines

½ cup sugar

½ cup light corn syrup

1 cinnamon stick (optional)

2 star anise (optional)

10 tennis-ball-sized tangerines (3½ pounds)

1 lime

Pinch of salt

SPECIAL TOOLS AND PANS

Fine-mesh strainer

Citrus reamer or electric juicer

Ice cream machine

See Ice Cream and Sorbet Guidelines (page 130).

YIELD

1 quart churned sorbet

This recipe takes advantage of the bounty of mandarin orange and winter tangerine varieties. Most people find this fruit hard to eat, with its thin skin and endless pits, but the juice and the zest are powerfully flavorful and not difficult to harvest from the fruit.

Make the simple syrup.

In a saucepan, combine the tangerine zest, ½ cup water, sugar, and corn syrup. Bring the mixture to a boil and immediately remove it from the heat. (If you allow the zest to boil, the simple syrup will have a bitter orange flavor.) Pass the syrup through a fine-mesh strainer into a bowl and discard the zest. Add the star anise and cinnamon stick, if you are using them. Set aside to infuse and cool.

Juice the tangerines.

Juice the 10 tangerines and the lime with a hand-held citrus reamer or an electric juicer. Pass the juice through a strainer to remove the seeds and extra pulp. You should have approximately 3 cups of strained juice.

Finish the sorbet.

Whisk the juice into the cooled simple syrup and transfer to the refrigerator to chill for a minimum of 1 hour. Once the mixture is cold, churn it in an ice cream machine according to the machine manufacturer's directions. The sorbet is finished once it has increased in volume and it holds whisk lines from the stirring mechanism and mounds like softly whipped cream. Transfer to the freezer for 4 hours to attain a scoopable consistency.

Serving Suggestions

Serve this sorbet with a crunchy cookie or wafer or some fresh fruit. I recommend the Hazelnut Shortbread (page 66) or the Walnut Cream Cheese Sandwich Cookies (page 61).

Storage

Sorbet does not maintain its texture if stored for too long in the freezer. As sorbet sits in the freezer, ice crystals begin to grow and increase in number and size. The sorbet is best if it is churned 4 hours before serving.

Muscat Grape Sorbet

Muscat grapes are available in the fall, but are also brought up from Chile during the spring (their autumn). They have a striking flavor: herbaceous, flowery, with an intense honey-like sweetness. You can find them with pits and without; either works for this sorbet, since you can strain the pits out.

If you have access to the white wine grapes that are sold in the fall, you can replace the Muscat grapes with Chardonnay, Sauvignon Blanc, or any other white wine grape. If you do this, make sure to match the wine you use in this recipe to the grapes; you may need to add 2 tablespoons of sugar if you use a dry wine, which does not have the native sweetness of Muscato.

Cook the grapes.
See BEYOND THE BASICS: *Enzymatic browning in fruit, page 143.*

Wash the grapes and remove them from their vines. In a stainless-steel saucepan, combine the grapes, 2 cups water, and sugar. Bring the mixture to a simmer over medium heat. Boil until the grapes turn an opaque yellow-green, 4 minutes, stirring frequently. Remove from the heat and let cool for 10 minutes.

Puree and strain the fruit.
Place the grapes and their cooking liquid in a food processor or blender and puree until smooth. Pass the puree through a fine-mesh strainer and into a stainless-steel bowl, pushing the fruit through the strainer with the back of a ladle or rubber spatula. Discard the pulp. Place the bowl in an ice bath to chill. Once the mixture is chilled, add the Muscat wine. Taste the sorbet base. If it seems too sweet, add a squirt of lime juice; if it needs more flavor, add a few teaspoons of superfine sugar. Transfer to the refrigerator to chill for a minimum of 1 hour or up to 2 days.

Churn the sorbet.
Churn the sorbet in an ice cream machine according to the machine manufacturer's directions. The sorbet is finished once it has increased in volume and it holds whisk lines from the stirring mechanism and mounds like softly whipped cream. Transfer to the freezer for 4 hours to attain a scoopable consistency.

Serving Suggestions
Serve this sorbet with a light, crisp cookie.

Storage
This sorbet is best if you serve it 4 to 6 hours after churning, but will keep in the freezer for up to 1 week.

---

2 pounds Muscat grapes

1¼ cups sugar

¼ cup Muscato (dessert wine)

Lime juice (optional)

Superfine sugar (optional)

SPECIAL TOOLS AND PANS

Food processor or blender

Fine-mesh strainer

Ice bath

Ice cream machine

See Ice Cream and Sorbet Guidelines (page 130).

YIELD

1½ quarts churned sorbet

Pineapple-Rosemary Sorbet

1 medium to large ripe pineapple (approximately 3 pounds plus 8 to 12 ounces)

1½ cups sugar

2 stalks fresh rosemary

Juice of 1 lime

Superfine sugar (optional)

SPECIAL TOOLS AND PANS

Food processor or blender

Fine-mesh strainer

Ice bath

Ice cream machine

See Ice Cream and Sorbet Guidelines (page 130).

YIELD

2 quarts churned sorbet

Rosemary is an excellent and versatile background flavor for any acidic or citrus fruit. For instance, you can use rosemary-infused simple syrup to spice up a summer lemonade or limeade, making the drink more refreshing, more hedonistic, and also somewhat mysterious. The rosemary in this sorbet lends a subtle undertone, transforming the pineapple flavor into something more complex and compelling.

Cook the pineapple.
With a sharp knife, remove the top and bottom of the pineapple. Stand the fruit up and carve the skin off in long, slow strokes. Slice the carved pineapple down the center and lay each half, flat side down, on a cutting board. Cut the halves into ¼ to ½ inch-thick semicircles. In a stainless-steel-lined saucepan, combine the sliced pineapple, sugar, and 2 cups cold water. Bring to a simmer and cook for 5 minutes. Add the rosemary and remove the pan from the heat. Make sure the rosemary is submerged in the liquid, cover the pan, and set it aside for 10 minutes.

Puree and strain the pineapple.
Remove and discard the rosemary. Scoop half of the pineapple and some of the cooking syrup into a food processor or blender and puree on the highest speed for 2 minutes. Transfer the puree to a bowl and repeat the process with the remaining pineapple. Pass the pureed pineapple through a fine-mesh strainer and into a stainless-steel bowl, pushing the fruit through the strainer with the back of a ladle or a rubber spatula. Discard the pulp. Place the bowl in an ice bath to chill. Once the mixture is chilled, add the lime juice. The sorbet base will be sweet. Some of the sweetness will be tamed by the freezing process, but if you find the sorbet base cloyingly sweet, add more lime juice. If the sorbet base does not

seem that sweet, try adding a few teaspoons of superfine sugar. Transfer to the refrigerator to chill for a minimum of 1 hour or up to 2 days.

Churn the sorbet.
Churn the sorbet in an ice cream machine according to the machine manufacturer's directions. The sorbet is finished once it has increased in volume and it holds whisk lines from the stirring mechanism and mounds like softly whipped cream. Transfer to the freezer for 4 hours to attain a scoopable consistency.

Serving Suggestions
Serve this sorbet with a crunchy cookie or wafer or some fresh fruit. It is delicious with the Meyer Lemon Curd Tart (page 18) or the Meyer Lemon Soufflé (page 114).

Storage
This sorbet is best if you serve it 4 to 6 hours after churning, but will keep in the freezer for up to 1 week.

Dark Chocolate Sorbet

This chocolate sorbet has been a staple on all my dessert menus, traveling with me through four different jobs over the last ten years. At Chanterelle we change the menu every four weeks, and this sorbet finds its way into a chocolate or fruit dessert on about half of our menus each year. When we are unveiling a new menu, our waiters meet and taste all the desserts for that particular menu and inevitably someone says to me, "This is chocolate sorbet? It's so creamy! Are you sure there's no dairy in this sorbet?" This frozen confection is a guaranteed showstopper. It is intensely chocolatey, with a velvety soft texture.

Make the sugar syrup.
Run a paring knife down the center of the vanilla bean. Split it open with your fingers and use the knife to scrape out the tiny black seeds into a heavy-bottomed saucepan. Add 2¼ cups water, the sugar, the corn syrup, and the vanilla pod and bring to a rolling boil over medium-high heat. Remove from the heat and allow the bean to steep for 15 minutes. Remove the pod, dry it, and save for another use. If you are using vanilla extract, add it after the syrup has been removed from the heat.

Prepare the chocolate.
See BEYOND THE BASICS: *Chocolate and water, page 47.*

Combine the chopped chocolate and cocoa powder in a medium-sized bowl. Gently whisk in ⅓ of the hot vanilla syrup. (The chocolate will begin to seize a bit.) Whisk in the remaining syrup, in two more parts, and continue to whisk until the sauce is shiny, thick, and smooth, about 4 minutes. Pass the chocolate sorbet base through a fine-mesh strainer to remove any lumps of cocoa powder. Place the sorbet base in an ice bath to cool completely. Transfer to the refrigerator for a minimum of 4 hours or up to 1 week.

Churn the sorbet.
Churn the sorbet in an ice cream machine according to the machine manufacturer's directions. The sorbet is finished once it has increased in volume and it holds whisk lines from the stirring mechanism and mounds like softly whipped cream. Transfer to the freezer for 4 hours to attain a scoopable consistency.

Serving Suggestions
Serve this sorbet with a crunchy wafer or a sprinkle of nuts.

Storage
This sorbet is best served the day it is churned.

1 vanilla bean or 1 teaspoon vanilla extract

¾ cup plus 1 tablespoon sugar

3 tablespoons corn syrup

6 ounces dark chocolate (61 to 65 percent cocoa solids), chopped into ½-inch pieces

4 ounces Dutch processed cocoa powder (approximately 1 cup)

SPECIAL TOOLS AND PANS

Fine-mesh strainer

Ice bath

Ice cream machine

See Ice Cream and Sorbet Guidelines (page 130).

YIELD

1 quart churned sorbet

BEYOND THE BASICS
Chocolate and cocoa as a starch-forming gel in sorbet

Chocolate and cocoa contain starch which, when mixed with water in the presence of certain amounts of heat, absorbs water and thickens, forming gels. As I discussed in the introduction to this chapter, water held in a gel does not form ice crystals or migrate out of the gel toward existing ice crystals at normal freezing temperatures. This gives ice creams and sorbets containing ingredients with starch, such as chocolate, a creamier, softer texture.

Strawberry and Tarragon Sorbet

3 pints (2 ½ pounds) strawberries

⅔ cup sugar

2 tablespoons corn syrup

1 ounce fresh tarragon

Superfine sugar (optional)

SPECIAL TOOLS AND PANS

Food processor or blender

Fine-mesh strainer

Ice bath

Ice cream machine

See Ice Cream and Sorbet Guidelines (page 130).

YIELD

1½ quarts churned sorbet

INGREDIENT
Superfine sugar

Superfine sugar, sometimes referred to as castor sugar in British or translated French cookbooks, is finely ground granulated sugar (sucrose derived from sugar cane and sugar beets). I recommend superfine sugar when you need to dissolve sugar in a liquid without heating or long periods of agitation.

This sorbet is a refreshing delight in spring or early summer. Use ripe strawberries at the peak of the season. I recommend just barely cooking the strawberries with the sugar and then icing the puree. I tend to bring most of my sorbets to a quick boil for two reasons: quick pasteurization preserves the flavor of the sorbet base for up to 2 days, and heating provides the opportunity to infuse the sorbet with other herbs, zests, and teas that serve as background flavors in the sorbet.

If you plan to make and serve this sorbet on the same day, you can achieve a wonderful, crisp, fresh strawberry flavor by just pureeing fresh, uncooked strawberries with 1 cup of superfine sugar and a squirt of lime juice, leaving out the corn syrup and the tarragon.

Prepare the strawberries.
Wash and dry the strawberries. Remove the stem and cut each strawberry in half. In a bowl, toss together the berries and the sugar. Combine the berries, corn syrup, and ½ cup water in a saucepan and bring to a boil. As soon as the fruit comes to a boil, add the tarragon and cook for 1 minute. Immediately remove from the heat and let the tarragon steep in the fruit for 5 minutes and then remove it with a fork.

Blend and strain the fruit.
Place the strawberries and their cooking liquid in a food processor or blender and puree until smooth. Pass the puree through a fine-mesh strainer and into a stainless-steel bowl, pushing the fruit through the strainer with the back of a ladle or rubber spatula. Discard the seeds and pulp. Place the bowl in an ice bath to chill. Once the mixture is chilled, taste it. If it seems overly tart, add a few teaspoons of superfine sugar. Transfer to the refrigerator and chill for a minimum of 1 hour or up to 2 days.

Churn the sorbet.
Churn the sorbet in an ice cream machine according to the machine manufacturer's directions. The sorbet is finished once it has increased in volume and it holds whisk lines from the stirring mechanism and mounds like softly whipped cream. Transfer to the freezer for 4 hours to attain a scoopable consistency.

Serving Suggestions
Serve this sorbet with a crisp cookie.

Storage
This sorbet is best if you serve it 4 to 6 hours after churning, but will keep in the freezer for up to 1 week.

Green Apple
and Muscato Sorbet

Muscato and green apple has always been one of my favorite flavor combinations. Together these two ingredients form their own sweet, honey-like, crisply refreshing flavor that is entirely unique and seemingly organic.

The skin and the seeds of the apple lend flavor, body, and a certain amount of natural pectin to the sorbet mixture, making an ultra-creamy white sorbet. The alcohol in the wine lowers the freezing point, keeping this sorbet, more than others, in a softer, scoopable state in the freezer.

Cook the apples.
See BEYOND THE BASICS: *Enzymatic browning in fruit, page 143.*

Wash and dry the apples. Pull off the stems and then quarter the apples, without peeling them or coring them. Combine the sugar, ½ cup of the wine, and 1½ cups water in a heavy-bottomed saucepan and bring to a boil. Add the apples, cover, and simmer for 10 minutes, stirring occasionally to make sure they cook evenly. If, after 10 minutes, pieces of the apple still seem hard and the skin is bright green, continue simmering for another 5 minutes. (Make sure all of the apples are cooked; otherwise the apple puree will turn brown as it cools. At the same time do not overcook the apples or they will lose their bright flavor.) Transfer the pan to an ice bath for 5 minutes to cool.

Puree the fruit.
Place the apples and their cooking liquid in a food processor and puree until the mixture is smooth. Pass the puree through a fine-mesh strainer and into a stainless-steel bowl, pushing the fruit through the strainer with the back of a ladle or rubber spatula. Discard the solids. Place the bowl in an ice bath to chill. Once the puree is chilled, add the remaining Muscat wine and taste. If it seems overly tart, add a few teaspoons of superfine sugar. Transfer to the refrigerator and chill for a minimum of 1 hour or up to 2 days.

Churn the sorbet.
Churn the sorbet in an ice cream machine according to the machine manufacturer's directions. The sorbet is finished once it has increased in volume and it holds whisk lines from the stirring mechanism and mounds like softly whipped cream. Transfer to the freezer for 4 hours to attain a scoopable consistency.

Serving Suggestions
Serve this sorbet with a crisp wafer.

Storage
This sorbet is best served the day it is churned, but will keep in the freezer for up to 1 week.

---

5 medium-sized Granny Smith apples (approximately 2½ pounds)

1 cup sugar

¾ cup sweet Muscato wine

Superfine sugar (optional)

SPECIAL TOOLS AND PANS
Ice bath

Food processor or blender

Fine-mesh strainer

Ice cream maker

See Ice Cream and Sorbet Guidelines (page 130).

YIELD
1 quart churned sorbet

Quince Sorbet

1½ cups sugar

2¼ pounds ripe, fragrant, yellow skinned quince (approximately 6 small quinces)

2 slivers (⅓ inch wide by 1 inch long) lemon peel

Superfine sugar (optional)

Lemon juice (optional)

SPECIAL TOOLS AND PANS

Fine-mesh strainer

Ice bath

Ice cream machine

See Ice Cream and Sorbet Guidelines (page 130).

YIELD

1 quart churned sorbet

I've been known to wax a bit too rhapsodic about the pleasures of quinces. As I note in my sidebar on quinces (page 151), this obdurate, difficult fruit releases the most seductive flavor, color, and texture when its hidden qualities are teased out through cooking.

The high pectin content in quince seeds gives the puree in this sorbet a smooth creaminess that is unequaled among fruit sorbets. The beautiful rusty rose color, the intensely earthy flavor, and that peerless creaminess all add up to an unforgettable frozen dessert.

Cook the quince.
In a large saucepan, combine 3 cups of water and the sugar and bring to a boil. Peel the quince and slice ½ inch off the top and bottom to remove the stem and the hairy bottom. Quarter the fruit, leaving the core and seeds attached. Add the quince to the pan and bring to a simmer. Cook the fruit slowly for 1½ hours. Once the quince begins to take on a rose-rust color, add the lemon peel and continue to cook for 20 minutes. Remove from the heat and set aside for 10 minutes. Remove the lemon peel and discard.

Strain the quince.
Place the quinces and their cooking liquid in a food processor or blender and puree until the mixture, aside from the bits of core and seeds, seems smooth.

Pass the puree through a fine-mesh strainer and into a stainless-steel bowl, pushing the fruit through the strainer with the back of a ladle or rubber spatula. Discard the seeds and pulp.

Place the bowl in an ice bath to chill. Taste the sorbet base. If it seems tart add a few teaspoons of superfine sugar. If it seems overly sweet, add lemon juice or a tablespoon or two of water. Transfer to the refrigerator and chill for a minimum of 1 hour or up to 2 days.

Churn the sorbet.
Churn the sorbet in an ice cream machine according to the machine manufacturer's directions. The sorbet is finished once it has increased in volume and it holds whisk lines from the stirring mechanism and mounds like softly whipped cream. Transfer to the freezer for 4 hours to attain a scoopable consistency.

Serving Suggestions
Serve this sorbet with a crisp cookie.

Storage
This sorbet is best served the day it is churned, but will keep in the freezer for up to 1 week.

BEYOND THE BASICS
The magical qualities of quince

Color: From light yellow to rusty red

Quinces contain pigment-precursor chemicals called proanthocyanidins (pro for "precursor to"). Anthocyanins are a class of vibrant pigments that color raw eggplants (purple), red cabbage (red), and blueberries (blue), as well as apple peels (red) and peach skins (orange). Proanthocyanidins, by contrast, are colorless, but when heated with acid in air they form anthocyanins, which lend their ruby color to cooked quince.

Anthocyanin pigments are generally unstable which is why red cabbage sometimes turns blue when cooked—but acidic or very sugary conditions increase the pigment's stability and redness. Cooking quinces in highly sugary syrup will therefore enhance and set the quinces' final ruby hue.

Flavor: From tannic and mouth puckering to round honey, apple, and pineapple

Proanthocyanidins form a subclass of tannins, the molecules responsible for astringency and puckering in the mouth. Raw quinces thus have a tannic, astringent aspect that smothers their flavor. When cooked, however, the proanthocyanidins turn to anthocyanins, which are unrelated to tannins. So cooked quinces have no tannic quality. The delicate, rich, flowery aroma of a raw quince is realized through this cooking process.

Quince Sorbet

Guava Sorbet

1 ½ cups sugar

2 ¼ pounds fresh ripe (soft and fragrant) guavas (approximately 8 fruits)

Juice of 1 lime

SPECIAL TOOLS AND PANS

Fine-mesh strainer

Ice bath

Ice cream maker

See Ice Cream and Sorbet Guidelines (page 130).

YIELD

1 quart churned sorbet

Guavas are one of the natural treasures from tropical climates that often get overlooked by Western palates. Though they have a mealy, slimy texture with numerous hard seeds, the guava's aroma and taste are quite sensuous and seductive. When I cook guavas downstairs in the pastry kitchen at Chanterelle, the sexy smell pervades the entire restaurant. Making sorbet is one way to harness this tantalizing flavor without having to actually eat the fruit.

Cook the guavas.
In a saucepan, combine the sugar and 2 cups of water and bring to a boil. Peel the guavas with a paring knife or a peeler and chop into small ½-inch pieces. Add the guava to the syrup and simmer until the fruit is falling apart and separates from the seeds easily, 30 to 45 minutes, stirring every 5 minutes. Remove from the heat.

Strain the fruit.
Pass the cooked guava and syrup through a fine-mesh strainer and into a stainless-steel bowl, pushing the fruit through the strainer with the back of a ladle or rubber spatula. Discard the seeds and pulp. Place the bowl of guava puree in an ice bath to chill. Add the lime juice and taste. If the puree seems overly sweet, add more lime juice or a tablespoon or two of water. Transfer the sorbet base to the refrigerator and chill for a minimum of 1 hour and up to 2 days.

Churn the sorbet.
Churn the sorbet in an ice cream machine according to the machine manufacturer's directions. The sorbet is finished once it has increased in volume and it holds whisk lines from the stirring mechanism and mounds like softly whipped cream. Transfer to the freezer for 4 hours to attain a scoopable consistency.

Serving Suggestions
Serve this sorbet with a crisp wafer. It is delicious with the Passion-Fruit Curd Tart (page 21) or the Meyer Lemon Curd Tart (page 18).

Storage
This sorbet is best served the day it is churned, but will keep in the freezer for up to 1 week.

Candied Kumquat Mascarpone Parfait

Kumquats are small oval citrus fruits that resemble an orange in color. Their skins are bursting with flavor, and their seeds are loaded with pectin, which is why they are commonly candied and jellied. I have candied kumquats in my refrigerator 365 days a year at Chanterelle. We use the candied fruit as a fruit tart garnish and in Florentine cookies and Christmas stollen; and we use the syrup in numerous sorbets and mousses and to soak cakes and make cheesecake.

My favorite recipe is this parfait, with flavors that bring to mind the Creamsicles of childhood, but with a depth and subtlety of flavor that make this an entirely more pleasurable frozen treat. At Chanterelle, we pour this kumquat-mascarpone mousse into cylindrical molds, freeze them, and serve the parfaits unmolded, enrobed in macadamia nuts, surrounded with seasonal citrus segments and blood orange caramel sauce, and garnished with blood orange chips. Candying a few kumquats will take at most ½ hour, and this recipe is well worth the effort.

Prepare the ingredients.
In a bowl, whip the cream to soft peaks and set it aside in the refrigerator. In a small bowl, dissolve the gelatin in 1 tablespoon of cold water.

Cook the kumquat sabayon.
See BEYOND THE BASICS: *Egg yolk foams and sabayons, page 216.*

In the bowl of a bain-marie, whisk together the egg yolks, kumquat syrup, and salt until well combined. Place the bowl over the simmering water and whisk briskly until the mixture has thickened and tripled in volume and barely holds the lines of the whisk, 5 to 10 minutes. Remove from the heat.

Finish the parfait.
Whisk the dissolved gelatin and chopped candied kumquats into the sabayon until evenly distributed. Set aside to cool to slightly warmer than room temperature. Vigorously whisk in the mascarpone until the mascarpone is evenly distributed and the mixture is smooth. Add the lightly whipped cream. Place the spatula in the center of the bowl, scrape the bottom, and bring the bottom over the top. Rotate the bowl 45 degrees and continue folding the mixture until the cream is just incorporated.

Mold and freeze.
Pour the sabayon into the molds, cups, tall glasses, or decorative bowls and freeze until set. Or pour the parfait into Popsicle molds, insert sticks into the center of each, and freeze.

Serving Suggestions
Unmold the frozen sabayon and enrobe it in ground macadamia nuts—they add a crunch and complement the creamy citrus flavor beautifully. Or serve the parfait frozen in a dish or tall glass and top it off with whipped cream and Blood Orange Caramel Sauce (page 212), or simply freeze the parfait in Popsicle molds and enjoy a truly great Creamsicle.

Storage
This dessert will keep in the freezer for 1 week.

½ cup heavy cream

1 teaspoon powdered gelatin

6 egg yolks

¾ cup Candied Kumquat Syrup (page 198)

Pinch of salt

3 tablespoons chopped Candied Kumquats (page 198)

1 pound mascarpone cheese, at room temperature

SPECIAL TOOLS AND PANS
Bain-marie (see page 10)

Whisk, preferably a balloon whisk (the head of the whisk is more rounded than the long variety)

Unmolded: 6 to 8 disposable aluminum molds or cups or Popsicle molds and sticks

Molded: 6 to 8 tall glasses or decorative bowls

YIELD
4 cups, serves 6 to 8

Cardamom and Honey
Pistachio Nougat Glacé

10 cardamon pods

3 cups heavy cream

1 recipe Almond Toffee, substituting pistachios (page 194), or ¾ cup chopped pistachios

9 egg whites (1⅛ cups), at room temperature

Pinch of cream of tartar

⅔ cup honey

⅓ cup sugar

SPECIAL TOOLS AND PANS

Food processor

Stand mixer

Candy thermometer

8 to 12 (6 to 8 ounces) parfait dishes or freezable molds

YIELD

2 quarts (8 cups), serves 8 to 12

This dessert is a twist on a French classic. But this version surpasses every nougat glacé that I can remember. The cardamom-infused cream adds depth to this frozen honey mousse, while the pistachio praline adds crunch and yet another layer of flavor. It is a very soft, creamy parfait because the addition of a whipped meringue to the frozen dessert adds a significant amount of air. Air prevents ice crystal formation, leaving a very creamy frozen dessert.

1 hour ahead of time: Infuse the cream.
Using the bottom of a small frying pan, crush the cardamom pods so that they split open. In a heavy-bottomed saucepan over medium heat, combine the cardamom pods and seeds and the cream and bring the mixture to a simmer. Remove from the heat and allow the cardamom to steep for 10 minutes. Pass the hot cream through a strainer and into a stainless-steel bowl. Discard the pods. Transfer to the refrigerator and chill for at least 1 hour or for up to 2 days.

Grind the toffee.
Either by hand or in a food processor, chop the hard pistachio toffee into ⅛-inch bits. Set aside.

Whip the cream.
Whip the chilled cardamom-infused cream until it forms soft peaks. Return it to the refrigerator.

Making the honey meringue.
See BEYOND THE BASICS: *Acid in egg white foams, page 123.*

Place the egg whites in the bowl of a stand mixer and whisk on medium-high speed. Once the egg whites begin to foam up, add a pinch of cream of tartar.

When the egg whites foam and hold the lines of a whisk, begin making the syrup. Combine the honey and all but 1 tablespoon of the sugar in a small heavy-bottomed saucepan. Attach a candy thermometer to the side of the pan and bring to a boil over high heat.

While the syrup is coming to a boil, slowly drizzle the remaining 1 tablespoon of sugar into the beating egg whites, 1 teaspoon at a time. As you add the sugar the egg whites will become shiny and gain volume.

Once the syrup reaches 248°F, remove from the heat and, with the mixer running on medium-high, pour it in a steady stream down the side of the bowl into the egg whites. The egg whites will gain more volume and take on a satiny light golden color. Beat the meringue until it is stiff and glossy, and has reached room temperature, 5 to 10 minutes.

Fold the mousse together.
Scrape the meringue over the lightly whipped cardamom-infused cream. Sprinkle the chopped pistachios or pistachio toffee over the meringue. Place a spatula in the center of the mixture, scrape the bottom, and bring the bottom over the top. Rotate the bowl 45 degrees and continue folding until all the egg whites are incorporated. Scoop the glacé into parfait glasses or molds and freeze for at least 4 hours or for up to 2 days.

Serving Suggestions
Serve frozen by itself or with some fresh seasonal fruit.

Storage
This frozen mousse keeps in the freezer for 1 week.

Passion-Fruit Soufflé Glacé

If you like passion fruit, this dessert has the most intense flavor this fruit can offer. I call this a soufflé glacé (frozen soufflé) because the egg yolk base is lightened with whipped egg whites, like a soufflé, rather than with only whipped cream, which is typical of a parfait. Both the whipped egg whites and the underlying custard are made with passion-fruit puree, creating a buttery, tart, creamy, yet light passion fruit–flavored extravaganza.

Make the curd base.
In the bowl of a bain-marie, whisk together the egg yolks and sugar. Add the passion-fruit puree and salt and place the bowl over the simmering water. Whisk briskly until the mixture has thickened, doubled in volume, and holds the lines of a whisk, 5 to 10 minutes. Remove from the heat and place in an ice bath to cool until just warm. Add the butter and whisk until thoroughly combined.

Whip the cream.
In a bowl, whip the cream to soft peaks. Set it aside in the refrigerator.

Make the meringue.
See BEYOND THE BASICS: *Acid in egg white foams, page 123.*

Place the egg whites in the bowl of a stand mixer and whisk on medium-high speed. Once the egg whites begin to foam up, add a pinch of cream of tartar.

When the egg whites foam and hold the lines of a whisk, begin making the passion-fruit syrup. Combine the passion-fruit puree and ½ cup plus 2 tablespoons sugar in a small heavy-bottomed saucepan. Attach a candy thermometer to the side of the pan and bring to a boil over high heat.

While the syrup is coming to a boil, slowly drizzle the remaining 1 tablespoon of sugar into the beating egg whites, 1 teaspoon at a time. As you add the sugar the egg whites will become shiny and gain volume.

Once the syrup reaches 245°F, remove from the heat and, with the mixer running on medium-high, pour it in a steady stream down the side of the bowl into the egg whites. Beat the meringue until it is stiff and glossy, and has reached room temperature, approximately 6 minutes.

Fold the mousse together.
Scrape the chilled whipped cream into the passion-fruit curd base. Place a spatula in the center of the mixture, scrape the bottom, and bring the bottom over the top. Rotate the bowl 45 degrees and continue folding until thoroughly incorporated. Scrape the meringue over the top and repeat the folding process until combined. Pour the mousse into parfait glasses, molds, or decorative dishes and freeze for 4 hours.

Serving Suggestions
At Chanterelle I serve this frozen soufflé unmolded in the Pineapple Fruit Soup with Mango and Passion Fruit (page 173) with chewy Candied Kumquats (page 198) and crunchy fresh passion-fruit pulp. Passion fruit and pineapple are a great combination. If you don't have time to make the fruit soup, serve the soufflé with some fresh sliced pineapple and a squirt of lime juice.

Storage
This frozen mousse will keep in the freezer for 1 week.

CURD BASE

8 egg yolks

⅓ cup sugar

½ cup plus 3 tablespoons passion-fruit puree

Pinch of salt

8 tablespoons (4 ounces) butter, at room temperature

MERINGUE

1 cup heavy cream

4 egg whites

Pinch of cream of tartar

6 tablespoons passion-fruit puree

½ cup plus 3 tablespoons sugar

SPECIAL TOOLS AND PANS

Bain-marie (see page 10)

Whisk, preferably a balloon whisk (the head of the whisk is more rounded than the long variety)

Ice bath

Candy thermometer

8 to 12 (6- to 8-ounce) parfait dishes or freezable molds

YIELD

2 quarts, serves 8 to 12

Lavender and Honey
Crème Fraîche Parfait

8 egg yolks

½ cup plus 2 tablespoons sugar

⅓ cup honey

1½ tablespoons dried lavender
or 4 fresh stalks

Pinch of salt

3 cups crème fraîche

SPECIAL TOOLS AND PANS

Stand mixer

Candy thermometer

Eight 5-ounce decorative dishes
for freezing the parfait or terrine
pan (optional)

YIELD

1¾ quarts, serves 8 to 10

I love desserts that feature lavender as a subtle background flavor, but this strong-flavored herb can be too assertive if used with a heavy hand. Sometimes lavender is at its best when you can't even identify it—you just sense some mysterious and intoxicating flavor.

In this dessert, the tartness of the crème fraîche helps to temper the potency of the lavender, and the combination of honey and lavender, of course, is a classic. If you use lavender honey, don't bother infusing the syrup with fresh or dried lavender.

Whip and cook the yolks.
Place the egg yolks and 2 tablespoons of the sugar in the bowl of a stand mixer and whisk at medium speed. Simultaneously, in a small saucepan, combine the remaining ½ cup sugar, honey, ¼ cup water, and lavender (if you are using fresh lavender, just use the flowers and leaves). Attach a candy thermometer to the side of the pan and cook over medium-high heat until it reaches 248°F. Pass the hot sugar syrup through a fine mesh strainer into a measuring cup. Discard the lavender. With the mixer set on medium-high speed, quickly pour the hot syrup into the egg yolks in a continuous stream. Add the salt. Whisk the yolks until they become pale, have tripled in volume, and are just slightly warm.

Whip the crème fraîche.
Whip the crème fraîche until it holds the lines of a whisk and forms soft peaks.

Finish the parfait.
Scrape the whipped crème fraîche into the whipped yolks. Place a spatula in the center of the bowl, scrape the bottom, and bring the bottom over the top. Rotate the bowl 45 degrees and continue folding until the mixture is well combined. Scoop into the molds or terrine pan and freeze for at least 4 hours.

Serving Suggestions
This parfait can be served with any fruit in season. Gently toss the berries with a bit of sugar and let them macerate 10 minutes before serving. This dessert is especially good complemented by fresh sliced melon or a melon puree.

Storage
This frozen mousse will keep in the freezer for 1 week.

Lavender and Honey Crème Fraîche Parfait

Vanilla Bean and Lemon Verbena Parfait with Summer Raspberries

1 vanilla bean (Tahitian
or Bourbon)

3 cups cream

1 tablespoon lemon verbena tea
or 4 fresh lemon verbena leaves

8 egg yolks

⅔ cup sugar

Pinch of salt

SPECIAL TOOLS AND PANS

Strainer

6 to 8 (4- to 6-ounce)
decorative parfait dishes

Candy thermometer

Stand mixer

YIELD

2 quarts, serves 12

VARIATIONS

This parfait can be flavored
with any herb or spice. Just
steep the herb or spice of choice
in the hot cream.

Fig Leaf Parfait: Replace the
lemon verbena with 2 chopped
fig tree leaves.

Black Mint Parfait: Replace
the lemon verbena with
1½ ounces black mint leaves

**Black Walnut or Hazelnut
Parfait:** Replace the lemon
verbena with 4 ounces
(¾ cup) ground black walnuts
or blanched hazelnuts. Do
not strain and remove the nuts.
Allow them to stay in
the cream while you whip it.

When I prepare vanilla desserts at Chanterelle, I often add a bit of dried lemon verbena. Vanilla has a complicated, multidimensional but subtle flavor. Lemon verbena provides a background, bringing out the intense vanilla flavor.

At Chanterelle, I serve this basic parfait recipe in countless ways by infusing the cream with different herbs, spices, and toasted nuts. It's an extremely adaptable base and technique you can apply to any flavor combination.

1 hour ahead of time: Infuse the cream.
Slice open the vanilla bean and scrape out all the tiny seeds. Set the seeds aside on a small plate. In a saucepan, combine the cream, vanilla pod, and lemon verbena and cook over medium-high heat. When the cream is almost at a boil, remove from the heat, cover, and let the cream infuse for 20 minutes. Pass the hot cream through a strainer and into a bowl. Discard the solids. Transfer to the refrigerator and chill until the cream is cold enough to whip, at least 1 hour.

Whip and cook the yolks.
Place the egg yolks and 2 tablespoons sugar in the bowl of a stand mixer and whisk at medium speed. In a small saucepan, combine the remaining sugar, 3 tablespoons water, and the reserved vanilla bean seeds. Cook the syrup over medium-high heat until it reaches 248°F. With the mixer set on medium-high speed, quickly pour the hot syrup into the egg yolks in a continuous stream. Add the salt. Whisk the yolks until they become pale, have tripled in volume, and are just slightly warm.

Whip the infused cream.
Chill a stainless-steel mixing bowl in the refrigerator. Pour the cold infused cream into the bowl and whisk the cream until soft peaks form.

Finish the parfait.
Scrape the whipped cream into the yolks. Place a spatula in the center of the bowl, scrape the bottom, and bring the bottom over the top. Rotate the bowl 45 degrees and continue folding until the mixture is well combined. Pour into the parfait dishes and freeze for at least 4 hours.

Serving Suggestions

This parfait can be served with any fruit in season. Gently toss the berries with a bit of sugar and let them macerate 10 minutes before serving. For a crunchy accompaniment, sprinkle some nut brittle over the parfait or serve a crispy wafer on the side.

Storage
This frozen mousse will keep in the freezer for 1 week.

INGREDIENT
Vanilla beans

Vanilla orchids—two types

Edible vanilla beans are the fruit from two distinct species of orchid: *vanilla tahitensis* and *vanilla planifolia*. The first, most commonly referred to as the Tahitian vanilla bean, is grown primarily, as the name would imply, on the islands of Tahiti. The second species has many commercial names: Bourbon, Mexican, Madagascar, and others. It is grown in Indonesia, the Bourbon Islands (Madagascar, Réunion, Seychelles, and Comoro), and Mexico. The two varieties of orchids produce vanilla beans that are distinct in flavor and appearance. The Tahitian bean is short and plump; its flavor is fruity and acidic, with exotic hints of cherry, prune, and licorice. The Bourbon bean is long and thin with a smooth, intense, buttery vanilla flavor. Like wine, vanilla beans exhibit *terroir*, subtle variations of flavor based on the islands where they are grown. The most common mistake is to confuse the provenance of the bean with its species.

How do vanilla orchids grow and pollinate?

Vanilla orchids are perennial vines that grow up the trunks of trees or poles; they reach maturity when they are ten to twelve feet high, though they can grow as long as thirty feet. The orchid flowers bloom for only one day and must be hand-pollinated on that day to produce their fruit, the vanilla bean. A good worker on a vanilla farm hand-pollinates fifteen hundred flowers a day during the blooming season.

Harvesting and curing vanilla beans

Vanilla beans are green—like string beans—when they are picked off orchid vines. They are fermented through a long and intense drying, heating, and sweating process that can last up to thirty and sometimes forty days, as the beans change from green to brown in this curing process. The beans are then dried for two to three more weeks, at which point they take on their trademark black appearance to which we are accustomed. Fermentation yields beans that vary enormously in flavor and aroma.

How do you select good-quality vanilla beans?

The best way to select a good vanilla bean is to examine it and smell it before you purchase it. It should be moist and fragrant. The bean should be black, not brown. If you cannot smell the bean at the time of purchase, seek out a reputable supplier. Mr. Recipe and Neilsen Massey both sell good-quality beans. Vanilla beans have over 250 different flavor compounds, of which the most obvious to our olfactory sense is vanillin. Commercially, machines are used to read the vanillin count in vanilla beans, and they are sorted and graded based on their vanillin count. These vanillin counts are not passed on to the consumer.

Imitation vanilla

In the supermarket one commonly encounters "imitation vanilla extract." This product is flavored with vanillin synthesized from other compounds. For example, it comes from eugenol, a compound in the oil of cloves. Vanillin is also a by-product of the breakdown of lignin in the manufacturing of paper from wood pulp. Natural vanilla extract is made from extracting some flavor from vanilla beans, but the process and proportions of vanilla do not fit the FDA profile for pure vanilla extract.

What do you do with a good vanilla bean?

Once you have purchased a good vanilla bean, keep it sealed in a dry area. You do not need to refrigerate the bean. Vanilla beans stand up to multiple uses. At Chanterelle, we first slice, scrape, and infuse the beans in custards, oils, butters, and ice cream bases. Once we have infused it in a fat or liquid, we lightly rinse the bean and let the pod dry out over the oven for an hour or two. At this point you can do many things with your vanilla bean. If you have collected a few you can immerse them in plain vodka and let them sit in the alcohol for a month in a dark place, making your own vanilla extract. Storing the dry bean in a canister with sugar infuses the sugar grains with the scent of vanilla. Or you can let the bean dry out for a few more hours and then grind it with granulated sugar in a food processor to make your own vanilla sugar.

A cluster of fresh vanilla beans growing on an orchid vine (top). Vanilla beans drying in the sun (bottom).

ROASTED FRUITS AND FRUIT SOUPS

Granny Smith Apple, Dried Fig, and Dried Cherry Winter Fruit Compote

1½ vanilla beans or 1 teaspoon vanilla extract

1 cup sugar

Pinch of cream of tartar

½ cup dry white wine

3 Granny Smith apples (1½ pounds)

14 dried figs (10 ounces)

1 cup (6 ounces) dried cherries

YIELD

1 quart fruit compote, serves 5 to 8

I didn't develop a taste for fruit compotes until I was well into my twenties. My father oohed and aahed over them during my childhood, much to my confusion, but now, belatedly, I love them as much as he does. More than that, I love to create new combinations, full of both expected and unexpected flavors, to accompany the staples of my pastry kitchen such as vanilla cake, ice cream, and panna cotta.

Unlike most fruit compotes, in this one, the fruit is soaked in a caramel-vanilla syrup with white wine. With these background flavors, the fruits really show their essence while melding together into a whole that is greater than its parts.

Make the caramel-vanilla and white wine poaching syrup.

See BEYOND THE BASICS: *Cooking caramel successfully, page 107.*

Run a paring knife down the center of 1 vanilla bean. Split it open with your fingers and use the knife to scrape the tiny black seeds into a heavy-bottomed medium-sized saucepan. (If you are using vanilla extract, add it to the syrup as directed below.) Add the vanilla pod, sugar, cream of tartar, and ⅓ cup water. Swirl the ingredients together with the tip of your finger until all the sugar is moist. Cover the pan and cook over high heat for 1 minute. Remove the cover and cook until the sugar caramelizes and turns light golden brown.

Remove from the heat, stand back, and carefully add ¼ cup of cold water. The mixture will bubble and steam furiously. Wait until the syrup has stopped boiling and add the white wine. Put the pan back on the heat and boil rapidly for 2 minutes. Remove from the heat and set aside.

Prepare the fruit.

Peel the apples and slice into 12 wedges. Remove the core and seeds from each wedge. Trim the stems off of the dried figs and quarter them.

Cook the compote.

Bring the syrup to a simmer over low heat and add the apples and the vanilla extract if you didn't use the vanilla bean. Place the apples in the syrup and cook at a slow simmer until the apples soften and become a bit translucent, while still holding their shape, 10 minutes. Add the figs and simmer for another 2 minutes. Add the cherries and remove from the heat. Set aside to cool.

Serving Suggestions

You can serve the compote right away while the fruit is still warm. I prefer to refrigerate it for 1 day to allow the flavors to meld and the fruit to soften further, soaking up the fragrant syrup. Serve with a dollop of whipped cream, crème fraîche, or vanilla ice cream. I also recommend serving this compote with the Spiced Mandarin Ice Cream (page 136), Vanilla Panna Cotta (page 99), Honey and Yogurt Panna Cotta (page 102), or the Vanilla, Brown Butter, and Almond Tea Cake (page 37).

Storage

This compote will keep, refrigerated, for 1 week.

Vanilla, Brown Butter, and Almond Cake with warm crème brûlée custard filling
Granny Smith Apple, Dried Fig, and Dried Cherry Winter Fruit Compote

Dates

The date tree, incredibly tall, a sponge for water, yet easily chopped down, exists in arid climates producing a tiny calorie-laden fruit that enables people to survive in a desert landscape with depleted food resources and water. Medjool date palms were brought to this country from the Middle East in the 1920s and are currently grown in the hot desert areas of Southern California and Arizona. They are an incredibly labor-intensive fruit to grow and harvest. The trees are tall and have enormous thorns that grow along the trunk. The thorns must be removed so that workers can climb the trunks safely in order to manage the fruit throughout the growing season. Once the trees are de-thorned, they have to be hand-pollinated, because the native Middle Eastern bee that typically pollinates the flowers does not live here.

Dates grow in enormous clusters, and as they develop into pea- to grape-size fruits, the workers must pick out a third of the underdeveloped fruits to thin the bunches out so that the remaining dates can grow into larger fruits. Because these clusters are still crowded, workers must insert metal rings into the bunches to spread out the fruit and allow air to circulate through and around all the fruit. Date clusters, toward the end of their maturity, are yellow or red, hard and crunchy, sweet yet somewhat astringent, and full of water. In Middle Eastern countries dates are often picked and sold at this point in their maturity.

"Dried dates" as we know them are allowed to stay on the tree and further ripen. Workers wrap the date clusters with a cheesecloth-like material or cover them with brown bags, which protect the dates not only from birds, some insects, and excess rain or humidity but also from some sun, yielding the unique texture of a fruit matured and "dried" on the tree—moist, creamy, yet slightly wrinkled, chewy, and browned. Unlike other dried fruits, once dates are harvested, there is no further drying process, so they're ready to eat once picked.

Roasted Medjool Dates Stuffed with Cashews, Currants, and Candied Citrus

Dates are loaded with natural sweetness, but it is challenging to actually taste their flavor. To bring out the underlying flavor of dates, I like to cook them in a slightly sweet Madeira, a Portuguese fortified wine.

The dates in this recipe are just barely infused with Madeira and vanilla, preserving the dates' intrinsic and delectable creamy texture. The candied citrus is a necessary extra step, but candied fruit will last in the refrigerator for months. The filling, with its candied Meyer lemon and kumquats, currants, and cashews, provides an acidic, fruity, crunchy, and nutty counterweight to the richness and sweetness of the dates.

Prepare the dates.
Preheat the oven to 325°F. With a paring knife, make a slit down the long side of each date. Gently pry open the date and remove the pit. Place the dates, cut side down, in a baking dish.

Run a paring knife down the center of 1 vanilla bean. Split it open with your fingers and use the knife to scrape out the tiny black seeds into a small saucepan. Add the vanilla pod (or vanilla extract), Madeira, and sugar and simmer over medium heat for 4 minutes. Pour the hot syrup over the dates and cover the baking dish with aluminum foil. Bake for 20 minutes. Remove the dates from the oven, flip them over so that the cut side faces up, cover, and bake for another 10 to 15 minutes. Remove from the oven, uncover, and allow the dates to cool. Remove the vanilla bean, dry it, and save it for another use.

Prepare the filling.
Grind the cashews in a food processor or coffee grinder. Place the currants in a bowl and sprinkle the rum over them. Add the cashews, candied citrus, and candied citrus syrup and mix together to form a paste.

Stuff the dates.
Remove the dates from the syrup and arrange them on a tray, cut side up. Stuff a small portion of filling into the cavity of the date, allowing some filling to mound on the top. Press the 2 halves of the date together around the filling.

Serving Suggestions
Serve these dates warm, with the Madeira cooking syrup drizzled on the plate. A small dollop of crème fraîche will complement these sweet dates perfectly. At Chanterelle we serve these dates with the Goat Cheesecake (page 42).

Storage
The stuffed dates will keep, wrapped and at room temperature, for 3 days or refrigerated for 1 week.

FOR THE DATES
12 to 14 Medjool dates
(12 ounces)

1 vanilla bean or
1 teaspoon vanilla extract

½ cup Madeira,
medium sweetness

¼ cup sugar

FOR THE CASHEW CITRUS FILLING
½ cup (2 ½ ounces) roasted, unsalted cashews

¼ cup (1 ounce) packed currants

1 teaspoon dark rum

1 tablespoon chopped candied kumquat (or candied orange)

1 tablespoon chopped candied Meyer lemon

1 tablespoon candied Meyer lemon syrup

SPECIAL TOOLS AND PANS
Small glass or metal baking dish large enough to hold the dates in one layer

Food processor or coffee grinder

YIELD
Serves 12 to 14

Bartlett Pears
Poached in Muscat Wine

6 cardamom pods

One 1 ½-inch-long piece
of fresh ginger

Two ½-inch-wide and
1 ½-inch-long strips of
tangerine peel

2 cups sugar

One bottle (750 milliliters)
Muscat wine

6 ripe Bartlett pears (2 pounds)

SPECIAL TOOLS AND PANS

Medium-sized stainless-steel-
lined saucepan

Fine-mesh strainer

YIELD

6 poached pears

Pears, unlike most fruits, maintain their shape while soaking up flavor during the poaching process. The ginger and cardamom in the syrup infuse the pears with a spiced floral flavor. Select pears that are just ripe, with some yellow in their skin and a nice pear perfume. Overripe pears, fruits that bruise easily and seem soft, will not stand up to poaching.

Serve these pears at room temperature so that you can appreciate all the subtle flavor notes. This is a recipe that can easily be prepared a few days ahead of time.

Prepare the poaching syrup.
Crack the cardamom pods open with the back of a spoon or a small sauté pan. Peel and slice the ginger into ¼-inch-thick coins. Using a peeler, remove 2 long strips of tangerine zest. Combine the sugar, wine, cardamom pods, ginger, and tangerine zest in a medium-sized saucepan and bring to a boil over medium heat.

Peel and poach the pears.
Peel the pears, leaving the stems on if possible. Carefully place the pears in the saucepan of boiling syrup. Put a small heat-proof dish over the pears to weight them down so they are immersed in the syrup; turn the heat down and simmer the pears until a paring knife is easily inserted into the center of the pear, 30 minutes. Remove from the heat and allow the pears to cool in their syrup.

Finish the pears.
If you plan on serving these pears the day you poach them, remove them from the syrup and strain the poaching syrup. Boil the poaching syrup until it is reduced by half, to 2 cups. If you drizzle some of the hot syrup on the counter, it should hold its shape and have the consistency of maple syrup.

If you plan to serve the pears in a day or two, store them in the refrigerator in the poaching liquid; strain and reduce the poaching liquid on the day you serve the pears. Allow the refrigerated pears to come to room temperature before serving.

If you would like to remove the core of the pear before serving, use a small melon baller and scoop the core out from the bottom of the pear. Or you can cut the pear in half right down through the center of the stem and scoop the core out of each half with the melon baller.

Serving Suggestions
Serve the pears at room temperature with some reduced poaching syrup poured over the top of the pears. The pears are also delicious with a dollop of whipped cream or brandied crème fraîche.

Storage
The poached pears will keep, in their cooking liquid, for 1 week.

Rhubarb Consommé with Summer Berries

For years, I've been making rhubarb chips as a garnish for strawberry-rhubarb desserts. I poach half a case of thinly sliced rhubarb in plain sugar syrup and then bake the strips of rhubarb in a low-temperature oven. Somehow I had never taken notice of the remaining lustrous rosy-pink clear poaching liquid that oozed with the flavor of rhubarb. Tasting it, not only was I stunned by the intense flavor and the luminous color, I became fascinated with the clarity and lightness of the liquid.

Up until this point I had not put many fruit soups on my menu at Chanterelle because I'm not a fan of the thick fruit puree most people call fruit soup, but this rhubarb consommé went on my menu the very next week, and it now appears once a year in May, when gorgeous red rhubarb first comes in from Oregon and Washington. In June I make a strawberry consommé using the same technique, followed by a nectarine consommé and a spiced red apple consommé in the fall.

This soup is a flavor powerhouse and will come in handy for a quick, light dessert or a predinner cocktail.

Approximately 8 medium-length stalks (2 pounds) dark red rhubarb

1 cup sugar

SPECIAL TOOLS AND PANS

1-foot-square piece of cheesecloth

Strainer

Ice bath

YIELD

3 cups (24 ounces), serves 6

Cook the rhubarb.

Wash and dry the rhubarb. Trim off the ends of each stalk and chop the stalks into ½-inch pieces. In a medium saucepan, combine the rhubarb, 1½ cups water, and sugar. Bring to a boil and simmer the rhubarb for 3 minutes. Do not stir the rhubarb. Remove from the heat and let it sit for 10 minutes.

Strain and chill the rhubarb.

Drape a piece of cheesecloth over a strainer and suspend the strainer over a stainless-steel bowl. Pour the rhubarb into the strainer and allow the liquid to drain for 15 minutes. Remove the strainer and place the bowl in an ice bath to chill. You will have a little more than 1 cup of rhubarb pulp remaining in the cheesecloth. Freeze the rhubarb and save it for the Strawberry-Rhubarb Crisp recipe (page 169).

Serving Suggestions

Serve this soup with sliced strawberries, fresh blueberries, and a dollop of crème fraîche or vanilla ice cream. If you have time, I recommend making the Honey and Yogurt Panna Cotta (page 102). Place the panna cotta in the center of a serving bowl and pour 4 ounces of the consommé over the custard into the bowl. See photo (page 103). At the restaurant I add a few teaspoons of fresh passion-fruit pulp, some diced mango, and cubes of guava Jell-O. Add whatever fresh berries or stone fruit are available to complement the custard and the tangy rhubarb.

Storage

The soup will keep, refrigerated, for 1 week or in the freezer for 2 weeks.

Strawberry-Rhubarb Crisp

Strawberry-Rhubarb Crisp

This dessert is a timeless classic. This recipe is almost identical to the one my mom made every summer with the rhubarb from our garden in Queens, with one exception: I now make rhubarb soup out of the strained juice and use the strained pulp rather than raw rhubarb in the crisp, which significantly reduces the water content of the baked fruit and the need to use flour as a thickener, thus intensifying the flavor of the fruit gel beneath the crisp topping.

Preheat the oven to 350°F.

Make the streusel topping.
In a bowl, toss together the flour, sugars, and salt. Cut the butter into ¼-inch cubes and add to the flour mixture. Using two knives or a pastry blender, chop and toss the butter simultaneously until the butter is pea-sized and coated with flour. Do not let the dough come together in a ball. Set the streusel aside at room temperature, uncovered.

Prepare the fruit.
Wash, dry, and quarter the strawberries. In a bowl toss together the strawberries, rhubarb pulp, flour, sugar, and salt. Pack the fruit mixture evenly on the bottom of the baking dish and top with the streusel. Do not pack the topping down.

Bake the crisp.
Bake until the crumb topping has browned and the fruit is bubbling beneath, 30 to 40 minutes. Allow the crisp to cool for at least 20 minutes before serving.

Serving Suggestions
Serve this crisp warm with vanilla ice cream, whipped cream, or crème fraîche. I also recommend the Basil Ice Cream (page 142), Coconut Cream Cheese Ice Cream (page 135), or Vanilla Bean and Lemon Verbena Parfait (page 158).

Storage
This crisp is best eaten the day it is made but will keep, refrigerated, for 4 days.

STREUSEL TOPPING

1 ¼ cups flour

⅓ cup sugar

⅓ cup packed, moist dark brown sugar

¼ teaspoon salt

10 tablespoons (5 ounces) butter, chilled

FRUIT MIXTURE

2 pints (1½ pounds) strawberries

Rhubarb pulp from the Rhubarb Consommé with Summer Berries recipe (page 167)

1 tablespoon plus 1 teaspoon flour

2 tablespoons sugar

¼ teaspoon salt

SPECIAL TOOLS AND PANS

Pastry knife (optional)

12 x 8 x 1¾-inch baking pan

YIELD

Serves 10

VARIATIONS

Hazelnut Streusel Topping: Omit 2 tablespoons of the flour and substitute ¼ cup (1 ounce) ground hazelnuts in the dry ingredients.

Cinnamon or Cardamom Streusel Topping: Add ½ teaspoon of ground cinnamon or ground cardamom to the dry ingredients.

Oatmeal Streusel Topping: Omit ¼ cup of the flour and substitute ½ cup raw oats in the dry ingredients.

Fresh Cherry Vanilla Compote

2 pounds fresh cherries

1 vanilla bean or
1 teaspoon vanilla extract

½ cup Madeira,
medium sweetness

½ cup sugar

SPECIAL TOOLS AND PANS

Cherry pitter (optional)

Ice bath

YIELD

4 cups (32 ounces),
serves 6 to 8

When cherries are at the peak of the season, I like to eat them straight out of the baskets they come in. One of the special properties of cooked cherries, though, is the way they maintain their firmness and body while the cooking process accentuates and deepens their flavor.

Pit the cherries.
Wash and dry the cherries. Using a cherry pitter or the tong of a fork, remove the pits.

Simmer the cherries.
Run a paring knife down the center of the vanilla bean. Split it open with your fingers and use the knife to scrape the tiny black seeds into a medium-sized saucepan. Add the pitted cherries, Madeira, sugar, and vanilla bean (or vanilla extract). Bring to a boil over medium heat, stirring every 2 minutes, to move the cherries from the bottom to the top. Reduce the heat and simmer, uncovered, for 25 minutes. Remove from the heat and transfer the compote to a bowl. Place the bowl in an ice bath to cool. Place in the refrigerator until you are ready to serve. Remove the vanilla bean before serving.

Serving Suggestions
Serve this compote with a scoop of vanilla or chocolate ice cream and chopped almonds. I also recommend the Dark Chocolate Sorbet (page 147) and the Vanilla Panna Cotta (page 99). Of course, the hot Chocolate Soufflé (page 119) is my favorite.

Storage
This compote will keep, refrigerated, for 1 week.

Fresh Fig and Madeira Compote

1 vanilla bean or
1 teaspoon vanilla extract

1 cup Madeira,
medium sweetness

1 cup sugar

2 pounds (21 large) fresh figs

Pinch of salt

SPECIAL TOOLS AND PANS

Ice bath

YIELD

4 cups (32 ounces),
serves 6 to 8

I use this compote as a sauce to accompany the Fresh Huckleberry and Fig Tart (page 24), and I also love to eat it with the Chocolate Bête Noire (page 47), as this dessert complements chocolate very well. You can also eat it without accompaniment, as my husband does whenever I bring some of this home and leave it in the refrigerator.

Prepare the compote.
Run a paring knife down the center of the vanilla bean. Split it open with your fingers and use the knife to scrape the tiny black seeds into a medium-sized saucepan. Add the Madeira, sugar, vanilla bean, and salt. Bring to a boil over medium heat and simmer for 5 minutes.

Meanwhile, slice the hard tips off the figs and divide each fig into 4 even wedges. Add the fruit to the Madeira, as well as the vanilla extract if you aren't using a vanilla bean. Simmer the figs over low heat for 15 to 20 minutes, stirring occasionally. Remove from the heat and transfer the compote to a bowl. Place the bowl in an ice bath to cool. Place in the refrigerator until you are ready to serve. Remove the vanilla bean before serving.

Serving Suggestions
Serve this compote with a scoop of vanilla or chocolate ice cream. I also recommend the Dark Chocolate Sorbet (page 147) and Vanilla Panna Cotta (page 99). The warm flourless Chocolate Bête Noire cake (page 47) is wonderful also.

Fresh Fig and Madeira Compote

Roasted Glazed Peaches

8 small to medium (2 pounds) fresh ripe peaches

⅓ cup white wine

½ cup sweet Muscat wine

¼ cup honey

5 tablespoons sugar

SPECIAL TOOLS AND PANS

Stainless-steel roasting pan big enough to hold 16 peach halves in one layer

YIELD

Serves 8

Like other oven-roasted and -basted fruits, these peaches are beautiful when they come out of the oven: they feature a whole range of oranges and reds, with caramelized brown lines throughout. The cooking liquid, a honey peach caramel, is suffused with the essence of peach.

At the height of summer, when fresh local peaches are in abundance, this is a relatively simple but utterly sublime way to pay homage to the bounty of the season.

Preheat the oven to 375°F.

Prepare the peaches.
Slice the peaches in half through the stem and around the pit. Hold each peach gently in your palms and slowly rotate both halves in opposite directions. One half should slide off the pit and one half should still hold the pit. Lay the peach halves down (with the pits still in place), cut side up, in your roasting pan. Pour all the remaining ingredients, except 2 tablespoons of the sugar, over the peaches.

Roast and glaze the peaches.
Roast the peaches for 30 minutes. Take them out of the oven and gently, with the tip of a paring knife, remove the pits from the 8 halves. If the pits seem well rooted in the peach flesh, you can try to pull them out later in the cooking process. Flip the peaches over and continue to roast for another 30 minutes. Remove the peaches from the oven again and flip them over. Remove any remaining pits. Once all of the peaches are without pits, ladle some of the cooking liquid over the peaches.

Raise the oven temperature to 400°F. Sprinkle the remaining sugar over the peaches and bake for 20 minutes. Baste and continue to bake until the peaches are reduced in size,

shiny, and are deep orange with some areas of caramelization, 20 minutes. If they are not done, baste and continue baking for 10 to 15 minutes. When they are done, baste the peaches one last time. Remove from the oven and allow the peaches to cool in the roasting pan.

Serving Suggestions
Place 2 peaches on each plate and drizzle the cooking syrup over the peaches. Serve with whipped cream or the Sauternes Sabayon (page 217). The Hazelnut Cake (page 39) is delicious with the peaches and their cooking juices. For a crunchy note, try the Hazelnut Streusel Topping (page 169).

Storage
These roasted peaches are best eaten the day they are made but will keep, refrigerated, for 4 days. Reheat the peaches in a 350°F oven for 10 minutes before serving.

Pineapple Fruit Soup
with Mango and Passion Fruit

This is a simple fruit soup to serve during the winter months when tropical fruits are widely available. I created this soup to go with the Passion-Fruit Soufflé Glacé (page 155), but it is equally delicious served with some fresh, crunchy passion-fruit pulp and diced kiwi, mango, papaya, or whatever other fresh fruit you can get your hands on.

Cook the pineapple.

Run a paring knife down the center of the vanilla bean. Split it open with your fingers and use the knife to scrape out the tiny black seeds and place the seeds and pod in the saucepan. With a sharp knife, remove the top and bottom of the pineapple. Stand the fruit up and carefully carve the skin off in long strokes. Slice the pineapple down the center and lay each half, flat side down, on the cutting board. Chop the halves into ¼- to ½-inch-thick semicircles. Add the pineapple, sugar, and 1 ½ cups cold water to the saucepan. Bring the mixture to a simmer and cook for 5 minutes.

Puree and strain the pineapple.

Remove the vanilla pod, dry it, and save for another use. Scoop half of the pineapple and some of the cooking liquid into a blender and puree it on the highest speed for 2 minutes. Transfer the puree to a bowl and repeat the process with the remaining pineapple. Pass the pureed pineapple through a fine-mesh strainer and into a container, using the bottom of a small ladle to push as much of the fruit through the strainer as possible. Discard the pulp. Transfer the soup to the refrigerator to chill.

Serving Suggestions

Serve this soup with some fresh diced mango, fresh passion-fruit, and strawberries. For a creamy center, add a scoop of vanilla ice cream or Vanilla Panna Cotta (page 99). At Chanterelle we serve this soup with the Passion-Fruit Soufflé Glacé (page 155) and garnish it with a pineapple chip.

Storage

This soup will keep, refrigerated, for 5 days or frozen for 2 weeks.

1 vanilla bean

1 medium pineapple
(8-count, meaning 8 pineapples
in a standard box)

1 cup sugar

SPECIAL TOOLS AND PANS

Blender

Fine-mesh strainer

YIELD

5 cups, 6 servings

Spiced Plum Compote with Plum Pit Cream

COMPOTE

14 medium (3¼ pounds) ripe plums (black or red)

2 cinnamon sticks

3 star of anise

¾ cup sugar

PLUM PIT CREAM

14 plum pits, crushed

1 cup heavy cream

2 tablespoons sugar

SPECIAL TOOLS AND PANS

Fine-mesh stainer

Ice bath

Meat tenderizer, hammer, or solid rolling pin

YIELD

4 cups (32 ounces), serves 8 to 10

When I was a child, my grandmother used to come to stay with us in the summer. Inevitably, she would cook up a pot of stewed plums. I don't think I ever dipped a spoon in them. But she was on to more than I realized at the time: gently braised plums, cooked for a short period of time with sugar and spices, make for a particularly lovely cold dessert during the hot summer months. I use the almond flavor of the plum pits to make an especially complementary cream.

If you are fortunate to live near a summer farmer's market, the many small plum varieties available, which never make it into commercial groceries, are perfect for this recipe.

Make the plum compote base.
Using a knife, quarter 8 plums, reserving the pits. In a small saucepan bring the plum flesh and skins, the spices, and the sugar to a simmer and cook until the fruit begins to dissolve in the cooking liquid, 10 to 15 minutes. Pass the plums through a fine-mesh strainer, using the bottom of a small ladle to push as much of the fruit through the strainer as possible. Return the compote to the saucepan.

Finish the compote.
Using a knife, carefully halve the remaining 6 plums and cut each half into 3 wedges, reserving the pits. (Do not worry if a little bit of fruit remains stuck to the pit.) Place the plums in the compote base over medium heat and simmer until the fruit is tender but not falling apart, 4 to 6 minutes. Remove from the heat, transfer to a bowl, and place it in an ice bath to chill.

Make the plum pit cream.
See INGREDIENT: *Plum pits and other stone fruit pits, page 175.*

Wash the plum pits and remove any plum flesh that is clinging to them. Using a small sandwich bag or some plastic wrap, seal 3 or 4 pits in plastic. Hold the plastic down firmly on the counter so the plum pits don't move around as you gently smash them with a meat tenderizer, rolling pin, or hammer. Place the smashed pits in a small saucepan and add the cream and sugar. Over medium heat, simmer for 5 minutes. Remove from the heat, and let the cream sit for 10 minutes. Pass the cream through a strainer into a bowl. Discard the pits. Place the bowl in an ice bath to cool. Transfer to the refrigerator to chill until the cream is cool enough to whip. Whip the infused cream before serving.

Serving Suggestions
Present the compote in a small bowl with a dollop of the infused cream in the middle. Vanilla or cinnamon ice cream is also delicious with this compote.

Storage
The compote and cream will keep, refrigerated, for 1 week.

INGREDIENT
Plum pits and other stone fruit pits

BEYOND THE BASICS
Browning and caramelization

Plum pits and most stone fruit pits (peach, nectarine, cherry, and apricot) surround a seed that is an almond look-alike, with a wonderful floral almond flavor commonly associated with marzipan. The seeds found in the shells of stone fruits should not be confused with the nuts known as bitter almonds, though this is often the case because they both contain a glucoside—amygdalin. Amygdalin is a dry, colorless substance that, in the presence of water, breaks down into cyanide, a poison if taken in large enough quantities, and benzaldehyde, an aldehyde with the intense floral almond flavor of marzipan. Natural almond extract contains benzaldehyde taken from cassia bark, a type of cinnamon, and artificial extract contains benzaldehyde synthesized in a lab.

If you simmer a bunch of crushed plum pits in cream, the amygdalin will be broken down into glucose, benzaldehyde, and hydrogen cyanide, a volatile colorless gas that disperses or evaporates into the air around the pot. So simmer the crushed stone fruit pits on a ventilated stove with a hood or in a well-ventilated kitchen with multiple open windows. The cream is left with benzaldehyde, lending it a rich marzipan-like flavor. If you would like to make a floral almond-infused ice cream, save your plum, cherry, or apricot pits and store them in a plastic bag in the freezer. Once you have accumulated 20 pits, smash them with a hammer or meat tenderizer. Follow the Basil Ice Cream recipe (page 142), leaving out the basil leaves and substituting the smashed almond look-alike seeds. Simmer the cream with the smashed seeds for 5 minutes over a ventilated stove. Alternatively, you can easily and safely substitute natural almond extract, using 2 teaspoons in the Basil Ice Cream recipe instead of fresh basil. Add the extract after you have cooked and strained the crème anglaise.

Like many words initially borrowed from science, the word "caramelization" in common usage is taken to mean two somewhat opposing things; oddly, one is too broad, the other too specific. Technically, caramelization is the process by which any carbohydrate breaks down in the presence of heat into component molecules and molecule fragments that we describe experientially as "caramel," in other words, dark, rich sweetness with greater depth than sugar, and color that ranges from light amber to dark brown.

Yet we tend to think of "caramel" as only one thing: sugar—sucrose, specifically—that is boiled until it becomes caramel. But this concept is too specific; any sugar, any starch, any carbohydrate at all, can "caramelize" in the presence of heat.

On the other hand, we often describe the process of searing a piece of meat or fish to bring out a depth of flavor while browning the outer flesh as "caramelizing" the protein. This is also inaccurate; while there is some actual caramelization occurring, what is predominantly happening in the browning of protein is a bunch of far more complex processes called Maillard reactions, in which carbohydrates react with nitrogen, usually supplied in this case by protein, in the presence of heat. Maillard reactions produce a wide and complex range of flavors, aromas, and colors, depending on the kind of protein supplying the nitrogen, which is one reason the browning of hangar steak and the browning of salmon produce such different flavors.

The reason this discussion is particularly relevant to the roasted pear dessert is that the extraordinary range of colors and flavors produced by the pear roasting process results mainly from actual caramelization of multiple carbohydrates—of the added sucrose (table sugar), of the fructose and glucose from the honey, and of the fructose, glucose, and starch in the pears—but also, to a lesser extent, from Maillard reactions due to the protein in the pears.

Honey-Glazed Roasted Pears

1 lemon

10 medium (approximately 5 pounds) ripe pears (Anjou, Comice, Bartlett, or Bosc)

2 tablespoons (1 ounce) butter

¾ cup sugar

¾ cup honey

1 recipe Sauternes Sabayon (page 217), optional

SPECIAL TOOLS AND PANS

12 x 8-inch metal roasting pan, preferably aluminum or copper

Cookie sheet

YIELD

10 roasted pears, serves 10

I make this dish for my family every year at Rosh Hashanah, the Jewish New Year. The holiday usually falls in September when the first pears come on the market, so this dish ushers in the fall fruit harvest. When the pears in this recipe are cooked, they produce an orange-amber honey-pear caramel that is perfectly symbolic of the sweet new year to come, encompassing the traditional symbols of the holiday, honey, and fall fruit. When the pears come out of the oven, they are absolutely beautiful: shiny and caramelized with a multitude of colors.

Select pears that are fragrant and firm but have some give when you press on them; underripe pears take a very long time to cook and the final product is sometimes mealy, and overly ripe pears will disintegrate during the cooking process.

This pear dish is somewhat labor intensive and requires the use of a hot oven for about 2 hours, so I'd recommend roasting these pears while you plan to be in the kitchen working on another dish. If you have a convection oven, use it, because the pears will roast faster and take on a bit more color.

Preheat the oven to 425°F. Set the rack on the top shelf of the oven.

Prepare the pears.
Peel the lemon zest into 4 long strips. Peel the pears and leave the stems on if they have not already fallen off. Cut a slice 1 inch in diameter and ⅓ inch thick off the bottom of each pear so it will stand up in the roasting pan. Place the pears in the roasting pan and add the remaining ingredients, including the lemon zest. You do not need to mix the ingredients together ahead of time because they will all melt together into a syrup in the oven.

Braise the pears.
Place the roasting pan on a cookie tray just in case the juices boil over. Bake until all the sugar and honey have dissolved and the tops of the pears are beginning to brown, 30 minutes.

Remove the pan from the oven. Using a rubber spatula, push the pears over so they are lying on their sides. Return to the oven and bake for 20 minutes. Rotate the pears to the opposite side and bake another 20 minutes. The pears will continue to take on color. Do not be alarmed if the tops of the pears become a very dark brown. You want them to caramelize.

Roast the pears.
See BEYOND THE BASICS: *Browning and carmelization, page 175.*

The pears are poached when a knife inserted into the center slides in easily and the pear is somewhat soft to the touch. If the pears seem hard and uncooked, bake them lying down for another 20 minutes.

Once the pears are poached, stand them back up and bake for 15 minutes. Remove the pan from the oven and baste the pears with the caramelized juices (which will continue to reduce and thicken into a syrup). Return the pears to the oven and repeat this process three more times for a total of 45 more minutes. The pears are done when the tops are almost black and the flesh is a shiny, deep caramel color. You might need to roast the pears for another 10 to

20 minutes to get this beautiful caramel shine. Remove the pears from the oven and baste one last time. The basting liquid should by now have become a thick syrupy caramel.

Finish the pears before serving.
Remove the pears from the roasting pan and place them on a tray or plate to cool. Save the caramel sauce, discarding the lemon zest. Once the pears have cooled, remove the core from the bottom with a small melon baller or paring knife. You need to carve out a cone shape from the bottom to remove the pear's seeds. To serve, reheat the pears in the oven.

Serving Suggestions
Place each pear on a plate with a dollop of whipped cream or crème fraîche or Sauternes Sabayon and a drizzle of the pear caramel sauce (the cooking liquid from the pears).

Storage
These roasted pears are best eaten the day they are made but will keep, refrigerated, for 4 days.

Roasted Apple Beignets with Cinnamon Sugar

ROASTED APPLES

4 large (2 pounds) tart apples
(Granny Smiths work well)

3 tablespoons (1 ½ ounces)
butter

2 tablespoons sugar

BEIGNET BATTER

4 eggs

¾ teaspoon salt

¼ cup vegetable oil

¾ cup light beer

1 ½ cups flour

Pinch of cream of tartar

2 teaspoons sugar

FOR FRYING

3 cups vegetable oil

½ teaspoon cinnamon

¾ cup sugar

SPECIAL TOOLS AND PANS

Apple corer

Cookie sheet

10-inch round sauté pan with
at least 3-inch sides

YIELD

Serves 8

VARIATION

Roasted Pear Beignets:
Substitute 4 large ripe Anjou
pears for the apples and follow
the same directions.

This is not a traditional doughnut, because the batter is not leavened with yeast or baking powder. Rather, it is something akin to a sweet tempura: a quick, light, crispy dough that gains its lightness from the addition of beer and whipped egg whites.

Beignets are a fun party dessert. Your guests will love to stand around the kitchen waiting for each succulent beignet to emerge and be dunked in cinnamon sugar and drizzled with caramel sauce.

Preheat the oven to 350°F. Grease the cookie sheet or line it with parchment.

Prepare and roast the apple slices.
Peel and core the apples with a corer. With a sharp knife, slice each apple into 4 even doughnut-shaped cross sections. Lay the apples on the prepared cookie sheet and dot each slice with butter, dividing the butter evenly among the apple slices. Sprinkle the sugar on top and bake until the apples are puffed and slightly soft to the touch, and a knife inserted meets no resistance, about 30 minutes. If the apple slices seem firm and uncooked, bake for 10 minutes and check again. Remove from the oven and allow them to cool.

Make the beignet batter.
While the apples are baking, prepare the beignet batter. Separate the eggs, reserving the whites. Place 3 egg yolks in a medium bowl; discard the remaining one or use it for something else. Whisk together the egg yolks, salt, oil, and beer. Add the flour and whisk the batter, by hand, until it is smooth and thick. In another bowl with a clean whisk, whisk the egg whites until frothy. Add the cream of tartar and continue whisking until the whites have foamed and hold soft peaks. While continuously whisking, add the sugar and beat the whites until they have become shiny, increase in volume, and hold slightly stiff peaks.

Using a rubber spatula, scrape the egg whites into the egg yolk batter. Place the spatula in the center of the bowl, scrape the bottom, and bring the bottom over the top. Rotate the bowl 45 degrees and continue folding until all the egg whites are incorporated. Cover the batter and refrigerate until you are ready to fry the apples. Do not leave the batter unused for more than 1 hour.

Fry the apples.
Heat the oil in a frying pan over medium heat to 325°F but no higher than 340°F. If you do not have the size pan I recommend, make sure the oil in the pan you do use is at least 1 inch deep. While the oil is heating, mix together the cinnamon and sugar in a small bowl and place it next to the stove. Line a plate with 3 paper towels to drain the beignets before dipping them in the sugar. Also have ready a second plate on which to place the finished beignets.

To test that the oil is hot enough, drop ½ teaspoon of beignet batter into the hot oil. The batter should puff immediately and the oil should bubble vigorously around the batter. When the oil is ready, dip each roasted apple in the batter, coating both sides, and gently lay it down in the hot oil. Cook 6 to 8 apple slices at a time. Using a slotted spoon or small spatula, flip each apple over and cook it until the batter has taken on a golden brown on both sides. Remove the beignets and rest them on the paper towel for 1 minute before dredging in the cinnamon sugar.

Serving Suggestions
Serve immediately. Place 2 beignets on a plate with a dollop of whipped cream and a drizzle of the Rum Caramel Sauce (page 213), if desired.

Roasted Apple Beignets with Cinnamon Sugar

Lemon Verbena Poached Nectarines

Lemon Verbena Poached Nectarines

There is nothing as pleasurable as eating a peak-of-season nectarine, infused with flavor, dripping with succulent juice. This is a dessert to make when you find yourself with such an abundance of nectarines that you cannot possibly eat them all fresh. The light poaching preserves the seductive fragrance and outrageous sweetness of ripe nectarines for a few days, allowing you to savor this ineluctably delicious summer treat for a bit longer than the fruit itself would last.

Poach the nectarines.
In a medium-sized saucepan combine the wine, sugar, lemon verbena leaves, and 2 cups water and bring to a boil. Wash the nectarines. Gently place the fruit in one even layer in the boiling syrup. Bring to a simmer and cook until a knife slides into the center with no resistance, 20 to 30 minutes. Use a spoon to gently turn the nectarines over once or twice during the cooking process. If you taste the cooking liquid, it might seem overly sweet. This sweet sensation is tamed through the chilling and preserving process.

Chill the cooked fruit.
Gently transfer the nectarines and the cooking liquid to a stainless steel bowl and place in an ice bath to cool. When the nectarines are cool enough to handle, use a knife to peel off the loosened skin. Transfer the chilled fruit and the syrup to a container and refrigerate them for a minimum of 1 hour or up to 1 week.

When ready to serve, slice the nectarines in half and remove the pits. Serve the two halves in a bowl with some of the cooking liquid ladled over the top with a dollop of whipped cream or vanilla ice cream.

Serving Suggestions
A crunchy cookie complements the dish perfectly. I recommend the Hazelnut Shortbread (page 66).

Storage
These nectarines and cooking liquid will keep, refrigerated, for 1 week.

1 cup dry white wine

1½ cups sugar

10 fresh lemon verbena leaves

8 ripe, fragrant nectarines (approximately 2 ¼ pounds)

SPECIAL TOOLS AND PANS

Saucepan at least 8 inches in diameter

Ice bath

YIELD

Serves 8

Stuffed Roasted Fall Apples

10 medium (approximately
3 pounds) Empire apples

8 tablespoons (4 ounces) butter

6 tablespoons sugar

1 vanilla bean or
1 teaspoon vanilla extract

½ cup finely chopped dried
figs, tightly packed

SPECIAL TOOLS AND PANS

Melon baller

Pastry brush

2 baking pans

10- to 12-inch sauté pan

YIELD

Serves 8

This recipe is a bit labor intensive, because it requires carefully removing the flesh from an apple, cooking it, and then reconstructing it for serving—but the presentation embodies the fall season, in both flavor and appearance. It is best to use apples you have had sitting around the house for a week, since the softer flesh is easier to remove without destroying the shape of the apple.

Preheat the oven to 375°F. Grease 2 baking pans or line them with aluminum foil or parchment.

Roast the apples.
Wash and dry the apples. With a sharp knife, slice off ½ inch of the top (stem end) of 8 apples. Lay the apple tops, flesh side down, on one of the prepared baking pans. With a melon baller, scoop out the core and seeds of the 8 topless apples and place these apples on the second baking pan. Melt 2 tablespoons of the butter. With a pastry brush, coat all the apple tops and bottoms with a thin layer of butter. Evenly sprinkle 2 tablespoons of the sugar over the apple tops and bottoms. Place both baking pans in the oven and bake the tops for 10 minutes and the bottoms for 20 to 25 minutes. The flesh of the apples should be rising a bit out of the skin. Remove from the oven and set aside to cool. As the apples cool, the skin will wrinkle and separate from the flesh.

Remove the flesh from the apples.
When the apple bottoms have cooled, using a tablespoon or a teaspoon, gently insert the spoon between the outer flesh and the skin, loosening the entire apple from its skin, then carefully scoop out the flesh in small spoonfuls without ripping the bottom of the apple. Leave a small portion of the apple flesh attached to the core on the bottom. You will be left with 8 hollowed-out standing apple skin vessels. (See photo on page 160.)

Chop the apples.
Chop the scooped apple flesh into ¼-inch pieces. Peel and core the 2 remaining raw apples and chop the apples into ¼-inch pieces.

Sauté the apples with the figs and the vanilla.
See TECHNIQUE TIP: *Browning butter, page 51.*

Run a paring knife down the center of the vanilla bean. Split it open with your fingers and use the knife to scrape out the tiny black seeds. Place the remaining 6 tablespoons of butter and the vanilla seeds and pod in a 10- to 12-inch sauté pan over medium-high heat. Once the butter begins to brown, add the chopped apples, the vanilla extract (if you are not using a vanilla bean), and the figs. Sauté for 1 minute, stirring with a heat-proof spatula or a wooden spoon. Add the remaining 4 tablespoons sugar and cook for 5 minutes, stirring every minute or so. Turn down the heat to medium and cook until the fruit is tender, 10 to 15 minutes. If the apples seem dry and are burning on the bottom, add ¼ cup of water to steam them a bit. When the apples and figs are cooked, scrape them out of the sauté pan onto a cookie sheet or baking dish to cool. Remove the vanilla bean. Rinse it, dry it, and save it for another use.

Stuff the apples.
Spoon the cooked apple and fig mixture into the hollowed-out apple skins, dividing the mixture evenly among the 8 skins. Top each stuffed apple with a roasted apple top. Roast the stuffed apples for 10 to 12 minutes at 350°F before serving.

Serving Suggestions
Serve these apples warm with vanilla ice cream or whipped cream, the Brandied Crème Fraîche Sauce (page 213), the Cider Caramel Sauce (page 212), or the Toffee Sauce (page 214).

Storage
These apples can be kept, well wrapped and at room temperature, for 36 hours.

Stuffed Roasted Fall Apples

CHOCOLATES
AND CANDIES

CHAPTER EIGHT

White Chocolate and Grapefruit Truffles with Hazelnuts

TRUFFLE

¼ cup plus 2 tablespoons (3 fluid ounces) heavy cream

½ cup ground hazelnuts (from 2 ounces whole blanched nuts)

1 tablespoon grapefruit zest (from 1 grapefruit)

8 ounces white chocolate

1 tablespoon (½ ounce) butter, at room temperature

TRUFFLE COATING

3 ounces white chocolate

¾ cup ground hazelnuts (from 3 ounces whole blanched nuts)

SPECIAL TOOLS AND PANS

Fine-mesh strainer

Bain-marie (see page 10)

Small melon baller, ⅞ inch or 22 millimeters in diameter

YIELD

50 to 54 small truffles

So many discoveries in the kitchen stem from serendipity. This truffle recipe was an accidental discovery fueled by the unavailability of oranges for Chanterelle's classic orange-hazelnut white chocolate truffle. We did have grapefruits in the kitchen, so I substituted them for the oranges, and the new flavor became so popular that it replaced the old classic.

Infuse the cream.
In a small saucepan, combine the cream and zest and cook over medium heat to almost boiling. Remove from the heat and let steep for 10 minutes. Pass the cream through a strainer and discard the zest.

Melt the white chocolate.
In the bowl of a bain-marie, melt the white chocolate, stirring with a rubber spatula as it melts. Do not overheat the chocolate—it should never be so hot that you cannot stick the tip of your finger in it. (White chocolate has an even lower melting point than dark chocolate, and will lump up if overheated.)

Emulsify the chocolate and the cream to make ganache.
Remove the melted chocolate from the heat and slowly whisk in the infused cream. (At first the chocolate might seize up and separate—do not worry.) Continue to whisk until the mixture (now a ganache) is smooth, creamy, and holds the lines of a whisk. Slowly whisk in the butter until incorporated and then add the hazelnuts. Scrape the ganache into a small bowl and refrigerate for 2 hours.

Scoop the truffles.
Fill a glass with very hot tap water. Dip a small melon baller into the hot water and tap on the counter to remove any excess water. Plunge the melon baller into the chilled ganache far enough down so that it sits completely in the ganache. Rotate the melon baller clockwise 360 degrees and remove from the ganache. Tap the melon

baller to release the ball onto a plate or tray. Repeat this process until all the ganache has been scooped into balls. Transfer the plate to the refrigerator and chill.

Make the truffle coating and dip the truffles.
In the bowl of a bain-marie, melt the white chocolate, stirring with a rubber spatula as it melts. Remove from the heat and cool for 15 minutes.

Set up an assembly line on your counter. From left to right, place the chilled ganache balls, the bowl of melted chocolate, a tray with the ground hazelnuts, and a container to hold your finished truffles.

With your left hand, pick up 2 ganache balls and dip them quickly into the melted chocolate and roll them around until coated. Drop the balls with your left hand into the ground hazelnuts. With your right hand roll the balls until completely enrobed. Pick up the finished candies with your right hand and place them in the container.

Serving Suggestions
Serve these truffles at room temperature on a tray with coffee for dessert.

Storage
The truffles will keep, in a sealed container and refrigerated, for 2 weeks.

BEYOND THE BASICS
Tempered chocolate

Tempering chocolate refers to the process by which the fat in pure chocolate—cocoa butter, which is made up of a few triglycerides (fats and oils composed of three fatty acid molecules attached to a glycerol molecule)—solidifies and cools in a tightly packed crystal formation at room temperature, leaving the chocolate with gloss, a snap, and a wonderful melt-in-your-mouth quality. If not melted, coaxed, and cooled properly, the triglycerides will settle into crystal structures that are unstable, have poor appearance and texture, and melt easily.

Chocolate is always cooled and tempered into bars and chips before it leaves the chocolate factory. For most chocolate recipes—brownies, cakes, soufflés, custards, ice creams, and tarts—you do not need to worry about tempering chocolate. If you are planning on making dipped strawberries or cookies, chocolate candies, or chocolate garnishes, you must retemper chocolate after you melt it. That is, you must carefully modulate the cooling process so that the triglycerides in the cocoa butter take shape into three-dimensional crystal structures, forming a stable solid.

White Chocolate, Cardamom, and Pistachio Truffles with Coconut

TRUFFLE

10 cardamom pods

¼ cup plus 2 tablespoons
(3 fluid ounces) heavy cream

8 ounces white chocolate

1 tablespoon (½ ounce) butter,
at room temperature

½ cup (2 ounces) ground
pistachios

TRUFFLE COATING

3 ounces white chocolate

¾ cup shredded unsweetened
coconut

SPECIAL TOOLS AND PANS

Small melon baller, ⅞ inch
or 22 millimeters in diameter

Bain-marie (see page 10)

YIELD

50 to 54 small truffles

The flavor of these truffles is derived from my intense passion for sweets (candies and rice puddings) flavored with milk, cardamom, coconut, and often pistachios—tastes that I sampled during a visit to India and Nepal. White chocolate ganache is a welcoming vessel for this flavor combination, transmuting the often overly sweet vanilla flavor in white chocolate to a luxurious blend of crunchy coconut, creamy cardamom, and chunky pistachio. Some chocolate manufacturers make a nice white chocolate that is less sweet and is made with some good-quality vanilla; I particularly recommend Valrhona.

Infuse the cream.
Using the back of a small frying pan, crush the cardamon pods to release the black seeds. In a small saucepan, combine the cardamom pods, seeds, and cream and cook over medium heat to almost boiling. Remove from the heat, cover, and let steep for 10 to 30 minutes. Pass the cream through a strainer and discard the cardamom pod and seeds.

Melt the white chocolate.
In the bowl of a bain-marie, melt the white chocolate, stirring with a rubber spatula as it melts. Do not overheat the chocolate—it should never be so hot that you cannot stick the tip of your finger in it. (White chocolate has an even lower melting point than dark chocolate, and will lump up if overheated.)

Emulsify the chocolate and the cream to make ganache.
Remove the melted chocolate from the heat and slowly whisk in the infused cream. (At first the chocolate might seize up and separate—do not worry.) Continue to whisk until the mixture (now a ganache) is smooth, creamy, and holds the lines of a whisk. Slowly whisk in the butter and pistachios until incorporated. Scrape the ganache into a small bowl and refrigerate for 2 hours.

Scoop the truffles.
Fill a glass with very hot tap water. Dip a small melon baller into the hot water and tap on the counter to remove any excess water. Plunge the melon baller into the chilled ganache far enough down so that it sits completely in the ganache. Rotate the melon baller clockwise 360 degrees and remove from the ganache. Tap the melon baller to release the ball onto a plate or tray. Repeat this process until all the ganache has been scooped into balls. Transfer the plate to the refrigerator and chill.

Make the truffle coating and dip the truffles.
In the bowl of a bain-marie, melt the white chocolate, stirring with a rubber spatula as it melts. Remove from the heat and cool for 15 minutes.

Set up an assembly line on your counter. From left to right, place the chilled ganache balls, the bowl of melted chocolate, a tray with the shredded coconut, and a container to hold the finished truffles.

With your left hand, pick up 2 ganache balls and dip them quickly into the melted chocolate and roll them around until coated. Drop the balls with your left hand into the shredded coconut. With your right hand roll the balls until completely enrobed. Pick up the finished candies with your right hand and place them in your container.

Serving Suggestions
Serve these truffles with coffee for dessert.

Storage
The truffles will keep, in a sealed container and refrigerated, for 2 weeks.

Assorted Truffles at Chanterelle

Dark Chocolate, Cinnamon, and Espresso Truffles with Walnuts

TRUFFLES

½ cup plus 2 tablespoons heavy cream

½ teaspoon ground fresh cinnamon

8 ounces bittersweet chocolate (61 to 66 percent cocoa solids)

2 tablespoons (1 ounce) butter, at room temperature, diced into 6 pieces

1 tablespoon coarsely ground fresh dark coffee

TRUFFLE COATING

3 ounces bittersweet chocolate

1¼ cups ground walnuts (from 5 ounces whole nuts)

SPECIAL TOOLS AND PANS

Small melon baller, ⅞ inch or 22 millimeters in diameter

Bain-marie (see page 10)

YIELD

50 to 54 small truffles

Cinnamon and chocolate is a classic Mexican flavor combination. Cinnamon and coffee is another, and chocolate and coffee is yet another. Why not combine them all and enrobe these flavors in chopped walnuts, adding yet another dimension of flavor and a light crunch? I find these truffles addictive, the perfect ending to any meal.

If you are short on time, you can roll the scooped ganache in cocoa powder and skip the truffle coating section.

Infuse the cream and melt the chocolate.
In a small saucepan, combine the cream and cinnamon and cook over medium heat to almost boiling. Remove from the heat, cover, and let the cream steep for 10 minutes.

Meanwhile, in the bowl of a bain-marie, melt the chocolate, stirring with a rubber spatula as it melts. Do not overheat the chocolate—it should never be so hot that you cannot stick the tip of your finger in it.

Emulsify the chocolate and the cream to make ganache.
Remove the melted chocolate from the heat and slowly whisk in the infused cream. (At first the chocolate might seize up and separate—do not worry.) Continue to whisk until the mixture (now a ganache) is smooth, creamy, and holds the lines of a whisk. Slowly whisk in the butter and the ground coffee until incorporated. Scrape the ganache into a small bowl and refrigerate for 2 hours.

Scoop the truffles.
Fill a glass with very hot tap water. Dip a small melon baller into the hot water and tap on the counter to remove any excess water. Plunge the melon baller into the chilled ganache far enough down so that it sits completely in the ganache. Rotate the melon baller clockwise 360 degrees and remove from the ganache. Tap the melon baller to release the ball onto a plate or tray. Repeat this process until all the ganache has been scooped into balls. Transfer the plate to the refrigerator and chill.

Make the truffle coating and dip the truffles.
In the bowl of a bain-marie, melt the bittersweet chocolate, stirring with a rubber spatula as it melts. Remove from the heat and cool for 15 minutes.

Set up an assembly line on your counter. From left to right, place the chilled ganache balls, the bowl of melted chocolate, a tray with the ground walnuts, and a container to hold the finished truffles.

With your left hand, pick up 2 ganache balls and dip them quickly into the melted chocolate and roll them around until coated. Drop the balls with your left hand into the ground walnuts. With your right hand roll the balls until completely enrobed. Pick up the finished candies with your right hand and place them in the container.

Serving Suggestions
Serve these truffles on a tray with coffee for dessert.

Storage
The truffles will keep, in a sealed container and refrigerated, for 2 weeks.

Five-Spice
Chocolate Truffles

Five-spice mix is a traditional Asian spice combination that is featured in Chinese and Vietnamese cuisine. The classic spice blend is made of Sichuan peppercorns, cinnamon sticks, fennel seeds, cloves, and whole star anise, which are either ground into a powder or tied up in a small piece of cheesecloth and used to infuse braised dishes and broths.

If you are short on time, you can roll the scooped ganache in cocoa powder and skip the truffle coating section.

Infuse the cream and melt the chocolate.
In a small saucepan, combine the cream and spices and cook over medium heat to almost boiling. Remove from the heat and let the cream steep for 15 minutes. Pass the cream through a strainer and discard the solids.

Meanwhile, in the bowl of a bain-marie, melt the chocolate, stirring with a rubber spatula as it melts. Do not overheat the chocolate—it should never be so hot that you cannot stick the tip of your finger in it.

Emulsify the chocolate and the cream to make ganache.
Remove the melted chocolate from the heat and slowly whisk in the infused cream. (At first the chocolate might appear grainy and sludge-like—do not worry.) Continue to whisk until the mixture (now a ganache) is smooth, creamy, and holds the lines of a whisk. Slowly whisk in the butter until incorporated. Scrape the ganache into a small bowl and refrigerate for 2 hours.

Scoop the truffles.
Fill a glass with very hot tap water. Dip a small melon baller into the hot water and tap on the counter to remove any excess water. Plunge the melon baller into the chilled ganache far enough down so that it sits completely in the ganache. Rotate the melon baller clockwise 360 degrees and remove from the ganache. Tap the melon baller to release the ball onto a plate or tray. Repeat this process until all the ganache has been scooped into balls. Transfer the plate to the refrigerator and chill.

Make the truffle coating and dip the truffles.
In the bowl of a bain-marie, melt the bittersweet chocolate, stirring with a rubber spatula as it melts. Remove from the heat and cool for 15 minutes.

Set up an assembly line on your counter. From left to right, place the chilled ganache balls, the bowl of melted chocolate, a bowl of cocoa powder, and a container to hold the finished truffles.

With your left hand, pick up 2 ganache balls and dip them quickly into the melted chocolate and roll them around until coated. Drop the balls with your left hand into the cocoa powder. With your right hand roll the balls until completely enrobed. Pick up the finished candies with your right hand and place them in the container.

Serving Suggestions
Serve these truffles on a tray with coffee for dessert.

Storage
The truffles will keep, in a sealed container and refrigerated, for 2 weeks.

TRUFFLES

½ cup plus 2 tablespoons heavy cream

1 cinnamon stick

3 star anise

12 Sichuan peppercorns (or black peppercorns), crushed lightly

3 cloves

12 fennel seeds

8 ounces semisweet chocolate (56 to 64 percent cocoa solids)

2 tablespoons (1 ounce) butter, at room temperature

TRUFFLE COATING

3 ounces dark chocolate (60 to 66 percent cocoa solids)

1 ounce cocoa powder

SPECIAL TOOLS AND PANS

Small melon baller, ⁷⁄₈ inch or 22 millimeters in diameter

Bain-marie (see page 10)

YIELD

50 to 54 small truffles

Almond Honey Caramel Chews

Almond Honey Caramel Chews

I don't think I've been to a single family event in the last five years to which I haven't brought a tray of these candies, sometimes made with pecans, sometimes with hazelnuts, and from time to time with added flavor from candied citrus or zest. They're intensely chewy, lightly crunchy, and full of a caramelized honey sweetness that enhances the flavor of whatever nut you are using. They keep really well, and, best of all, they're not particularly hard to make.

Toast the almonds.
Preheat the oven to 350°F. Place the almonds on a cookie sheet and bake until they are brown and emit a nutty aroma, 10 to 15 minutes. Transfer the nuts to a bowl. Leave the oven on. Grease the baking pan and line the bottom with a piece of aluminum foil or parchment.

Cook the caramel.
Place all the remaining ingredients except the toasted almonds in a heavy-bottomed saucepan with a candy thermometer attached to the side. Bring the mixture to a boil over medium-high heat. When the mixture changes from beige to a light golden brown (5 to 8 minutes) turn the heat down to medium-low and continue to cook, stirring the candy with a heat-proof spatula every 2 minutes. The candy will continue to thicken and darken. Cook the caramel until it registers 260°F on the thermometer. If you do not have a thermometer, dip a clean fork quickly into the caramel and drizzle a drop or two on a clean counter surface. If the candy holds its domed drop shape and scrapes off the counter cleanly without sticking, it is ready. Remove the pan from the heat.

Finish the candy.
Fold in the toasted almonds with the heat-proof spatula and scrape the mixture into the prepared baking pan. Bake until the candy flattens out and air bubbles appear throughout the caramel, 12 minutes. Remove from the oven and allow the candy to cool for at least 4 hours before cutting. Cut the candy into squares, diamonds, or rectangles.

Serving Suggestions
Serve this candy as dessert or on a tray of cookies and candies. Make some around the holidays and send it to your friends.

Storage
This candy will keep, in a well-sealed container and at room temperature, for 2 weeks.

---

14 ounces (approximately 4 cups) sliced, blanched almonds

1 cup heavy cream

1 cup whole milk

16 tablespoons (8 ounces) butter

¾ cup honey

1 ½ cups sugar

1 tablespoon light corn syrup

SPECIAL TOOLS AND PANS

12 x 8-inch cookie sheet or baking pan with at least ½-inch sides

Medium-sized heavy-bottomed saucepan with at least 4-inch sides

Candy thermometer (optional)

YIELD

50 small squares of candy

VARIATIONS

Hazelnut, Walnut, Pistachio, or Peanut Honey Chews: Substitute the same amount of any of these nuts for the almonds. Make sure you chop the nuts before incorporating them into the caramel.

Chocolate-dipped Nut Chews: Melt 3 ounces of bittersweet chocolate and follow the tempering instructions on page 195 and the temperature guidelines for dark chocolate on page 195. Dip the bottom of each cut caramel chew in the chocolate and allow the dipped candies to dry dipped side up.

Milk Chocolate and Almond Toffees

ALMOND TOFFEE

½ cup (1.5 ounces) sliced almonds

8 tablespoons (4 ounces) butter

½ cup sugar

3 tablespoons light corn syrup

MILK CHOCOLATE AND ALMOND COATING

1½ cups (4.5 ounces) sliced almonds

4 ounces milk chocolate (36 to 44 percent cocoa solids)

SPECIAL TOOLS AND PANS

13 x 9-inch piece of parchment paper

2 baking pans lined with parchment, aluminum foil, or wax paper

Bain-marie (see page 10)

Digital candy thermometer

YIELD

Forty-five ¾ x 1-inch candies

VARIATION

Hazelnut, Walnut, or Pistachio Toffee: Substitute ½ cup chopped toasted hazelnuts, walnuts, or pistachios for the almonds.

Homemade hard butter toffee is delicious, but it often absorbs humidity and becomes unpleasantly tacky and chewy in the mouth. One solution to this problem—and a tasty one as well—is to place a vapor barrier between the toffee and the air. The cocoa butter in the milk chocolate forms an almost impassable barrier to the air, preserving the crunchiness of the toffee and lending the candy an extra layer of flavor, texture, and snap.

Toast the nuts.
Preheat the oven to 350°F. Place the almonds on a baking sheet and toast for 10 minutes. Remove from the oven and cool. Tape a piece of parchment onto a cutting board.

Cook the toffee.
In your heavy-bottomed saucepan, combine the butter, sugar, corn syrup, and 1 tablespoon water. Bring to a boil over medium-high heat, stirring with a heat-proof spatula, scraping the bottom every minute or so. The mixture will foam slightly and change from beige to a golden brown. Whisk the boiling candy vigorously to make sure the mixture is caramelizing evenly. When the candy is a rich golden brown, remove from the heat and whisk in ½ cup of the toasted almonds. If the toffee seems separated—the caramel appears to be curdled and floating in clear fat—whisk it briskly and it will smooth out and come together. Quickly pour the toffee onto the parchment and spread it into as large and thin a rectangle as it will make.

Shape the candy into rectangles.
While the candy is hot, use a chef's knife to cut the toffee into ¾ x 1½-inch rectangles. The toffee might be so hot that the lines do not hold, especially toward the center. This is normal. Let the candy cool for 2 minutes and cut over the same lines again. You need to cut the toffee repeatedly because if you wait until the candy is cool, it will be so crunchy and brittle that it will snap and you won't get even, rectangular candies. (If you are planning to chip or grind the toffee into small pieces to be used as a crunchy topping, you do not need to cut it.)

Temper the milk chocolate.
Follow the instructions on page 195 to temper the chocolate. *See* BEYOND THE BASICS: *Tempered chocolate, page 187.*

Dip the toffees.
Using your hands, crush the remaining 1½ cups of almonds and put them on a plate. Set up an assembly line on your counter. From left to right, place the cut and cooled toffee pieces, the bowl of tempered milk chocolate, the crushed almonds, and a clean tray, lined with aluminum foil or parchment, to hold the finished candies.

With your left hand, pick up a piece of toffee and dip it quickly into the tempered chocolate. Flip the toffee over so both sides are coated and scrape against the side of the bowl to remove any excess chocolate. Still using your left hand, lay the dipped toffee on top of the crushed almonds and, with your right hand, sprinkle crushed almonds on top of the candy until it is completely enrobed. Pick up the finished candy with your right hand and place it on your lined tray to set and dry. If the chocolate is well tempered and the room you are working in is around 66 to 70 degrees, the candies should dry within 5 minutes.

Serving Suggestions
Serve these candies on a tray with coffee for dessert.

Storage
These candies will keep, sealed and in a cool, dry place, for 2 weeks.

Milk Chocolate Crunch Candies

If you can get your hands on good-quality milk chocolate, like Scharffen Berger, Valrhona, or Michel Cluizel, this candy is the ideal version of the Nestlé Crunch bar.

Temper the milk chocolate.
Follow the instructions on this page to temper the chocolate. *See* BEYOND THE BASICS: *Tempered chocolate, page 187.* Once it is ready, add the Rice Krispies and fold the cereal into the chocolate until all of it is coated.

Shape the candies.
Using two small teaspoons, scoop and scrape the candies into small mounds on the lined cookie sheets. Try to make the mounds higher and not wider by adding small amounts of chocolate crispies to the top of the candy. Place the candies in a cool, dry place to set. Do not refrigerate. If the chocolate is well tempered and it is not too hot in the room you are working in, the chocolate should become shiny and dry within 5 to 10 minutes.

Storage
These candies will keep, sealed and in a cool, dry environment, for 1 week.

7 ounces milk chocolate
(37 percent cocoa solids or more)

2 cups Rice Krispies

SPECIAL TOOLS AND PANS

Bain-marie (see page 10)

Digital candy thermometer

2 cookie sheets lined with parchment, aluminum foil, or wax paper.

YIELD

40 to 48 candies

TECHNIQUE TIP
How to temper chocolate

You will need a digital thermometer to temper chocolate. The room you are working in needs to be between 62°F and 72°F. If the temperature is significantly higher than 72°F, it will be difficult to temper chocolate, so I don't recommend attempting this process in the heat of the summer. Make sure your cutting board, knife, bowl, and rubber spatula are clean and completely dry. Foreign particles and water will prevent the fat from crystallizing in the optimal formation. Prepare a bain-marie. Chop the chocolate into ½-inch pieces. Scrape 90 percent of the small pieces of chocolate into the bowl of the bain-marie. Melt the chocolate, stirring every minute or so, and remove from the heat when it reaches the temperatures listed on the chart below for the chocolate that you are using. Add the reserved 10 percent of the chopped chocolate. This chocolate will function as a seed crystal—it is already tempered, and the fat molecules in the melted chocolate will follow the same crystal formation. Stir and scrape the chocolate with a rubber spatula every 4 minutes until it cools to the temperature on the chart below.

Test the chocolate to see if it is ready by smearing a small droplet on a clean counter surface or piece of parchment or wax paper. If the room you are working in is not too warm (over 72°F), the smeared chocolate should dry within 5 minutes. If you have smeared it on paper, you should be able to peel the paper off the chocolate. If you smeared it on the counter, it should scrape off easily. If it is not drying and setting, stir the chocolate and allow it to cool another degree or two before testing it again.

Allow the bain-marie to continue to simmer as you dip your cookies. As the tempered chocolate cools, you can reheat it very gently within the temperature range listed on the chart.

Chocolate	Heat to	Cool to
Dark	120°F	82–87°F
Milk	112°F	81–84°F
White	110°F	81–84°F

Milk Chocolate Crunch Candies

Pectin's gelling power

Quince

Pectin is a polysaccharide, a large molecule made up of numerous sugar molecules consecutively linked together. Pectin is used to thicken jellies and set candies because of its ability to trap water molecules. In order for pectin to properly gel jellies and candies, it must be used with sugar in an acidic environment. Pectin exists naturally in the cell walls of most fruits and it is extracted from these plants by boiling.

When you are making fruit candies or *pâté de fruit*, you cook the fruit puree with an equal amount of sugar (by weight). This sugar absorbs some of the water naturally present in the fruit puree. Fruit pectin is added and it absorbs a portion of the water as well—in the case of quince, enough natural pectin is extracted from the core and the seeds that no additional pectin is needed. You boil the sugar-saturated fruit puree until it reaches around 221°F to 225°F (depending on the fruit), a temperature range that indicates that enough water has boiled off and the solution is 74 to 76 percent dry matter. The pectin holds the remaining water molecules. Water holding pectin molecules, however, in most fruit-sugar solutions have a negative electrical charge and they are not attracted to each other. Acidic conditions (the addition of lemon juice or tartaric or citric acid) reduce the electrical charge and encourage the pectin molecules to join, encapsulating the water molecules and thus properly setting the jelly candies.

Quince may truly be the forbidden fruit. With its fuzzy yellow skin and its hard, dry tannic flesh, it is not meant to be eaten raw. Other than an alluring aroma it releases as it ripens, and the tree's golden yellow blossoms in the spring, raw quince grants no sensual pleasures.

But when cooked, candied, roasted, or jellied, quince undergoes an almost magical metamorphosis, transforming from the proverbial ugly duckling of the orchard into one of the most seductive, hedonistic fruits available.

Indeed, quince is one of my favorite fruits. Available domestically in the fall and occasionally in the spring when it is imported from South America, quince is most commonly found in the United States in specialty stores in the form of jelly and paste (these are generally used as condiments on cheese boards). In Korea, according to a culinary student of mine, quince is used only in perfumes and body creams, a testament to its compelling aroma and persnickety flavor when raw.

One quirky property of quince is the change in color it undergoes—from a golden yellow to a pale, rusty red—when it is cooked for a long period in water with a high concentration of sugar. I cook quince for hours to obtain this striking rusty red hue for syrups that I use with all my fall apple, quince, pear, and pomegranate desserts.

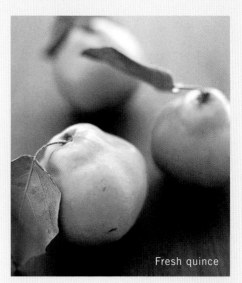

Fresh quince

Quince Fruit Jellies

Cooked quince has an incredibly earthy, round, rich, pear-honey-pineapple-like flavor. One of the best ways to savor its essence is to make quince jellies (in French, *pâté de fruit*). Ordinarily, *pâté de fruit* recipes call for pectin as a gelling agent. The core and seeds of the quince are naturally high in pectin, which—if cooked and extracted properly—is enough to set these candies. This recipe is, admittedly, a bit tricky, but these heavenly delights are worth the trouble.

TO MAKE THE QUINCE PUREE

Prepare and cut the quince.
Bring 3 cups of water and the sugar to boil in a large saucepan. Peel the quinces and cut off the fuzzy stem on the bottom of the fruit. Chop each quince into 8 pieces, leaving the core intact.

Add the quince to the pan and bring the fruit to a simmer. Cook the fruit slowly, uncovered, until the quince begins to take on a rose-rust color, 1½ to 2 hours. Add the lemon peel slivers and continue to cook for 20 minutes.

Process the quince.
Remove from the heat and take out the lemon peel. Pour the cooked quince and its syrup into a blender and puree. Pass the puree through a strainer and into a bowl, pushing and squeezing the fruit through with the back of a ladle or a rubber spatula. Discard the pulp and seeds. Pour the strained quince puree back into the saucepan.

TO MAKE THE QUINCE JELLIES

Cook the quince candy.
Add the sugar to the pan of quince puree and bring it to a boil over medium heat, whisking every 1 to 2 minutes. Cook the puree for 10 to 20 minutes on medium-high heat, stirring continuously with a whisk. During this time the puree will bubble, turn a darker red/rust color, and reduce in volume. About 10 minutes into the cooking process, put a thermometer into the puree. When the quince reaches 221°F, add the lemon juice and cook for 2 minutes to boil off the excess water in the lemon juice.

Test for doneness.
See BEYOND THE BASICS: *Pectin's gelling power, page 196.*

Test the quince candy by dribbling a tiny bit of hot quince on a clean, cool countertop and let cool for 1 to 2 minutes. If the candy does not peel off the counter cleanly, add another tablespoon of lemon juice and continue cooking the candy for 1 to 2 minutes. Test the quince candy again. When the candy is set, pour into the prepared pan and cool for 4 hours or overnight.

Shape and sugar the quince jellies.
Place the sugar in a small bowl. Cut the quince candy into rectangles or squares, or punch out circles with a cookie cutter and roll in granulated sugar.

Serving Suggestions
Serve these candies on a tray any time of the day.

Storage
The candies will keep, sealed and in a cool, dry place, for 1 month.

PUREE

3 cups sugar

4 large quinces (2½ pounds)

2 slivers of lemon peel, ½ inch wide x 1½ inches long

JELLIES

1 cup sugar

Juice of 3 lemons

1 cup sugar (for dipping the finished jellies)

SPECIAL TOOLS AND PANS

13 x 9-inch jellyroll pan

Blender

Candy thermometer

Fine-mesh strainer

YIELD

Approximately 4 dozen candies

Candied Kumquats and Candied Meyer Lemon Zest

**CANDIED KUMQUATS
AND KUMQUAT SYRUP**

¾ pound (2 cups) fresh
kumquats

1 cup sugar

2 tablespoons corn syrup

**CANDIED MEYER
LEMON ZEST AND
MEYER LEMON SYRUP**

4 Meyer lemons

1 cup sugar

2 tablespoons corn syrup

YIELD

Kumquats: 1 cup kumquat
syrup and ¾ cup chopped
candied kumquats

Meyer lemon zest: ½ cup
Meyer lemon zest syrup
and ½ cup candied Meyer
lemon strips

I use these candied fruits as garnishes on many desserts at Chanterelle, and they, along with their syrups, are a component in several of the recipes in this book.

Make the candied kumquats and syrup.
Slice off the ends of each kumquat, ¹⁄₁₆ inch round sliver. Slice the remaining fruit into 3 to 5 slices depending on its size. Combine the sliced kumquats, sugar, ⅓ cup water, and corn syrup in a small saucepan and bring the pan to a boil over medium-high heat. Immediately turn down the heat and slowly simmer until the kumquats become somewhat translucent, 6 to 10 minutes. Remove from the heat and allow to cool in the syrup.

These kumquats in their syrup keep, in a sealed container and refrigerated, for several weeks.

Make the candied Meyer lemon zest and syrup.
Using a peeler with a square head, remove the zest of the lemons in long, even strokes. Slice the zest into long thin strips to make ½ cup of julienned Meyer lemon zest (½ inch long x ¹⁄₁₆ inch thick). In a small saucepan, combine the zest and 2 cups cold water and bring to a boil. Strain out the zest and discard the water. Repeat this process 3 more times. Combine the blanched zest, sugar, ⅓ cup water, and corn syrup in the saucepan and bring to a boil. Turn down the heat and simmer the lemon peel for about 30 minutes.

This candied peel in its syrup will keep, in a sealed container and refrigerated, for several weeks.

BEYOND THE BASICS
Blanching citrus rind

What we experience as "bitter" flavor in foods (including citrus rinds) is often attributable to tannins. Tannins are found in many fruits—especially in the skin or rind—and some vegetables, among other foods.

Cooking fruits and vegetables in water, even for the brief time involved in blanching, causes the cell walls to soften, releasing undesirable tannins as well as desirable essential oils and acids. Since tannins are water-soluble but essential oils are not, tannins are more likely than oils to be leached out by blanching; so despite the loss of some flavor due to the loss of oils, the net effect of blanching is to decrease astringency more than to decrease flavor.

In the candied kumquat recipe, it is not necessary to blanch the kumquat slices. Kumquats are very rich in pectin, and in the process of simmering them with sugar, the naturally present pectin absorbs and binds with the proteins containing tannins, taking their flavors out of circulation.

Guava and Passion-Fruit Jellies

This is an intensely tropical treat. The guava and passion fruit complement each other and deepen the combined flavor. The guava is hard to coax into a *pâté de fruit*, or fruit jelly, because it has very little natural pectin and acidity, but passion fruit has both in abundance, so the combination gels without having to add any excess pectin and acid. Use fresh passion fruit and push the pulp through a fine strainer to obtain the juice or look in specialty stores or on the Web for passion-fruit puree. This puree is usually sold unsweetened or with 10 percent sugar.

4 cups sugar

7 medium fresh, ripe guavas (1¾ pounds)

3 tablespoons apple pectin

1 cup unsweetened passion-fruit juice

SPECIAL TOOLS AND PANS

13 x 9-inch pan

Fine-mesh strainer

YIELD

Approximately 4 dozen candies

Cook the guava.
In a large heavy-bottomed saucepan, combine 1 cup sugar and 1 cup water and bring to a boil. Peel the guavas with a paring knife or peeler and chop into ½-inch pieces. Place the pieces in the syrup and simmer for 30 to 45 minutes, stirring the pan every few minutes, until the fruit falls apart and separates from the seeds easily. Remove the pan from the heat.

Strain the fruit.
Pass the cooked guava and syrup through a fine-mesh strainer and into a bowl, pushing and squeezing the fruit through with the back of a ladle or a rubber spatula. Discard the pulp and seeds left in the strainer.

Cook the guava and passion-fruit jelly.
Place the pectin and ¼ cup of the sugar in a small dry container and shake to thoroughly mix and set aside. In a heavy-bottomed pan, combine the guava puree, passion-fruit juice, and 1¾ cups of the sugar and bring to a boil over medium heat, whisking every minute or so to prevent it from burning. Whisk in the reserved pectin and sugar mixture and cook, continuously whisking, for 10 minutes. The puree will bubble, turn a darker rusty rose color, and reduce in volume.

Test the jelly for doneness.
See BEYOND THE BASICS: *Pectin's gelling power, page 196.*

About 8 minutes into the process, test the consistency of the jelly by dribbling a tiny bit of hot jelly on a clean, cool countertop and let cool for 1 to 2 minutes. If the jelly does not peel off the counter cleanly, continue cooking for 1 to 4 minutes. Test the jelly again. When the jelly is set, pour into the prepared pan and cool for 4 hours or overnight.

Shape and sugar the guava and passion-fruit jellies.
Place the sugar in a small bowl. Cut the jelly candy into rectangles or squares, or punch out circles with a cookie cutter and roll in granulated sugar.

Serving Suggestions
Serve these candies on a decorative tray any time of the day.

Storage
The candies will keep, sealed and in a cool, dry place, for 1 month.

Huckleberry Fruit Jellies

PUREE

1½ pounds fresh or frozen huckleberries

½ cup sugar

JELLIES

2 tablespoons apple pectin

3 cups sugar

Juice of 1 lime

SPECIAL TOOLS AND PANS

9 x 7½-inch pan

Fine-mesh strainer

Blender

YIELD

Approximately 4 dozen candies

Huckleberries are very special—as I elaborate in the accompanying sidebar, they cannot be cultivated, only grow in the northwest United States, and have a short season—so making desserts with them is always a treat. Huckleberry *pâté de fruit* is so good—pure essence of huckleberry, in all its sweet, acidic, tart, and earthy splendor. Huckleberries also have a lot of natural pectin, so they gel easily. You can substitute frozen huckleberries for fresh ones.

Prepare the huckleberry puree.
In a heavy-bottomed saucepan, toss the huckleberries with the ½ cup sugar. Bring to a boil over medium heat, stirring occasionally. The sugar will pull the juice out of the berries, transforming the mixture into a liquid. Once the berries are suspended in liquid, simmer for 4 minutes and remove from the heat. Pour the berries and liquid into a blender and puree until smooth.

Strain the fruit.
Pass the huckleberry puree through a fine-mesh strainer and into a bowl, pushing and squeezing the fruit pulp through with the back of a ladle or a rubber spatula. Return the strained puree to the saucepan, and discard any seeds or fruit pulp remaining in the strainer.

Cook the huckleberry jelly.
Place the pectin and ⅓ cup sugar in a small dry container with a cover and shake to thoroughly mix. Set aside. Add 2 cups sugar to the huckleberry puree and bring to a rapid boil over medium heat, whisking every minute or so to prevent it from burning. Whisk in the reserved pectin and sugar mixture until combined. Add the lime juice. Cook the jelly, while continuously whisking, for 10 minutes. The huckleberry puree will bubble, turn a darker, more intense purple, and reduce in volume.

Test the jelly for doneness.
See BEYOND THE BASICS: *Pectin's gelling power, page 196.*

About 8 minutes into the process, test the consistency of the jelly by dribbling a tiny bit of hot jelly on a clean, cool countertop and let cool for 1 to 2 minutes. If the jelly does not peel off the counter cleanly, continue cooking for 1 to 4 minutes. Test the jelly again. When the jelly is set, pour into the prepared pan and cool for 4 hours or overnight.

Shape and sugar the huckleberry jellies.
Place the sugar in a small bowl. Cut the jelly candy into rectangles or squares, or punch out circles with a cookie cutter and roll in granulated sugar.

Serving Suggestions
Serve these candies on a decorative tray any time of the day.

Storage
The candies will keep, sealed and in a cool, dry place, for 1 month.

INGREDIENT
Huckleberries

Wild huckleberries, most frequently found in the mountainous wilderness of Montana, Idaho, Oregon, and Washington, are available fresh from about mid-August to early October. In appearance, they resemble wild blueberries (small and round) but are a darker shade of purple/blue. They are tart, earthy, and packed with flavor—similar to a combination of a Concord grape and a blackberry—and thus are perfect for pies, jellies, ice creams, candy, or sauces.

Horticulturists have been struggling for years to domesticate the huckleberry, making it available for farmers to grow. But most attempts have yielded plants that produce few to no berries. Huckleberry plants and cuttings from the wild, transplanted to other locations, usually die within a year or two. The berry's willingness to grow only in the wild at high altitudes contributes to its allure and mystique, making it highly sought after in late summer.

At the Sawtooth Berry Fields of the Gifford Pinchot National Forest in southwest Washington, you can find recreational pickers and families, members of the Yakima Indian tribe, and commercial pickers holding a Forest Service permit all competing for space around huckleberry patches. These berries are also a favorite of the black bear, though once a bear shows up there's not much competition around the berry bush.

The Yakima Indian Nation has a long and rich cultural history linked to the huckleberry season and harvest. The Forest Service grants this tribe exclusive access to the berry fields each August before commercial picking permits are released. Hundreds of migrant workers descend upon this region and areas of Oregon during the huckleberry season to pick berries, which are then sold on the open market. Recreational pickers can pick up to 3 gallons of berries without having to pay for and obtain a permit from the Forest Service.

Huckleberry and Guava Passion-Fruit Jellies

EDIBLE GARNISHES AND SNACKS

CHAPTER NINE

Thin and Delicate Peanut Brittle

1 cup sugar

1/8 teaspoon cream of tartar

1/2 cup finely ground peanuts

1/4 teaspoon finely ground
sea salt

SPECIAL TOOLS AND PANS

17 x 11-inch baking pan

Food processor or coffee grinder

Nonstick reusable silicone
baking pad (optional)

HINT

**Perfectly round disks
of peanut brittle.**
To give the brittle a more
finished look, before baking it
you can sprinkle the ground
caramel and nut mixture inside
a round cookie cutter (2 inches
in diameter) on a prepared
pan, 1/8 inch thick. Repeat this
process until you have 12 circles.
Carefully place the pan in the
oven and bake until the caramel
has melted and begins to bubble,
4 to 6 minutes. Remove from
the oven, cool completely, and
remove the disks. If you would
like to shape the disks, remove
them from the baking pan
before the caramel has cooled
completely and place them on
a desired form (a rolling pin
or inverted muffin cups, for
example). When completely
cooled, the disks will hold the
shape of the form.

This is one of the easiest recipes I make. It is also one of the most rewarding.
Brittle stands alone as a great, simple, crunchy end to a meal. In the
restaurant I prepare various nut brittles and use them in endless ways:
as a crunchy topping for ice cream, as a cookie, as a garnish for caramel
mousse. In a dessert, texture is as important as flavor. Nothing can replace
the satisfaction one feels from a blend of crispy and creamy on the tongue.
This recipe calls for peanuts, but you can easily substitute almonds,
hazelnuts, or pistachios.

Preheat the oven to 350°F. Line a 17 x 11-inch
baking pan with parchment, aluminum foil,
or a nonstick baking pad.

Cook the caramel.
See BEYOND THE BASICS: *Cooking caramel
successfully, page 107.*

In a small, heavy-bottomed saucepan combine
the sugar, 1/3 cup water, and the cream of tartar.
Cover and cook over high heat until the syrup
comes to a very rapid boil. Remove the cover and
continue to cook on medium-high heat until the
sugar has turned a golden brown caramel color.
Pour the caramel onto the prepared baking pan
and let cool.

Grind the caramel.
When the caramel is cool, break it into 1-inch
pieces. Place the pieces in a food processor or
coffee grinder and grind to the consistency
of granular sugar. Stir in the ground nuts.

Bake and shape the brittle.
Reline your baking sheet with parchment paper,
aluminum foil, or a nonstick baking pad.

Spread the caramel and nut mixture onto
the baking sheet in an even layer, approximately
1/8 inch thick. Bake until the caramel melts and
begins to bubble, 4 to 6 minutes. Remove from
the oven and immediately sprinkle the salt evenly
over the melted caramel. When the brittle is cool,
break it up into small pieces and serve.

Storage
This brittle will keep, sealed, in a cool, dry place,
for 2 weeks. Humid conditions cause the brittle to
lose its crunch and become sticky, overly chewy,
and generally unpleasing. Though you might
have the proper storage conditions, I do not
recommend making this brittle on a humid day.

Thin and Delicate Peanut Brittle

Fruit Chips

A fruit chip should be beautiful in its appearance, preserving the natural color of the fruit. It should have a crisp, light texture. And, most important, it should taste of the fruit's concentrated essence, maintaining the fruit's inherent acidity in order to highlight its flavor.

Fruit chips are a delightful garnish on any plated dessert. Or simply make them as a snack, great for nibbling in the late afternoon. At Chanterelle, I make them from many fruits: blood oranges, rhubarb, as well as all the ones below. The recipes for each chip are very similar, but each fruit requires a different technique for applying simple syrup—sugar and water—which helps to brighten the flavor and enhance the crispiness of the finished baked chip.

THE SWEET LIFE

Apple and Pear Chips

Preheat the oven to 225°F (200°F for a convection oven).

Boil the sugar syrup.
In a medium-sized saucepan, combine the sugar, 1 cup water, and cream of tartar and bring to a boil. Lower the heat and continue to simmer while you slice the apples.

Slice the apples.
Wash and dry the apples. Do not peel them or core them. Depending on how you would like the apple cross sections to appear, you can position the apple in either a vertical position, with the cheek facing the blade, or in a horizontal position, with the stem facing the blade.

Cut a slice about ½ inch thick off one end of the apple so that you begin slicing with a flat surface. With a slicing machine, slice the apples into $\frac{1}{16}$-inch cross sections. If you do not have a slicing machine, you can use a mandoline. Make sure you use a small apple that will fit on a mandoline. With either the mandoline or the slicer, you will be left with a ¾-inch-thick section of apple that you cannot slice. Discard these apple scraps.

Poach the apple slices.
See BEYOND THE BASICS: *Enzymatic browning in fruit, page 143.*

Immediately immerse the apple slices in the boiling sugar syrup and cook, stirring with a slotted spoon. When the syrup has resumed a rapid boil, remove the apple slices with a slotted spoon and transfer to a wire rack set over a pan to cool.

Bake the apple slices.
Lay the apple slices flat—without any wrinkles—on your baking pans, making sure that the slices do not touch or overlap one another. Bake for 30 to 45 minutes in a convection oven or 40 to 50 minutes in a regular oven, rotating the pans halfway through baking. To test if the apple chips are done, remove one from the oven and allow it to cool on the counter. If it is crispy once it has cooled, then it is done. If the apples are browning, take them out of the oven. Remove the apple slices from the pan while they are hot, and cool on a clean, dry countertop.

Serving Suggestions
Use these chips as a crunchy note and a garnish on any apple dessert. Or enjoy them alone as the most delightful snack ever made.

Storage
The chips will keep, sealed and in a cool place, for 2 weeks.

¾ cup sugar

¼ teaspoon cream of tartar

2 crisp red apples or underripe pears

SPECIAL TOOLS AND PANS

Food slicer or mandoline

2 nonstick baking pans or 2 baking pans lined with nonstick silicone baking pads

YIELD

20 to 30 apple or pear chips

Pineapple Chips

¾ cup sugar

1 medium pineapple

SPECIAL TOOLS AND PANS

Food slicer

Strainer

2 nonstick baking pans or
2 baking pans lined with
nonstick silicone baking pads

YIELD

30 pineapple chips

Preheat the oven to 225°F (200°F for a convection oven).

Make the sugar syrup.
In a small saucepan, combine the sugar and 1 cup water and bring to a boil. Boil for 2 minutes. Remove from the heat and let it cool to room temperature.

Carve the pineapple.
Slice the top and bottom off the pineapple. Slice the fruit in half, crosswise. Save half to eat fresh. Stand the other half up vertically and gently, with a serrated knife, just barely trim the outside rind; don't cut so much off that you remove the eyes. You need to leave a little bit of the rind to hold the thinly sliced pineapple cross sections together.

Slice the pineapple.
With a slicing machine, slice the trimmed pineapple into $1/16$-inch round cross sections. Immerse the slices in the cooled syrup and let sit for 1 hour at room temperature. Strain the fruit, allowing the pineapple slices to remain suspended in a colander or mesh strainer for 5 minutes to let all the excess liquid drain.

Bake the pineapple slices.
Lay out the pineapple slices—without any wrinkles—on the baking pans, making sure that the pineapple slices do not touch or overlap one another. Bake for 30 to 45 minutes in a convection oven or 40 to 50 minutes in a regular oven, rotating the pans halfway through baking. To test if the chips are done, remove one from the oven and allow it to cool on the counter. If it is crispy once it has cooled, then it is done. If the slices are browning, take them out of the oven. Remove the slices from the pan while they are hot, and cool on a clean, dry countertop.

Serving Suggestions
Use these chips as a crunchy note or a garnish on any tropical dessert. Or enjoy them alone as the most delightful snack ever made.

Storage
The chips will keep, sealed and in a cool place, for 2 weeks.

Strawberry Chips

Preheat the oven to 225°F (200°F for a convection oven).

Boil the sugar syrup.
In a small saucepan, combine the sugar and ¾ cup water and bring to a boil. Boil for 2 minutes. Remove from the heat and let it cool to room temperature.

Slice the strawberries.
Slice the stems off the strawberries so that the berries have a flat end. Slice the strawberries on a food slicer or mandoline as thinly as possible. Or line the berries up on a cutting board with the flat side down and thinly slice with a chef's knife. Slice ½ to ⅔ of each strawberry and use the remaining strawberry chunks for a fruit salad or a shake or a snack.

Bake the strawberry slices.
Lay out the strawberry slices on the baking pans. With a pastry brush, paint a thin layer of sugar syrup over each strawberry. Bake for 30 to 45 minutes in a convection oven or 40 to 50 minutes in a regular oven, rotating the pans halfway through baking. To test if the chips are done, remove one from the oven and allow it to cool on the counter. If it is crispy once it has cooled, then it is done. If the slices are browning, take them out of the oven. Remove the slices from the pan while they are hot, and cool on a clean, dry countertop.

Serving Suggestions
Use these chips as a crunchy note or a garnish on any creamy dessert. Or enjoy them alone as the most delightful snack ever made.

Storage
The chips will keep, sealed and in a cool place, for 2 weeks.

¾ cup sugar

12 large firm strawberries (1 pound)

SPECIAL TOOLS AND PANS

Pastry brush

Food slicer or mandoline (optional)

2 nonstick baking pans or 2 baking pans lined with nonstick silicone baking pads

YIELD

60 small strawberry chips

SAUCES AND CREAMY ACCOMPANIMENTS

CHAPTER TEN

Blood Orange Caramel Sauce

1 ¼ cups sugar

¼ teaspoon cream of tartar
or ½ teaspoon lemon juice

1 cup blood orange juice

YIELD

1 ½ cups sauce

This sauce has a beautiful, rusty red color, and its flavor marries well with most citrus desserts.

Make caramel and add the blood orange juice.
See BEYOND THE BASICS: *Cooking caramel successfully, page 107.*

In a heavy-bottomed saucepan combine the sugar with ¼ cup plus 2 tablespoons water and either the cream of tartar or the lemon juice. Cover and cook over high heat until the syrup comes to a very rapid boil. Remove the cover and continue to cook at medium-high heat until the sugar takes on a golden brown caramel color. Remove from the heat, stand back, and slowly add the blood orange juice. The mixture will bubble and steam furiously. When the bubbling has subsided, return to the heat. Whisk the caramel and then let mixture come to a rolling boil. Immediately remove from the heat. Transfer to a bowl and place in the refrigerator to chill before serving.

Serving Suggestions
Serve this sauce cold or at room temperature with any citrus or chocolate dessert. I also recommend the Candied Kumquat Mascarpone Parfait (page 153), Meyer Lemon Curd Tart (page 18), and Goat Cheesecake (page 42).

Storage
The sauce will keep, refrigerated, for 1 week.

Cider Caramel Sauce

5 cups apple cider

1 cup sugar

¼ teaspoon cream of tartar
or ½ teaspoon lemon juice

YIELD

1 ¼ cups sauce

This is a simple sauce to make when apple cider is abundant in the fall and goes well with any apple or pear dessert.

Reduce the apple cider.
In a heavy-bottomed saucepan, boil the apple cider until it reduces to 1½ cups. Set it aside.

Make the caramel and finish the sauce.
See BEYOND THE BASICS: *Cooking caramel successfully, page 107.*

In a heavy-bottomed saucepan combine the sugar, ¼ cup water, and either the cream of tartar or lemon juice. Cover and cook over high heat until it comes to a very rapid boil. Remove the cover and continue to cook at medium-high heat until the sugar takes on a golden brown caramel color. Remove from the heat, stand back, and slowly add the reduced apple cider. The mixture will bubble and steam furiously. When the bubbling has subsided, return to the heat. Whisk the caramel and then let the mixture come to a rolling boil. Immediately remove from the heat. Transfer to a bowl and place in the refrigerator to chill before serving.

Serving Suggestions
Serve this sauce warm with any apple, pear, or quince dessert. I recommend the Apple and Quince Tart (page 23), the Stuffed Roasted Fall Apples (page 182), the Roasted Apple or Pear Beignets (page 178), or the Spiced Apple and Sour Cream Cake (page 48). To reheat it, gently heat the sauce in a saucepan over low heat.

Storage
This sauce will keep, refrigerated, for 1 week.

Brandied Crème Fraîche Sauce

I love crème fraîche, and brandy rounds out the flavor, tempering the natural tanginess of the cream without undermining its essential characteristics. If you enjoy the flavor of crème fraîche as much as I do, you can serve this sauce as a complement to almost any dessert in this book.

1 cup crème fraîche

2 tablespoons sugar

1 tablespoon brandy

SPECIAL TOOLS AND PANS

Balloon whisk (optional)

YIELD

1 ¼ cups whipped crème fraîche

Whip the crème fraîche.
In a stainless-steel bowl, combine the crème fraîche, sugar, and brandy. Whisk the mixture until it thickens and holds the lines of a whisk with soft peaks. (The cream might loosen up a bit as you begin to whisk it.)

Serving Suggestions
Serve this sauce cold with any dessert.

Storage
Use this topping immediately or store in the refrigerator for up to 4 days.

Rum Caramel Sauce

The rum tempers the sometimes cloying sweetness of caramel, giving the sauce an addictive buttery richness.

1 cup sugar

Pinch of cream of tartar

½ cup heavy cream

2 tablespoons dark rum

YIELD

1 cup sauce

Caramelize the sugar and finish the sauce.
See BEYOND THE BASICS: *Cooking caramel successfully, page 107.*

In a heavy-bottomed saucepan combine the sugar, ¼ cup water, and the cream of tartar. Cover and cook over high heat until it comes to a very rapid boil. Remove the cover and continue to cook at medium-high heat until the sugar takes on a golden brown caramel color. Remove from the heat, stand back, and slowly add the cream. The mixture will bubble and steam furiously. When the bubbling has subsided, return to the heat. Whisk the caramel and then let the mixture come to a rolling boil. Immediately remove from the heat and add the rum.

Serving Suggestions
This sauce should always be served warm. To reheat this sauce after it has been refrigerated, either heat the sauce directly over the stove, stirring with a rubber spatula, or place the container of sauce in a bowl of hot water. It goes well with any of the chocolate desserts in this book, and with the Brandied Dried Fig and Vanilla Soufflé (page 124), Maple Walnut Soufflé (page 122), Pumpkin Soufflé (page 126), and Roasted Apple Beignets (page 178).

Storage
This sauce will keep, refrigerated, for 1 week.

Milk Chocolate Caramel Sauce

¾ cup sugar

Pinch of cream of tartar

½ cup cream

½ cup crème fraîche

3 ounces milk chocolate (36 percent cocoa solids or higher)

Pinch of salt

SPECIAL TOOLS AND PANS

Bain-marie (see page 10)

YIELD

1 ½ cups sauce

Served warm, this sauce is a delicious accompaniment to nearly any of the chocolate desserts in this book.

Make the caramel cream.
See BEYOND THE BASICS: *Cooking caramel successfully, page 107.*

In a heavy-bottomed saucepan combine the sugar, ¼ cup water, and the cream of tartar. Cover and cook over high heat until it comes to a very rapid boil. Remove the cover and continue to cook at medium-high heat until the sugar takes on a golden brown caramel color. Remove from the heat, stand back, and slowly add the cream. The mixture will bubble and steam furiously. When the bubbling has subsided, return to the heat. Whisk the caramel and then let the mixture come to a rolling boil. Whisk in the crème fraîche. Remove from the heat and cool for 10 minutes.

Melt the chocolate and finish the sauce.
Meanwhile, in the bowl of a bain-marie, melt the chocolate, stirring occasionally with a rubber spatula; this will take about 5 minutes. Add a ladleful of caramel cream to the melted chocolate, whisking until the mixture is smooth. Continue adding the cream, whisking thoroughly after each addition. Add the salt. The sauce should be shiny and smooth once you have added all the cream. Remove from the heat and serve warm or transfer to a bowl and refrigerate until using.

Serving Suggestions
Serve this sauce warm. Reheat the sauce directly over the stove, stirring with a rubber spatula, or place the container of sauce in a bowl of hot water.

Storage
This sauce will keep, refrigerated, for 1 week.

Toffee Sauce

4 tablespoons (2 ounces) butter

⅓ cup light brown sugar

¼ cup sugar

⅓ cup plus 1 tablespoon light corn syrup

⅓ cup heavy cream

1 ½ tablespoons rum, brandy, or bourbon

YIELD

1 ⅓ cups sauce

This sauce is an integral part of the recipe for Date Cake (page 45). This sauce differs from Rum Caramel Sauce (page 213) because it has brown sugar, giving it a subtle molasses flavor.

Cook the butter with the sugars.
In a heavy-bottomed saucepan, combine the butter, light brown sugar, white sugar, corn syrup, and 1 tablespoon of water and bring to a boil. Simmer for 2 minutes. Remove from the heat and let cool until it is slightly warm to the touch.

Finish the sauce with the cream and alcohol.
Add the cream, 2 tablespoons at a time, whisking after each addition. Once you have added all of the cream, whisk in the alcohol of choice. Remove from the heat and serve warm or transfer to a bowl and refrigerate until using.

Serving Suggestions
Serve this sauce warm. Reheat the sauce directly over the stove, stirring with a rubber spatula, or place the container of sauce in a bowl of hot water. It matches up well with the Date Cake with Toffee Sauce (page 45) and the Brandied Dried Fig and Vanilla Soufflé (page 124).

Storage
This sauce will keep, refrigerated, for 1 week.

Plum Caramel Sauce

The black plums give this sauce a particularly beautiful, rusty purple color.

Make the plum puree.

Quarter the plums and discard the pits. Combine the plums, 2 tablespoons sugar, and ¼ cup of water together in a medium-sized saucepan. Bring to a boil over medium-high heat, reduce the heat, and simmer for 10 to 15 minutes. Pass the cooked plums and their cooking liquid through a fine-mesh strainer, using the back of a ladle or rubber spatula to push as much of the fruit through as possible. Discard the skins. Set the puree aside to cool.

Caramelize the sugar.

See BEYOND THE BASICS: *Cooking caramel successfully, page 107.*

In a covered heavy-bottomed saucepan, combine the remaining sugar, cream of tartar, and 3 tablespoons water. Cover and bring to a boil over medium-high heat. After 1 minute of rapid boiling, uncover the pot. Cook the syrup until the sugar caramelizes and reaches a light golden brown color, about 5 minutes. Remove from the heat, stand back, and carefully add the plum puree. The caramel will erupt with bubbles and steam. Place the pot back on the stove over medium heat and whisk the plum puree until the caramel is completely dissolved and smooth. Remove from the heat and cool.

Serving Suggestions

Serve this sauce cold or warm. Or serve it at room temperature with the Roasted Apple or Pear Beignets (page 178), Plum and Almond Tart (page 26), or Vanilla Panna Cotta (page 99).

Storage

This sauce will keep, refrigerated, for 1 week.

¾ pound ripe black plums (approximately 4 medium plums)

⅔ cup plus 2 tablespoons sugar

Pinch of cream of tartar

SPECIAL TOOLS AND PANS

Fine-mesh strainer

YIELD

1 cup sauce

TECHNIQUE TIP
Sugar and egg yolks

BEYOND THE BASICS
Egg yolk foams and sabayons

There are numerous custard recipes in this book in which you will be instructed to first whisk sugar with egg yolks. Make sure you do not leave the sugar and yolk mixture unattended for very long or it will curdle. Sugar is hygroscopic—it pulls the water out of surrounding materials. When sugar is left sitting in egg yolks it will draw the water out of the raw egg yolks and cook or curdle your egg yolks. The result will be little bits of hard egg yolk in your custard. If these lumps do appear, fortunately they can be strained out later with a fine-mesh strainer. If you need to step away from your egg mixture, to avoid curdled yolks, make sure you whisk the sugar and the yolks together briskly for about 3 minutes.

The raw ingredients of a cooked sabayon, before the addition of whipped cream, are egg yolks, wine (some sabayons are made with another liquid flavoring element, not alcohol), salt, and sugar. These ingredients are whisked over a double boiler until they are transformed into an ethereal, creamy, light, flavorful custard. This transformation is a very interesting process.

This mixture of egg yolks, wine, salt, and sugar is whisked and heated simultaneously, causing most of the egg yolk proteins to unwind and bump into each other. The water (wine), sugar, and fat dilute and coat the proteins, slowing the process in which unwound proteins form elaborate scaffolding-like structures. With the help of continued and vigorous whisking over heat, the unwound protein strands link together around water and air molecules, sealing them into their structure and forming an egg gel. This gel becomes a thick and aerated custard as the air sealed in the scaffolding-like structure expands through exposure to more heat.

Traditional Italian zabaglione (the above-mentioned custard without cream) is served right away because, like a soufflé, this custard will deflate after it rests for a few minutes. The air, trapped in the egg gel, which expanded when it was heated, deflates as it cools.

Wine has a few key roles in the sabayon. Most important, the alcohol carries flavor. It also contributes water, which dilutes the proteins. If you use an alcoholic beverage with too high an alcohol content (anything over 20 percent), your sabayon will curdle and collapse very early in the whisking process. An alcoholic beverage such as Grand Marnier has much less water to dilute the proteins and the mixture coagulates too quickly at a lower temperature, leaving less time for whisking and aeration. So if you would like to make a sabayon with a liqueur instead of wine, dilute the liqueur with an equal amount of water.

Sometimes a sabayon with the right amount of alcohol will collapse and turn into a dense yellow mass in your bowl. This happens when the sabayon is cooked for too long. Too much heat and agitation can cause the protein scaffolding to collapse, releasing the air and water trapped inside.

Sauternes Sabayon

While the greatest of the Sauternes—such as Chateau D'Yquem, which runs in the hundreds of dollars per bottle—are meant only for drinking, one of my favorite dessert accompaniments is a sabayon, an egg yolk foam custard, flavored with Sauternes. A dollop turns any fruit—roasted, poached, or fresh—into a five-star dessert. If you prefer, you can substitute a Muscat wine, a sweet Riesling, champagne, or Marsala, each of which will add its own unique flavor to the custard. Most decent liquor stores carry a Sauternes that costs no more than $20, and this is the appropriate choice for the following recipe.

If you are interested in serving a nondairy dessert, you can omit the cream and serve the sauce as a classic zabaglione (whipped egg yolk foam). I do, however, love the added touch of the cream: it mellows the sauce and gives it body and sensuality.

Cook the sabayon.
See BEYOND THE BASICS: *Egg yolk foams and sabayons, page 216.*

In the bowl of a bain-marie, whisk together the egg yolks and sugar. Whisk in the sweet wine and salt and place the bowl over the simmering water. Whisk briskly until the mixture has thickened, tripled in volume, and holds the lines of a whisk, 5 to 10 minutes. As you whisk your sabayon you will smell the alcohol in the Sauternes evaporating.

Finish the sabayon.
Remove the sabayon from the heat and cool slightly. If you would like it finished with cream, allow the sauce to cool completely and fold in the lightly whipped cream.

Serving Suggestions
If you would like to serve it in the classic Italian style (zabaglione made tableside), then serve it immediately.

Storage
This sabayon will keep, refrigerated, for 1 day.

6 egg yolks

½ cup plus 2 tablespoons sugar

½ cup Sauternes

Pinch of salt

¾ cup cream, lightly whipped (optional)

SPECIAL TOOLS AND PANS

Bain-marie (see page 10)

Whisk, preferably a balloon whisk

INGREDIENT
Sauternes

Sauternes, one of the greatest dessert wines of the world, begins in paradox and ends in poetry. Grown in a small subregion of Bordeaux, the grapes are for the most part the same as those used in dry white Bordeaux wine— mostly Semillon, a touch of Sauvignon Blanc, with the addition of a small amount of Muscadelle. What makes these white wine grapes produce a Sauternes and not a dry white wine is rot. The grapes overripen on the vine, shriveling up like raisins. With the help of a noble mold that develops on the outside of the grapes, causing enzymatic reactions in the fruit, the flavor of these white wine grapes undergoes a divine transformation. While the process might sound a bit unappealing, the results are anything but. Drinking Sauternes is truly one of the great pleasures offered by food and wine; it has a honeyed, apricot, vanilla, caramel flavor that is unmistakable and irresistible.

Acknowledgments

Karen and David Waltuck are Chanterelle. For over a quarter century, they have devoted themselves to creating one of America's most extraordinary restaurants, and I have been fortunate enough to be a part of their team for the last six years. Without their personally managed, warm, supportive working environment, I could never have fine-tuned my recipes and my skills as a pastry chef. I am forever indebted to them for lending me their kitchen and trusting me with their clients.

My sous chef for my first six years at Chanterelle, Susan Punturieri, was my lifeline throughout the writing of this book. We came to the job together, and we had an inseparable partnership. I simply could never have done this job without her. Her down-to-earth realism about the daily demands of the job has been both an inspiration and a bedrock. I've never worked with anyone as skilled and focused as Susan, and I am humbled by her dedication and loyalty. Thank you, Susan.

The staff — kitchen, floor, and manage-rial — at Chanterelle are an amazing bunch. Hardworking, creative, steadfast, and full of life, they make Chanterelle what it is. Never, in the numerous restaurants at which I've worked, have I encountered a more loyal and professional team. I would be particularly remiss not to mention a few individuals at the restaurant: Roger Dagorn, our master sommelier, has been warmly supportive from the first; George Stinson, our GM, makes the restaurant run so smoothly and is a generous comrade to us all; Vincent Nicolai, our former maître d', made Chanterelle a happier place to work, and his assistance in translating from French was much appreciated.

My pastry staff: first and foremost, thanks to Yoko Paker, my new sous chef, who subbed for me so I could squeeze enough time out of my life to write this book. Her inquisitiveness and obsession with perfection have kept me on my toes and taught me so much. I cherish her dedication and friendship. To Tara Kruse and Atsuko Takahashi, for covering for me during my earlier maternity leave and for their endless good cheer and hard work. And to all my numerous students, externs, and stagières: thank you for being so gracious and interested in learning from me, because teaching you has taught me what it is that I wanted to communicate in this book.

Specifically, I owe a special thanks to the externs who tested many of the recipes for this book: Rachel Thebault, Lillian Chan, and Alex D'Addio, to name a few.

Everyone who works as a chef is the sum of the cooks they worked for and alongside through the years. In my own career, a few who stand out for their extraordinary talents are Lydia Shire and Susan Regis, Rick Katz, Brad Levy, Roland Passot, Eric Coesel, Lynn Sheehan, and David Pasternack.

Kirsten Hubbard, my science guru and a former student extern, encouraged me to write this book, but more important, she encouraged me to get it right. One of the great pleasures of tackling this project was our seemingly endless correspondence in which we struggled to make sense of the science in ways that were both simple and true. Everything that in the end we got right is due to her insight and attention to the smallest detail; anything we got wrong is due to my misinterpretations. And thanks are due to Brent Stockwell as well for coming in from the bullpen to answer a particularly thorny biochemistry question.

Finding and understanding good chocolate has been a central goal of mine, and I am very thankful to Robert Steinberg of Scharffen Berger Chocolate and to Pierrick Chouard of Plantations Chocolates, who both took time out of their busy schedules to discuss the sourcing and the process of making chocolate. Also I am grateful to Aaron Isaacson, the man behind Mr. Recipe, for helping me to untangle some facts about vanilla. Thanks as well to Toussaint Raharison, a photographer in Madagascar, who provided me with some lovely shots of cocoa and vanilla beans.

Tina Rupp took the beautiful photographs that make this book such a visual joy. Tina's extraordinary professionalism, clear vision, and calm amid the storm were a godsend. Alistair Turnbull, my prop stylist, came up with more gorgeous plates, colors, and accessories than I knew existed. And Gary Tooth, my book designer, not only has been the guiding creative force in bringing this book together, but has done so with warmth and a generous collaborative spirit.

I called on some friends and family to test my recipes in their own home kitchens, and I'm so grateful to Amy Margolis, Susan Karwoska, Roberta Moskowitz, and Tara Kruse for making my desserts for their families and friends.

Susan Ginsburg, my agent at Writers House, has been telling me to write cookbooks since I was eighteen years old. It only took me sixteen years, but I did it at last. Jill Cohen, Karen Murgolo, Karyn Gerhard, Matthew Ballast, Peggy Freudenthal, and the entire team at Bulfinch have been incredibly supportive of my work and of this book, and I am so grateful for their belief in me. Thanks are due as well to my publicists, Kim Yorio and Aimee Bianca at YC Media and Chloe Mata at Baltz & Company.

Thanks to my mom and my dad for standing behind me while I pursued this career. Thanks to my brothers, Aaron and Jonah, for being the first consumers of my desserts and for still eating them with relish all these years later.

I could never have written this book without the support and encouragement of my husband, Simon — my partner in life, my editor, my chief taster, and my writing coach. And to my kids, Chaim and Ruth, who in the midst of deadlines and hours of endless writing always made me smile and enjoy my sweet life.

Sources of Unusual Ingredients

Some of the ingredients in this book may not be available at your local grocery store. Below, I've listed stores in New York City where you can purchase these items. I've also noted online sources in every case.

Almond paste

Kalustyan's
123 Lexington Avenue
New York, NY
www.kalustyans.com

Chestnuts

Kalustyan's
123 Lexington Avenue
New York, NY
www.kalustyans.com

Online:
www.igourmet.com

Chocolate

Zabar's
2245 Broadway
New York, NY

Online:
www.chocosphere.com

Cocoa Nibs

Zabar's
2245 Broadway
New York, NY

Online:
www.chocosphere.com

Guavas

Garden of Eden
New York, NY
multiple locations

Online:
www.grovestand.net

Halva

Kalustyan's
123 Lexington Avenue
New York, NY
www.kalustyans.com

Hazelnut paste

Kalustyan's
123 Lexington Avenue
New York, NY
www.kalustyans.com

Huckleberries

SOS Chefs
104 Avenue B
New York, NY

Online:
www.nwwildfoods.com

Kumquats

Garden of Eden
New York, NY
multiple locations

Online:
www.ceresspecialtyfruit.com

Lemon Verbena

Takashimaya
693 Fifth Avenue
New York, NY

Online:
www.teagschwendner.com

Medjool Dates

Kalustyan's
123 Lexington Avenue
New York, NY
www.kalustyans.com

Online:
www.hadleyfruitorchards.com

Meyer Lemons

Garden of Eden
New York, NY
multiple locations

Online:
www.grovestand.net

Passion Fruit Puree

SOS Chefs
104 Avenue B
New York, NY

Online:
www.lepicerie.com

Sichuan Peppercorns

Kalustyan's
123 Lexington Avenue
New York, NY
www.kalustyans.com

Online:
www.thespicehouse.com

Truffle Honey

Kalustyan's
123 Lexington Avenue
New York, NY
www.kalustyans.com

SOS Chefs
104 Avenue B
New York, NY

Online:
www.caviarstar.com
www.cybercucina.com

Vanilla Beans

Kalustyan's
123 Lexington Avenue
New York, NY
www.kalustyans.com

SOS Chefs
104 Avenue B
New York, NY

Online:
www.bakerscatalogue.com

Index

A

acid
  in egg white foams, 123
  unique consistency of citrus curds, 20
almond paste, 64
almonds
  Almond Honey Caramel Chews, 193
  Almond Macaroons, 79
  Chocolate Almond Cracks, 63
  Coconut, Almond, and Brown Butter Macaroons, 70
  Fresh Apricot and Almond Tart, 26
  Milk Chocolate and Almond Toffees, 194
  Miniature Chocolate, Almond, and Lime Brown Butter Tea Cakes, 41
  Vanilla, Brown Butter, and Almond Tea Cake, 37–38
amygdalin, 175
apples
  Apple and Pear Chips, 207
  Apple and Quince Tart, 23
  Apple Cider and Caramel Ice Cream, 141
  Cider Caramel Sauce, 212
  Granny Smith Apple, Dried Fig, and Dried Cherry Winter Fruit Compote, 162
  Green Apple and Muscato Sorbet, 149
  Roasted Apple Beignets with Cinnamon Sugar, 178
  Spiced Apple and Sour Cream Cake, 48
  Stuffed Roasted Fall Apples, 182
apricots
  Apricot Pit Ice Cream, 143
  Fresh Apricot and Almond Tart, 26

B

bain-marie, 10
baked custards. See custards
baking pads, 10
baking pans, black steel, 69
baking powder, 46
baking soda, 46, 57
bananas
  Banana Cream Pie, 91
  Banana Cream with Crunchy Toffee, 91
  Banana Malt Ice Cream, 137
Bartlett Pears Poached in Muscat Wine, 166
Basil Ice Cream, 142
Beignets, Roasted Apple with

Cinnamon Sugar, 178
berries
  Rhubarb Consommé with Summer Berries, 167
  See also huckleberries; raspberries; strawberries
Bittersweet Chocolate Mousse, 108
Black Mint Ice Cream, 142
Black Mint Parfait, 158
Black Pepper Ice Cream, 143
black steel baking pans, 69
Black Walnut Parfait, 158
blanching citrus rind, 198
blenders, using, to puree hot liquids, 11
Blood Orange Caramel Sauce, 212
Brandied Crème Fraîche Sauce, 213
Brandied Dried Fig and Vanilla Soufflé, 124–125
Brioche Pudding with Truffle Honey, 101
browning, 51, 175
butter, 10
  browning, 51
  creaming, 67
  infusing with vanilla, 38
  room-temperature, 11

C

cacao beans, 31
  See also chocolate
cakes
  Chocolate Bête Noire, 47
  Chocolate Layer Cake with Milk Chocolate Frosting, 52–53
  Date Cake with Toffee Sauce, 45
  Goat Cheesecake Enrobed in Hazelnut Brittle, 42
  Hazelnut Cake, 39
  Miniature Chocolate, Almond, and Lime Brown Butter Tea Cakes, 41
  Spiced Apple and Sour Cream Cake, 48
  Vanilla, Brown Butter, and Almond Tea Cake, 37–38
  Whipped Brown Butter and Vanilla Birthday Cake, 49–50
Candied Kumquat Mascarpone Parfait, 153
Candied Kumquats, 198
Candied Meyer Lemon Zest, 198
  Roasted Medjool Dates Stuffed with Cashews, Currants, and Candied Citrus, 165
candies
  Almond Honey Caramel Chews, 193
  Candied Kumquats, 198

Guava and Passion-Fruit Jellies, 199
Huckleberry Fruit Jellies, 200
Milk Chocolate and Almond Toffees, 194
Milk Chocolate Crunch Candies, 194
Quince Fruit Jellies, 197
  See also truffles
caramel
  Almond Honey Caramel Chews, 193
  Apple Cider and Caramel Ice Cream, 141
  Blood Orange Caramel Sauce, 212
  Candied Meyer Lemon Zest, 198
  caramel sauce, liquid or solid, 98
  Cardamom Caramel Mousse, 106
  Chocolate Caramel Pot de Crème, 93
  Chocolate Caramel Tart, 29
  Cider Caramel Sauce, 212
  Cinnamon Caramel Mousse, 106–107
  Clove Caramel Mousse, 106
  cooking tips, 107
  Espresso Ice Cream, 138
  Milk Chocolate Caramel Sauce, 214
  Plum Caramel Sauce, 215
  Rum Caramel Sauce, 213
  Star Anise Caramel Mousse, 106
  Thin and Delicate Peanut Brittle, 204
  See also crème caramels
caramelization, 175
cardamom
  Cardamom and Honey Pistachio Nougat Glacé, 154
  Cardamom Caramel Mousse, 106
  Cardamom Ice Cream, 143
  Cardamom Streusel Topping, 169
  Cardamom-scented sweet tart dough, 15
  Creamy Coconut Cardamom Rice Pudding, 94
  Hazelnut, Cinnamon, Cardamom, and Raspberry Sandwich Cookies, 71–72
  White Chocolate, Cardamom, and Pistachio Truffles with Coconut, 188
cashews, Roasted Medjool Dates Stuffed with Cashews, Currants, and Candied Citrus, 165
castor sugar, 148
Cheesecake Enrobed with Hazelnut Brittle, Goat, 42
cherries
  Double Chocolate and Cherry Cookies, 58
  Dried Cherry and Chocolate Chip

Oatmeal Cookie, 68
  Fresh Cherry Vanilla Compote, 170
  Granny Smith Apple, Dried Fig, and Dried Cherry Winter Fruit Compote, 162
Chestnut and Amaretti Cookie Pudding, 97–98
chocolate
  about, 31–33
  Bittersweet Chocolate Mousse, 108
  Chocolate Almond Cracks, 63
  Chocolate Bête Noire, 47
  Chocolate Buttercream, 79
  Chocolate Caramel Pot de Crème, 93
  Chocolate Caramel Tart, 29
  Chocolate Crumb Crust, 65
  Chocolate-dipped Nut Chews, 193
  Chocolate Layer Cake with Milk Chocolate Frosting, 52–53
  Chocolate Soufflé, 119–120
  Crispy, Chewy Chocolate Chip Cookies, 57
  Crispy Bittersweet Chocolate Wafers, 65
  Crispy Malted Bitter Chocolate Meringues, 74–75
  Dark Chocolate, Cinnamon, and Espresso Truffles with Walnuts, 190
  Dark Chocolate Sorbet, 147
  Double Chocolate and Cherry Cookies, 58
  Five-Spice Chocolate Truffles, 191
  Milk Chocolate and Almond Toffees, 194
  Milk Chocolate Caramel Sauce, 214
  Milk Chocolate-coated Malted Meringues, 74
  Milk Chocolate Crunch Candies, 195
  Miniature Chocolate, Almond, and Lime Brown Butter Tea Cakes, 41
  Oatmeal Cookies with Golden Raisins and Milk Chocolate Chips, 68
  Sesame Milk Chocolate Mousse, 109
  tempering, 187, 195
  and water, 47
  White Chocolate and Grapefruit Truffles with Hazelnuts, 186–187
  White Chocolate, Cardamom, and Pistachio Truffles with Coconut, 188
Cider Caramel Sauce, 212
cinnamon
  Cinnamon Caramel Mousse, 106–107

Cinnamon Ice Cream, 143

Cinnamon Streusel Topping, 169

Cinnamon-scented sweet tart dough, 15

Dark Chocolate, Cinnamon, and Espresso Truffles with Walnuts, 190

Hazelnut, Cinnamon, Cardamom, and Raspberry Sandwich Cookies, 71–72

Maple Cinnamon Ice Cream, 139

Roasted Apple Beignets with Cinnamon Sugar, 178

Walnut, Currant, and Cinnamon Rugelach, 73

citrus

Roasted Medjool Dates Stuffed with Cashews, Currants, and Candied Citrus, 165

See also grapefruit; lemon; lime; orange

citrus curds, 20

citrus rinds, 198

Clove Caramel Mousse, 106

cocoa, in sorbet, 147

coconut

Coconut, Almond, and Brown Butter Macaroons, 70

Coconut Cream Cheese Ice Cream, 135

Creamy Coconut Cardamom Rice Pudding, 94

White Chocolate, Cardamom, and Pistachio Truffles with Coconut, 188

compotes

Fresh Cherry Vanilla Compote, 170

Fresh Fig and Madeira Compote, 170

Granny Smith Apple, Dried Fig, and Dried Cherry Winter Fruit Compote, 162

Spiced Plum Compote with Plum Pit Cream, 174

cookies

Chocolate Almond Cracks, 63

Coconut, Almond, and Brown Butter Macaroons, 70

Crispy, Chewy Chocolate Chip Cookies, 57

Crispy Bittersweet Chocolate Wafers, 65

Crispy Malted Bitter Chocolate Meringues, 74–75

Double Chocolate and Cherry Cookies, 58

Gingersnaps, 59

Hazelnut and Orange Macaroons,

78–79

Hazelnut, Cinnamon, Cardamom, and Raspberry Sandwich Cookies, 71–72

Hazelnut Shortbread, 66–67

Maple-Pecan Meringue Cookies, 76–77

Oatmeal Cookies with Golden Raisins and Milk Chocolate Chips, 68

Pignoli Amaretti Cookies, 64

Walnut Cream Cheese Sandwich Cookies, 60–63

Walnut, Currant, and Cinnamon Rugelach, 73

cream, heavy, 10

cream cheese

Coconut Cream Cheese Ice Cream, 135

Walnut, Currant, and Cinnamon Rugelach, 73

Walnut Cream Cheese Sandwich Cookies, 60–63

cream of tartar, 10

Creamy Coconut Cardamom Rice Pudding, 94

crème brûlées

Prune Armagnac Crème Brûlée, 89–90

Rice Pudding Brûlée, 96

crème caramels, 84

Espresso Crème Caramel, 87

Maple Crème Caramel, 88

Vanilla/Classic Crème Caramel, 86

crème fraîche

Brandied Crème Fraîche Sauce, 213

Lavender and Honey Crème Fraîche Parfait, 156

Crispy, Chewy Chocolate Chip Cookies, 57

Crispy Bittersweet Chocolate Wafers, 65

Crispy Malted Bitter Chocolate Meringues, 74–75

crusts

Chocolate Crumb Crust, 65

Flaky Tart Shell, 16

Hazelnut Tart Shell, 14

Sweet Tart Shell, 15

currants

Roasted Medjool Dates Stuffed with Cashews, Currants, and Candied Citrus, 165

Walnut, Currant, and Cinnamon Rugelach, 73

custards

cooking a stirred custard, 96

Banana Cream with Crunchy Toffee, 91

Brioche Pudding with Truffle Honey, 101

Chestnut and Amaretti Cookie Pudding, 97–98

Chocolate Caramel Pot de Crème, 93

guidelines, 82–83

Honey and Yogurt Panna Cotta, 102

stirred, 96

Vanilla Panna Cotta, 99

See also crème brûlées; crème caramels

D

Dark Chocolate, Cinnamon, and Espresso Truffles with Walnuts, 190

Dark Chocolate Sorbet, 147

dates, 164

Date Cake with Toffee Sauce, 45

Roasted Medjool Dates Stuffed with Cashews, Currants, and Candied Citrus, 165

disulfide bonds, 20, 123

Double Chocolate and Cherry Cookies, 58

E

eggs

egg white foams, 123

egg yolk foams and sabayons, 216

egg yolks, 216

raw egg yolks in pastry cream, 127

room-temperature, 11, 53

sugar and egg yolks, 216

emulsifiers, 53, 133

espresso

Dark Chocolate, Cinnamon, and Espresso Truffles with Walnuts, 190

Espresso Crème Caramel, 87

Espresso Ice Cream, 138

F

fat, 132–133

figs

Brandied Dried Fig and Vanilla Soufflé, 124–125

Fig Leaf Ice Cream, 142

Fig Leaf Parfait, 158

Fresh Fig and Madeira Compote, 170

Fresh Huckleberry and Fig Tart, 24–25

Granny Smith Apple, Dried Fig, and Dried Cherry Winter Fruit Compote, 162

Stuffed Roasted Fall Apples, 182

Five-Spice Chocolate Truffles, 191

Flaky Tart Shell, 16

flour, 10

French meringue, 75

Fresh Apricot and Almond Tart, 26

Fresh Cherry Vanilla Compote, 170

Fresh Fig and Madeira Compote, 170

Fresh Huckleberry and Fig Tart, 24–25

Frosting, Milk Chocolate, 52–53

frozen desserts

Black Mint Parfait, 158

Black Walnut Parfait, 158

Candied Kumquat Mascarpone Parfait, 153

Cardamom and Honey Pistachio Nougat Glacé, 154

Fig Leaf Parfait, 158

Hazelnut Parfait, 158

Lavender and Honey Crème Fraîche Parfait, 156

Passion-Fruit Soufflé Glacé, 155

Vanilla Bean and Lemon Verbena Parfait with Summer Raspberries, 158

See also ice cream; sorbet

fruit candies, 196

Candied Kumquats, 198

Candied Meyer Lemon Zest, 198

Guava and Passion-Fruit Jellies, 199

Huckleberry Fruit Jellies, 200

Quince Fruit Jellies, 197

fruit chips, 206–209

Apple and Pear Chips, 207

Pineapple Chips, 208

Strawberry Chips, 209

fruit compotes

Fresh Cherry Vanilla Compote, 170

Fresh Fig and Madeira Compote, 170

Granny Smith Apple, Dried Fig, and Dried Cherry Winter Fruit Compote, 162

Spiced Plum Compote with Plum Pit Cream, 174

fruit pits, 175

fruits

enzymatic browning of, 143

See also specific types

G

ginger

Bartlett Poached Pears in Muscat Wine, 166

Gingersnaps, 59

Maple-Ginger Ice Cream, 139

glacés

Cardamom and Honey Pistachio Nougat Glacé, 154

glacés (*continued*)

Passion-Fruit Soufflé Glacé, 155

goat cheese

Goat Cheese and Purple Basil Soufflé, 116–118

Goat Cheesecake Enrobed in Hazelnut Brittle, 42

Granny Smith Apple, Dried Fig, and Dried Cherry Winter Fruit Compote, 162

grapefruit, White Chocolate and Grapefruit Truffles with Hazelnuts, 186–187

Grape Sorbet, Muscat, 145

Green Apple and Muscato Sorbet, 149

guavas

Guava and Passion-Fruit Jellies, 199

Guava Sorbet, 152

H

halvah, 109

hazelnuts

Goat Cheesecake Enrobed in Hazelnut Brittle, 42

Hazelnut and Orange Macaroons, 78–79

Hazelnut Cake, 39

Hazelnut, Cinnamon, Cardamom, Raspberry Sandwich Cookies, 71–72

Hazelnut Honey Caramel Chews, 193

Hazelnut Parfait, 158

Hazelnut Shortbread, 66–67

Hazelnut Streusel Topping, 169

Hazelnut Tart Shell, 14

Milk Chocolate and Hazelnut Toffees, 194

White Chocolate and Grapefruit Truffles with Hazelnuts, 186–187

heavy cream, 10

Herb-infused or Spiced Panna Cotta, 99

honey

Almond Honey Caramel Chews, 193

Brioche Pudding with Truffle Honey, 101

Cardamom and Honey Pistachio Nougat Glacé, 154

Hazelnut Honey Caramel Chews, 193

Honey and Yogurt Panna Cotta, 102

Honey-Glazed Roasted Pears, 176–177

Lavender and Honey Crème Fraîche Parfait, 156

Peanut Honey Caramel Chews, 193

Pistachio Honey Caramel Chews, 193

Roasted Glazed Peaches, 172

Walnut Honey Caramel Chews, 193

huckleberries

about, 200

Fresh Huckleberry and Fig Tart, 24–25

Huckleberry Fruit Jellies, 200

I

ice baths, 10

ice cream

Apple Cider and Caramel Ice Cream, 141

Apricot Pit Ice Cream, 143

Banana Malt Ice Cream, 137

Basil Ice Cream, 142

Black Mint Ice Cream, 142

Black Pepper Ice Cream, 143

Cardamom Ice Cream, 143

Cinnamon Ice Cream, 143

Coconut Cream Cheese Ice Cream, 135

Espresso Ice Cream, 138

Fig Leaf Ice Cream, 142

guidelines, 130–134

Lemon Verbena Ice Cream, 142

Mandarin Ice Cream, 136

Maple Cinnamon Ice Cream, 139

Maple-Ginger Ice Cream, 139

Maple–Star Anise Ice Cream, 139

Maple Vanilla Ice Cream, 139

Plum Pit Ice Cream, 143

Port Plum Ice Cream, 140

Spiced Mandarin Ice Cream, 136

Star Anise Ice Cream, 143

See also sorbet

ice cream machines, 130, 131, 133–134

Italian meringue, 112–113

Italian zabaglione, 216

K

kumquats

Candied Kumquat Mascarpone Parfait, 153

Candied Kumquats, 198

L

Lavender and Honey Crème Fraîche Parfait, 156

leavening agents, 46

lecithin, 133

lemon

Candied Meyer Lemon Zest, 198

Meyer Lemon Curd Tart, 18

Meyer Lemon Soufflé, 114–115

lemon curds, 20

lemon verbena

Lemon Verbena Ice Cream, 142

Lemon Verbena Poached Nectarines, 181

Tangerine and Lemon Verbena Rice Pudding, 94

Vanilla Bean and Lemon Verbena Parfait with Summer Raspberries, 158

lids, 10

lime, Miniature Chocolate, Almond, and Lime Brown Butter Tea Cakes, 41

M

macaroons

Almond Macaroons, 79

Coconut, Almond, and Brown Butter Macaroons, 70

flourless, 70

Hazelnut and Orange Macaroons, 78–79

Maillard reactions, 175

mandarin

Mandarin Ice Cream, 136

Mandarin Orange Sorbet, 144

mango, Pineapple Fruit Soup with Mango and Passion Fruit, 173

maple

Maple Cinnamon Ice Cream, 139

Maple Crème Caramel, 88

Maple-Ginger Ice Cream, 139

Maple-Pecan Meringue Cookies, 76–77

Maple–Star Anise Ice Cream, 139

Maple–Star Anise Mousse, 104

Maple Vanilla Ice Cream, 139

Maple Walnut Soufflé, 122–123

maple syrup, reducing, 10

mascarpone, Candied Kumquat Mascarpone Parfait, 153

meringues, 112–113

Crispy Malted Bitter Chocolate Meringues, 74–75

Maple-Pecan Meringue Cookies, 76–77

Milk Chocolate-coated Malted Meringues, 74

Meyer Lemon Curd Tart, 18

Meyer Lemon Soufflé, 114–115

Meyer Lemon Zest, Candied, 198

Meyer Lemons, about, 18

milk chocolate

Milk Chocolate and Almond Toffees, 194

Milk Chocolate Caramel Sauce, 214

Milk Chocolate-coated Malted Meringues, 74

Milk Chocolate Crunch Candies, 195

Sesame Milk Chocolate Mousse, 109

See also chocolate

Miniature Chocolate, Almond, and Lime Brown Butter Tea Cakes, 41

mousse

Bittersweet Chocolate Mousse, 108

Cardamom Caramel Mousse, 106

Cinnamon Caramel Mousse, 106–107

Clove Caramel Mousse, 106

Maple–Star Anise Mousse, 104

Sesame Milk Chocolate Mousse, 109

Star Anise Caramel Mousse, 106

Muffins, Spiced Apple, 48

Muscat Grape Sorbet, 145

N

Nectarines, Lemon Verbena Poached, 181

nonstick silicone baking pads, 10

nuts. *See specific types*

O

oatmeal

Oatmeal Cookies with Golden Raisins and Milk Chocolate Chips, 68

Oatmeal Streusel Topping, 169

orange

Blood Orange Caramel Sauce, 212

Hazelnut and Orange Macaroons, 78–79

Mandarin Orange Sorbet, 144

ovens, 10

P

panna cotta

Herb-infused or Spiced Panna Cotta, 99

Honey and Yogurt Panna Cotta, 102

Vanilla Panna Cotta, 99

parfaits

Black Mint Parfait, 158

Black Walnut Parfait, 158

Candied Kumquat Mascarpone Parfait, 153

Fig Leaf Parfait, 158

Hazelnut Parfait, 158

Lavender and Honey Crème Fraîche Parfait, 156

Vanilla Bean and Lemon Verbena Parfait with Summer Raspberries, 158

passion fruit

Guava and Passion-Fruit Jellies, 199

Passion-Fruit Curd Tart, 21

Passion-Fruit Soufflé Glacé, 155

Pineapple Fruit Soup with Mango and Passion Fruit, 173

Peaches, Roasted Glazed, 172

peanuts

Peanut Honey Caramel Chews, 193

Thin and Delicate Peanut Brittle, 204

pears

Apple and Pear Chips, 207

Bartlett Pears Poached in Muscat Wine, 166

Dried Pear and Milk Chocolate Chip Oatmeal Cookies, 68

Honey-Glazed Roasted Pears, 176–177

Roasted Pear Beignets, 178

pecans, Maple-Pecan Meringue Cookies, 76–77

pectin, 196

Pie, Banana Cream, 91

Pignoli Amaretti Cookies, 64

pinch, 10

pineapples

Pineapple Chips, 208

Pineapple Fruit Soup with Mango and Passion Fruit, 173

Pineapple-Rosemary Sorbet, 146

pistachio

Cardamom and Honey Pistachio Nougat Glacé, 154

Milk Chocolate and Pistachio Toffees, 194

Pistachio Honey Caramel Chews, 193

White Chocolate, Cardamom, and

Pistachio Truffles with Coconut, 188
plum pits, 175
plums
    Plum and Almond Tart, 26
    Plum Caramel Sauce, 215
    Plum Pit Ice Cream, 143
    Port Plum Ice Cream, 140
    Spiced Plum Compote with Plum Pit
        Cream, 174
polyphenol oxidase (PPO), 143
polysaccharides, 132
Port Plum Ice Cream, 140
protein, 20, 51, 75, 83, 131–132
Prune Armagnac Crème Brûlée, 89–90
puddings
    Brioche Pudding with Truffle Honey,
        101
    Chestnut and Amaretti Cookie
        Pudding, 97–98
    Creamy Coconut Cardamom Rice
        Pudding, 94
    Rice Pudding Brûlée, 96
    Tangerine and Lemon Verbena Rice
        Pudding, 94
Pumpkin Soufflé, 126–127
Q
quince
    about, 151, 196
    Apple and Quince Tart, 23
    Quince Fruit Jellies, 197
    Quince Sorbet, 150
R
raisins, Oatmeal Cookies with Golden
    Raisins and Milk Chocolate Chips,
    68
raspberries
    Hazelnut, Cinnamon, Cardamom, and
        Raspberry Sandwich Cookies, 71–72
    Vanilla Bean and Lemon Verbena
        Parfait with Summer Raspberries,
        158
    Whipped Brown Butter and Vanilla
        Birthday Cake, 49
rhubarb
    Rhubarb Consommé with Tropical
        Fruit, photo 103. 167
    Strawberry-Rhubarb Crisp, 169
rice pudding
    Creamy Coconut Cardamom Rice
        Pudding, 94
    Rice Pudding Brûlée, 96
    Tangerine and Lemon Verbena Rice
        Pudding, 94
Roasted Apple Beignets with Cinnamon
    Sugar, 178
Roasted Glazed Peaches, 172
Roasted Medjool Dates Stuffed with
    Cashews, Currants, and Candied
    Citrus, 165
Roasted Pear Beignets, 178

rosemary, Pineapple-Rosemary Sorbet,
    146
Rugelach, Walnut, Currant, and
    Cinnamon, 73
Rum Caramel Sauce, 213
S
sabayon, 216
    Sauternes Sabayon, 217
salt, 131
sauces
    Blood Orange Caramel Sauce, 212
    Brandied Crème Fraîche Sauce, 213
    Cider Caramel Sauce, 212
    Milk Chocolate Caramel Sauce, 214
    Plum Caramel Sauce, 215
    Rum Caramel Sauce, 213
    Toffee Sauce, 45, 214
Sauternes, 217
Sauternes Sabayon, 217
Sesame Milk Chocolate Mousse, 109
Shortbread, Hazelnut, 66–67
skim milk powder, 132
sorbet
    Dark Chocolate Sorbet, 147
    Green Apple and Muscato Sorbet,
        149
    Guava Sorbet, 152
    guidelines, 130–134
    Mandarin Orange Sorbet, 144
    Muscat Grape Sorbet, 145
    Pineapple-Rosemary Sorbet, 146
    Quince Sorbet, 150
    Strawberry and Tarragon Sorbet, 148
soufflés
    Brandied Dried Fig and Vanilla
        Soufflé, 124–125
    Chocolate Soufflé, 119–120
    Goat Cheese and Purple Basil Soufflé,
        116–118
    guidelines, 112–113
    Maple Walnut Soufflé, 122–123
    Meyer Lemon Soufflé, 114–115
    Passion-Fruit Soufflé Glacé, 155
    Pumpkin Soufflé, 126–127
Spiced Apple and Sour Cream Cake, 48
Spiced Plum Compote with Plum Pit
    Cream, 174
Spiced Mandarin Ice Cream, 136
stabilizers, 132
star anise
    Maple–Star Anise Ice Cream, 139
    Maple–Star Anise Mousse, 104
    Star Anise Caramel Mousse, 106
    Star Anise Ice Cream, 143
starches, 90, 147
steam, 46
stone fruit pits, 175
strawberries
    Strawberry and Tarragon Sorbet, 148
    Strawberry Chips, 209
    Strawberry-Rhubarb Crisp, 169

streusels
    Cardamom Streusel Topping, 169
    Cinnamon Streusel Topping, 169
    Hazelnut Streusel Topping, 169
    Oatmeal Streusel Topping, 169
    Strawberry-Rhubarb Crisp, 169
Stuffed Roasted Fall Apples, 182
sugar, 11, 131
    and egg yolks, 216
    superfine, 148
    testing, 11
Sweet Tart Shell, 15
T
Tangerine and Lemon Verbena Rice
    Pudding, 94
tannins, 198
tarragon, Strawberry and Tarragon Sorbet,
    148
tarts
    Apple and Quince Tart, 23
    Chocolate Caramel Tart, 29
    Flaky Tart Shell, 16
    Fresh Apricot and Almond Tart, 26
    Fresh Huckleberry and Fig Tart,
        24–25
    Hazelnut Tart Shell, 14
    Meyer Lemon Curd Tart, 18
    Passion-Fruit Curd Tart, 21
    Sweet Tart Shell, 15
techniques
    blanching, 198
    browning butter, 51
    caramel sauce, 98
    creaming butter, 67
    French meringue, 75
    rolling tart dough, 17
    stirred custards, 96
    tempering chocolate, 195
    whisking sugar and egg yolks, 216
Thin and Delicate Peanut Brittle, 204
toffee
    Date Cake with Toffee Sauce, 45
    Milk Chocolate and Almond Toffees,
        194
    Toffee Sauce, 214
truffle honey, 101
truffles
    Dark Chocolate, Cinnamon, and
        Espresso Truffles with Walnuts, 190
    Five-Spice Chocolate Truffles, 191
    White Chocolate and Grapefruit
        Truffles with Hazelnuts, 186–187
    White Chocolate, Cardamom, and
        Pistachio Truffles with Coconut, 188
V
vanilla
    Brandied Dried Fig and Vanilla
        Soufflé, 124–125
    Fresh Cherry Vanilla Compote, 170
    Maple Vanilla Ice Cream, 139
    Vanilla Bean and Lemon Verbena

Parfait with Summer Raspberries,
    158
    Vanilla, Brown Butter, and Almond
        Tea Cake, 37–38
    with warm crème brûlée custard
        filling, 158, photo 163
    Vanilla Buttercream, 79
    Vanilla/Classic Crème Caramel, 86
    Vanilla Panna Cotta, 99
    Whipped Brown Butter and Vanilla
        Birthday Cake, 49–50
vanilla beans, 11, 159
W
walnuts
    Black Walnut Parfait, 158
    Dark Chocolate, Cinnamon, and
        Espresso Truffles with Walnuts, 190
    Maple Walnut Soufflé, 122–123
    Milk Chocolate and Walnut Toffees,
        194
    Walnut Cream Cheese Sandwich
        Cookies, 60–63
    Walnut, Currant, and Cinnamon
        Rugelach, 73
    Walnut Honey Caramel Chews, 193
Whipped Brown Butter and Vanilla
    Birthday Cake, 49–50
white chocolate
    White Chocolate and Grapefruit
        Truffles with Hazelnuts, 186–187
    White Chocolate, Cardamom, and
        Pistachio Truffles with Coconut, 188
Z
zabaglione, 216

Bulfinch Press

Hachette Book Group USA

1271 Avenue of the Americas, New York, NY 10020

Visit our Web site at www.bulfinchpress.com

First Edition: October 2006

Food science consultant, Kirsten Hubbard

Library of Congress Cataloging-in-Publication Data
Zuckerman, Kate.
    The sweet life : desserts from Chanterelle / Kate Zuckerman. — 1st ed.
        p. cm.
Includes index.
ISBN-10: 0-8212-5744-7 (hardcover)
ISBN-13: 978-0-8212-5744-9 (hardcover)
1. Desserts. I. Chanterelle (Restaurant : New York, N.Y.). II. Title.
TX773.Z83 2006
641.8'6 — dc22   2005033355

Design: Gary Tooth / Empire Design Studio

PRINTED IN SINGAPORE

NOV   2006